**BOCCONI
UNIVERSITY
PRESS**

Stefania Micaela Vitulli · Gabriele Ghini

CEO BRANDING
IN THE GLOBAL REPUTATION ECONOMY

Translator: Martina Gordon
Cover: Cristina Bernasconi, Milano
Typesetting: Corpo4 Team, Milano

Copyright © 2024 Bocconi University Press
EGEA S.p.A.

EGEA S.p.A.
Via Salasco, 5 - 20136 Milano
Tel. 02/5836.5751 – Fax 02/5836.5753
egea.edizioni@unibocconi.it – www.egeaeditore.it

First edition: September 2024

ISBN Domestic Edition	979-12-80623-40-9
ISBN International Edition	979-12-81627-23-9
ISBN Digital Domestic Edition	978-88-238-8881-4
ISBN Digital International Edition	979-12-81627-24-6

Stampa: Logo S.p.A. - Borgoricco (Pd)

Table of Contents

Acknowledgments

We would like to thank the following list of people for assisting in sourcing contents for this book and for being willing to collaborate:

1. Dr. Andrea Monzani: Head of Group Press Management and Head of Communication Italy – EURONEXT.
2. Dr. Roberto Race: Senior Advisor, Corporate Strategy and Reputation.
3. Ulrich F. Ackermann—Managing Partner TRANSEARCH Germany—Chairman of the Board of Directors TRANSEARCH International Partners Ltd.
4. Dr.-Ing. Carlo Mackrodt—Managing Partner TRANSEARCH Germany.
5. Bill Sakellaris—Managing Partner TRANSEARCH Australia.
6. Lars Tegelberg (LT): Partner, VP Northern Europe, Global Council Mem-ber TRANSEARCH.
7. Celeste Whatley—CEO TRANSEARCH International Partners Ltd.
8. Kim Bell—Global Head of Marketing TRANSEARCH International Partners Ltd.
9. TRANSEARCH Italian Team.

This book is a collaborative effort that could not have taken shape without the selfless support of many people who enabled the authors to complete the long journey that led to its creation. First and foremost, we are grateful to the CEOs who, with openness and willingness, have shared in this volume a wealth of managerial experience with a strong inspirational value that has never before been collected in this form. We would like to thank the team at Euronext - Borsa Italiana for believing in this initiative from the beginning, especially Marta Testi, Roberta Laveneziana and Elettra Pescetto. Thanks to Egea, who have supported us until the very end. The collaboration of Giorgia Altovino, Carolina Conti, Andrea de Luna, Nani Marchese, Giovanni Mordenti, Claudio Ricci, Rosa Serpico and the partners of TRANSEARCH International was invaluable for interviews and data processing. Thanks to Giorgio Del Mare, who encouraged us in our research and provided indispensable material on which to base our reflections: to him we express our deepest respect in memory. Thanks to Professor Edoardo Teodoro Brioschi, without whom the theoretical foundations of this book would not have been firmly rooted in the discipline.

Introduction

by Fabrizio Testa[1]

Since the first Italian edition of this book, Borsa Italiana, part of the Euronext Group, has closely followed the meticulous process of collecting and analysing data and testimonials that culminated in its publication. Particularly now, with its English edition, we are deeply interested in a subject like corporate reputation, not only in Italy but across all the markets where Euronext operates.

Corporate reputation is paramount due to its pivotal role in fostering trust, credibility, and competitive advantage. A positive reputation nurtures customer loyalty, attracts top talent, and instils investor confidence. Moreover, it helps companies in effectively managing crises and navigating regulatory challenges. Ultimately, a favourable reputation significantly influences a company's financial performance and long-term success, underscoring its importance as a valuable asset that necessitates careful cultivation and protection.

This volume authored by Gabriele Ghini and Stefania Vitulli includes significant testimonials on corporate reputation, striking an interesting balance between theoretical insights and practical "on-field experience." The selection of cases encompasses a diverse range of companies, both small and large, listed and unlisted, with varying managerial and en-

---

[1] Appointed Chief Executive Officer of Borsa Italiana, part of the Euronext Group, in November 2021, joined the Managing Board of Euronext NV in May 2022. From 2014 to 2021 Fabrizio held the position of CEO of MTS, the leading electronic market in Europe for trading fixed income securities. First years of his career in Bank of America in Milan and London, where he was part of the Treasury team responsible for trading government bonds.

trepreneurial cultures. It constitutes a valuable resource for individuals seeking to delve into the interpretation of reputational strategies in the corporate realm, whether for academic pursuits or professional endeavours.

Another pertinent observation highlighted in the book, corroborated by our own experiences, pertains to the impact of going public on corporate reputation. We agree that corporate reputation and listing are intricately linked. Indeed, while the former is a prerequisite for a successful listing, the latter exerts significant reputational influence. The enhanced corporate processes and internal controls mandated for listing, coupled with heightened transparency demanded by markets, contribute to the fortification, and sometimes establishment, of a genuine stakeholder management ethos. Continuous engagement with investors facilitates companies' improvement both in business performance and reputation enhancement.

Of particular interest to markets is the role of ESG (Environmental, Social, and Governance) factors in shaping a company's reputation capital, representing a strategic imperative. Reputation serves as a magnet for capital, necessitating companies to take a leading role in these initiatives for success.

Borsa Italiana is dedicated to ensuring that companies increasingly align with the expectations of all stakeholders, not just shareholders, but also the broader society, including the communities in which they operate. This book starts from the same assumption, and we anticipate it will further stimulate the attention every company should devote to the reputational theme. Enhancing corporate reputation is pivotal in fostering fruitful relationships with all stakeholders and, consequently, positions companies as attractive players in the capital market.

1 CEO and Brand: Embodying Competitive Advantage

by Stefania M. Vitulli

"Impression is for the now, trust is for the future."

Sentence on a teabag

1.1 For the sustainability of the CEO as a possible leader

If I had to indicate the two reasons that make a book such as this necessary, or in any case the discussion of this topic, I would certainly say, on a similar level, the predominance the ethical purposes of the business have assumed in the perceptions of citizens and consumers on one hand, and on the other, the incessant call to leadership that Generation Z and Light Millennials invoke against companies', or better still, brands. Companies which will know how to condense influence, credibility, and charisma into global and local reference figures with human approaches and intentions will have won the challenge of the next few years: Individuals seek other individuals they trust as transparent and visionary decision-makers, and this research does not take place in the political or no profit sphere, the educational field, the media, or the military, but as researchers have concluded, in the world of business. It is true that companies are blamed as being responsible for climate damage, but regardless, it is always the companies and not the non-governmental organizations (NGOs) or political parties that can represent the engine of change that could save us from catastrophe.

Companies are asked to:

- Take position.
- Keep dialog open 24/7.

- Focus on ethical goals.
- Be flexible and authoritative at the same time.

Achieving these goals, or at least attempting to, is not possible without being brave and shameless. Nassim Nicholas turned the business world upside down in mid-economic crisis in 2007 by publishing the book *Il Cigno Nero*[1] (The Black Swan), which put in check the mental rigidity shown up to then by political, economic, and financial global management, that is, the presumption of being able to predict the events that disrupt the world, from World War I, to 9/11, to the creation of Harry Potter. Ten years later, Taleb tried again with *Rischiare Grosso*[2] (*Skin in the Game*), a book that preaches to a world that grabs the winning poker chips by transferring the risk to those who has never even seen the counter, giving importance to putting at stake everything which has been earned, or expected to earn, but above all your essence without incentives, while accepting both losses and consequences.

This is an uncomfortable concept, also the only one that would allow a leader to look behind and find a crowd following him. The intention, however, constituting the indispensable kick-off, is not enough. Being willing to take a big risk is completely useless if nobody knows about it. Almost a century of literature on the subject of corporate communication marks that the 20s of the new Millennium are and will be a time in history where a lack of communication is not only pointless but counterproductive.

In summary, the new generations do not reject the concept of profit, provided that it is the reward for social responsibility exercised with fairness and an open mind, as long as they have the decision on who to reward. Therefore, we need leaders capable of acting clearly and communicating in a coherent and effective way in regard to the values and objectives of their organizations. CEO training to embody this idea of leadership is not only necessary for companies, but vital: Those who will not grasp this challenge in the short term will be swallowed by the media which prefers, even in visibility, relevance and coherence, or a strategic

---

[1] N.N. Taleb, *The Black Swan: The Impact of the Highly Improbable*, New York, Random House and Penguin Books, 2007.
[2] N.N. Taleb, *Skin in the Game: Hidden Asymmetries in Daily Life*, New York, Random House, 2018.

and adaptive vision. This training, however, must be able to work simultaneously on models derived from the management of complex situations and on the ability to understand psychological and cultural variables (in one word: human) that whoever is brave and shameless must be able to consider. A "plastic" CEO, a puppet governed solely by business reasons, as well as a self-centered CEO who responds only to himself and to mandatory and non-delegable principles, will receive the same refusal to engage from economic and ethical stakeholders, especially if younger. We are far from creating a simple list of purposes, skills, and objectives, so we can start from the theory: How CEO and business are aligned, how corrections are made to possible aberrations, and how medium and large companies in Italy are reacting to the demand of markets and individuals in looking for their own reputational routes.

1.2   CEO branding as a strategic tool: reasons for this book

CEO branding is a relatively recent theme in the discipline of brand management at the corporate communication level. In the early days of its diffusion, the business world was touched in a very superficial way, neither intentionally nor strategically, from the organizational conceptual flow relating to this theme for the areas relating to image and reputation. However, a series of macrotrends of contemporaneity and their synergy and global interconnections have led to an essential exponential development[3] for organizations, therefore of the theories around the management of organizations, and consequently of the theory and practice around this subject.

Here we mention a few, for the benefit of an overall structure:

1. Digital acceleration.
2. Media recognition and exposure of the executive line and the company board.
3. Cocreation of value in intangible assets by stakeholder communities.

---

[3] I. Salim, M.S. Malone, Y. Van Geest, *Exponential organizations. Why new organizations are ten times better, faster, and cheaper than yours (and what to do about it)*, Diversion Books, 2014.

4. Multi-stakeholder engagement in corporate communication strategies.
5. Birth and development of *Corporate Activism*.
6. Call of companies to citizenship by Light Millennials and Generation Z.

Consequently, in less than 10 years, thanks also to the *best and worst practice* media practices of some CEO superstars who have had a founding character (see Chapter 2), CEO branding has become one of the corporate communication tools on which internal resources of communication, external consultancy activities, and the academy are being exercised on a strategic level, both for building trusted models and to historicize what has happened and what is expected.

This is why discussing this topic and providing pragmatic managerial guidelines of reference, with a pull approach on the adoption of these practices in companies of all sizes including start-ups, becomes a priority as well as a necessity, for which purpose this book was created. In the first few chapters we want to frame the "state of things" thus what it is, why to consider CEO branding, in which corporate purposes it finds ground for development, and who has been the Superstar CEOs so far. Together, we will direct the discussion toward the "state of art" which will be reached in the following chapters, where scenarios and case studies leave almost entirely the place for the description of the Italian reality, both in small- and medium-sized enterprises, as well as in the thinking of some of the most illustrious Italian CEOs, who direct some of the largest companies and turnover.

1.3   CEO and brand: understanding osmosis

When observing the role of CEOs as part of communication strategy, or the management of the organization in its most exclusive and authoritative responsibilities,[4] there is a wider potential than usual. Its figure be-

---

[4] For the adoption of a shared vocabulary, we specify here that the CEO (Chief Executive Officer) is the person to whom the powers of the board of directors have been delegated. The CEO has an executive function, at the top of the hierarchical career within a company organization, and its role also depends on the

comes a means to involve stakeholders and earn their approval. *The CEO creates a brand of himself and behaves like a brand: promoting itself with the aim of creating engagement*[5] *with stakeholders, be pleasant with them, gain approval, creating, maintaining, and improving its reputation.*[6]

This embodiment, however, is neither an automatism nor can it become a predefined model once and for all. Instead, it is a dynamic process with several complex steps that lead to a possible communication plan that invests the CEO in the role of cocatalyst of stakeholder engagement, and, if studied strategically as the last decade demonstrates, will have positive effects on corporate reputation.

Before focusing more on the dynamics related to the CEO branding phenomenon, it is essential to understand what defines a brand, since it is from this area that the dynamics themselves are borrowed. If we want to refer to the "classic," a first definition of a brand is given by the American Marketing Association, according to which "a brand is a name, term, symbol, design, or a combination of all these variables, intended to identify the goods or services of a seller or a group of sellers, and to differentiate from those of competitors."

Of course, since the 1960s, the definitions have multiplied and the concept has evolved, to the point that this definition today could be considered not only too simplistic, but incomplete or even inaccurate. However, it already contains supporting elements that today make us think of the CEO as a possible multiplier of any communication effort that

---

size of the company in which they operate. In Italy, Portugal, and Belgium, the acronym CEO translates into AD, while in France it corresponds to the general manager, in England to the Managing Director, and in Germany to the Chairman of the management board.

[5] 'Client's participation to the processes of communication, production and innovation' (Kotler, 2017).

[6] Again, for the purpose of adopting a shared vocabulary, we would like to make the distinction between self-brand and personal brand. The first, and original concept, provides that the individual, in feeling represented by a brand, expresses a part of themselves toward it. The concept then expanded to include those techniques (especially web and social) that allow you to convey and advertise yourself as a brand, always with the aim of self-representation. From this to *personal brand*, there is still a long way order to be fully aware of them and to be able to build around that strategy that includes marketing and communication actions. The expression *personal branding* was introduced by Tom Peters in 1997 to underline how the term "brand" cannot refer only to products or services, but in the new Millennium even more toward the personality of individuals.

the company puts in place to create and maintain a positive reputation with the stakeholders on which it depends[7]: creation and maintenance of identification and differentiation of a good or service. The brand is an intangible, holistic, and strategic resource and bearer of value for the organization, allowing it to gain a competitive advantage.

Keeping this perspective in mind, we will therefore have to understand the logic of branding applied to the CEO: If, thanks to the brand, the market is able to recognize a product or service and differentiate it from the competition, this is the potential which must be built, nurtured, and exploited also in the CEO in the moment in which we decide to adopt the CEO branding tool within our strategic corporate communication.

Naturally, as we previously stated, the definition given by the AMA of brand finds itself today exploded in complexity that provides the brand with multidimensional and synergistic functions. According to the most recent interpretations, which we will not go into excessive detail, but to which we refer to for completeness, in the mind of the stakeholder, the brand is no longer just a name or a symbol but has multiple functions all capable of impacting both the relationship with the stakeholder and the value of the company:

1. Recalls through its attributes, *qualities, strengths, and weaknesses* of the goods or service.
2. Contains distinctive values and culture, representative of those of the company.
3. Suggests a personality that allows stakeholders to identify themselves, and companies to confidently address certain users rather than others (Kotler 2002).
4. It is perceived as an entity that arouses sensations and feelings in the consumer.
5. It is a facilitator in building the relationship, thanks to the brand personality.
6. Amplifies value thanks to brand equity.[8]

---

[7] On the concept of reputation and its management, as well as on company stakeholder interactions, see the different founding theories.

[8] Now quantified in an increasingly precise and relevant way in the operations of M&A and other corporate economic negotiations. On the measurement model of the CBBE (Customer Based Brand Equity) for an initial reference, see in any case.

7. It plays a fundamental role in decision-making and the intentions behind a consumer's purchase, thanks to brand awareness.
8. It is able to evoke stratified and complex associations within stakeholders, linked to types, preferences, strengths, and uniqueness, thanks to the brand image.

If we decide that CEO branding is one of our main tools of communication, all of these features and others we will see will be designed in a strategic way when planning the CEO's contribution to corporate communication. Clearly, the theoretical framework of the brand is so broad and relevant that it is impossible to give an exhaustive account here. However, recalling some of its basics is useful in understanding how the implementation process of the CEO branding, despite being historically born from "below," or rather from behavioral models tactically introduced into the communicative flow by CEOs themselves (often those who later become Superstar CEO's), if wanted to be used effectively and efficiently in the company's competitive strategy must now, on one hand, benefit from everything which has been understood and resolved about the brand, and, on the other, everything which the constant monitoring of the most attractive brands and their affirmation strategies have to offer[9].

1.4   The branding activity: a no-limits evolution

As has been known for over a century, branding in companies, understood not only in building a brand, but as a defense and support of the brand, is carried out by top management and therefore certainly also by CEOs. It started with the aim of using it to differentiate the product, but later during the 1980s, the focus widened to the entire organization, up to the creation of corporate branding which provides the adoption of a pan-company perspective, where the customer-centric vision expands to include all the stakeholders from which the organization depends. Thus, if product branding resided exquisitely in the dimension of customer

---

[9] In this regard, to cite only one of the most popular sources, see all Interbrand reports, starting with the annual reports on the Best Global Brands, to those with a specific territorial or thematic focus (interbrand.com).

marketing, corporate branding requires the involvement and commitment of the entire organization, from the CEO to the bottom line[10].

In this way, corporate branding becomes, more than a marketing lever, a management philosophy. It must be treated as such and must give the following results:

1. Contribute to the corporate images of the organization that are perceived by all stakeholders, not just customers but employees, investors, suppliers, partners, legislators, municipalities, local authorities, and NGOs.
2. Provide a key endorsement, through a coherent and transparent projection of the corporate identity, of the involvement and identification of the same stakeholders.[11]
3. Reach individual stakeholder groups in a targeted manner, balancing the corporate images for each of them.

With this same logic, the branding business can invest places, cities, human resources,[12] or specific individuals for which branding aims to build a personal brand.

The process of building personal branding can take place for any member of the organization at any level, from the entrepreneur to the employee, to the freelancer. The construction of an image that is positive, outstanding, and full of distinctive features to the point of being perceived as unique can, in fact, be beneficial and translatable firstly into a demonstration and later into an enrichment of one's professional value, including on an individual level, both with peers and superiors, both in the current workplace and in the one it is aimed at.[13]

To summarize, we can say that among the countless descriptions of

---

[10] R.C. Gambetti, S.P. Quigley, *Managing Corporate Communication: A Cross-Cultural Approach*, New York, Palgrave Macmillan, 2013.

[11] A. Ries, L. Ries, <<The 22 Immutable Laws of Branding>>, *Symphonya. Emerging Issues in Management*, University of Milano-Bicocca, issue 1 Brand E., 2001.

[12] See Chapter 4 of this volume for the part of employer branding relating to the impact of the CEO on talent attraction.

[13] P. Montoya, *The Personal Branding Phenomenon*, Santa Ana, CA, Personal Branding Press, 2002.

the process of personal branding developed over time, there are some common characteristics:

1. The strategic approach.
2. The person-centered view.
3. The desire to convey a positive and engaging image.

If this is the process, the result is a personal brand or the "set of characteristics of an individual (attributes, values, beliefs etc.) represented with a true and symbolic narrative to establish a competitive advantage in the perception of the target audience."[14] Ultimately, like all brands, even the personal brand is a promise.

1.5 The concept of CEO branding between theory and practice

Regardless of age, regardless of position, regardless of the business we happen to be in, all of us need to understand the importance of branding. We are CEOs of our own companies: Me Inc. To be in business today, our most important job is to be head marketer for the brand called "you."

Tom Peters

If the CEO branding is a personal branding activity centered on the CEO, and based on everything we have so far described in relation to the brand and the process of its construction with specific reference to the person, the key quality promised to the CEO brand is that it does not only relate to the resulting image from the combination of skills, values, and personality of the CEO himself, but to the overall figure which the person embodies, so much so that the *CEO brand can be conceptualized as a multidimensional affective cognitive phenomenon*, which therefore also requires multidimensional measurement scales[15].

It is becoming clear that the potential for study and application of per-

---

[14] S. Gorbatov, S.N. Khapova, E.I. Lysova, "Personal Branding: Interdisciplinary Systematic Review and Research Agenda", *Frontiers in Psychology*, vol. 9, 2018.

[15] H.-M. Chen, H.-M. Chung, "How to Measure Personal Brand of a Business CEO", *Journal of Human Resource and Sustainability Studies*, vol. 4, 2016, pp. 305–324.

sonal branding in general, and CEO branding in particular (a study and application to which this book tries to make a contribution) are certainly underestimated at the moment, and consequently underdeveloped than those of product branding and corporate branding. At the moment, this is surely not only pathological but also a clear source of business opportunities through the intangible assets for those in the company who decide to approach these processes strategically, shunning those superficial intentions that they want to see, for example in stellar reputational performance linked to the CEOs of some companies, only meteors destined to leave behind a media trail leading to rapid consumption and oblivion.

Corporate branding and CEO branding must necessarily be aligned, in a holistic and strategic vision of corporate communication. From a dynamic perspective, one or the other of the two brands may prevail, that of the CEO or the corporate one. The CEO can be at the top at a time when the company suffers a decline in popularity, or vice versa, the company may disclose a strategic maturity in its branding which the CEO has not yet arrived at with the branding of himself. What matters, however, is awareness by the organization that research of an alignment through analysis and appropriate corrections is essential, especially in an era where thinking about a brand and who manages it is now inevitable.

These practical evidences are wisely the symptom of the blossoming of numerous contemporary studies, related to the theme of this volume. Apart from those already mentioned, we would like to give a short space to what was probably the progenitor of these studies, at least for its purpose of wanting to provide a theoretical construct of the daily life of a real CEO: Almost half a century ago, in 1973, Henry Mintzberg published *The Nature of Managerial* Work,[19,16] in which he represented the results of a research conducted on the observation of *working behavior* of five CEOs. Based on his observations, Mintzberg formulated 10 possible managerial roles in the volume and 13 propositions designed to define the characteristics of managerial work based on the theoretical assumption that it is the structural conditions that largely determine managerial behavior. For example, Mintzberg examined a week's work of five American CEOs in profoundly different contexts (including the director of a hospital, the president of a manufacturing company, and the CEO of a

---

[16] Mintzberg Henry, *The Nature of Managerial Work*, New York, Harper & Row, 1973.

consulting company). The observation led Mintzberg to outline behavioral patterns that are still considered reliable today, although outdated by recent studies which enrich and broaden the perspective with new models: A part of the CEO's duties are involved with interpersonal relationships and includes legal and ceremonial duties ("figurehead"); another part is being devoted to motivating, challenging, and incentivizing the employee ("Leader"); while another creates links with the environment outside the organization ("Liaison"). Lastly, there is the "monitor" function, aimed at observing the company and collecting data from their personal network, organized in order to promote a better understanding of the dynamics of the organization, and so on with the functions of "entrepreneur," "spokesperson," "resource allocator," and "negotiator." These are all intuitively understandable and identifiable, even in the behavior of contemporary CEOs, whatever the size and turnover of the company they manage.

Mintzberg's study[17] had and still has the merit of having revealed the *multifunctional and multifactorial components of the CEO figure,* giving the initiation of specific studies on each of them, but most importantly to the study on how the CEO figure is indissoluble from the benefits that he can bring to the company that he directs. Therefore, the complexities of the CEO person must be evaluated not only in situations of risk such as failures, misunderstandings, or instability, but as an extraordinary opportunity to provide corporate communications with a multidimensional prospect. Fundamentally, Mintzberg's study communicates the perspective of CEO branding embodying *total business communication.*[18] This is done through interconnected methods of public objectives to be achieved and complementary tools, as each of the functions of a CEO is suitable for multiplying the results of single media exposure on different audiences. If discussions on the functions of the CEO from the time of Mintzberg have multiplied exponentially, that of CEO branding is, as we have already stated, at its very beginning. Yet the acceleration in the ways of relating to the stakeholders and the media exposure to which this func-

---

[17] Study passed, commented and implemented by Mintzberg himself as well as fifteen years later by H.Mintzberg. For a more recent reference on the functions see M.B Glick.

[18] E. T. Brioschi, *Total business communication. Profiles and problems for the new century*, Vita e Pensiero, Milano, 2006.

tion is subjected require ever more prompt answers and flexible models. It is worth mentioning at least a few current milestones in the literature on CEO branding.

It is not surprising that the CEO is a crucial factor for the success of a company, they are a "vision builder who runs the company, gives it motivations, has specific duties toward it, is familiar with analyzing and determining the direction it must go in."[19] The CEO applies management skills within their company and coordinates behavior in an adequate coherent manner, bringing their vision and ability of innovation.[20] The CEO is not only a vision setter, a motivator, an analyst, and a task manager,[21] but is also the figure that knows how to take leadership in vision, strategy, financial politics, market orientation, goods and services, corporate culture to differentiate one's own company from those in competition, and preserve the position of acquired strength.[22] Therefore, we can now say that the personal brand of a CEO reflects their core values, passions, and skills, and that the branding of their leadership must reveal competence, standard, and style of a leader. Consequently, we can define a CEO's personal brand as *an individual representation of his personality, values, skills, and leadership that set him apart from other CEOs*. A CEO's personal brand will guide their decisions and will give them the ability to influence other people. Lastly, the personal brand of a CEO reflects the way in which people experience their own relationships with the CEO himself.[23] We can, therefore, consider the CEO brand *a particular category of human brand, which qualifies in a unique manner as CEOs are subject to different needs of stakeholders. They are influenced by their role and identity as manager and are obliged to consider their relationship with the corporate brand.*

---

[19] W. Arruda, "Brand connection", *Executive Excellence*, 21(4), 4, 2004.

[20] D.C. Hambrick, G.D.S. Fukutomi, "The seasons of a CEO tenure", *Academy of Review*, 16, 1991, pp. 719–720.

[21] S.L. Hart, R.E. Quinn, "Roles executives play: CEOs, behavioral complexity, and firm performance", *Human Relations*, 46(5), 1993, pp. 543–574.

[22] A. Atalay, A.S. Yucel, "'CEO' applications in modern sports", *International Journal of Academic Research*, Part B, 5(3), 2013, pp. 19–25.

[23] For a systemization of the literature on the subject see: Chen H.-M, Chung H.-M., "A scale for CEO personal brand measurement", *South African Journal of Business Management*, Volume 48, 2017.

1.5.1 *The Bendisch Model*

In 2013, Bendisch[24] developed what is perhaps the largest conceptual models relating to the CEO brand to date: Understanding both in the perspective of the creator and the stakeholder the constitutive elements in the managerial and human aspects of the CEO, and its purpose in being an adequate tool, understanding which variables and with what mechanisms to constantly carry out a monitoring of the CEO's reputation. As can be seen in Figure 1.1, the "creator" perspective refers to the *CEO brand identity*, where managerial and personal identity converge, while that of the stakeholder sees both of these projected in the *CEO brand reputation*. The alignment of these two perspectives contributes decisively to determining the positioning and equity of the CEO brand: From the combination of input CEO brand identity and output CEO brand reputation, CEO brand positioning is derived. This is essentially how the CEO brand positions itself in the mind of stakeholders, which relates directly to the CEO brand equity, thus the added financial value from the CEO brand.

The creator's perspective is the point on which Bendisch insists, as in the case of the individual and more specifically the CEO, that the nature of human identity is positioned on a scale between two extremes: fixed and stable or fluid and uncertain. Instead, the theoretical framework and management practices are traditionally based on tangible products and services that are relatively fixed and stable. Humans are complex beings, whose nature and character vary according to a long list of factors: role, age, context, emotional state, time, and so on, as a result determining an identity that is changeable, questionable, multifaceted, and socially and historically situated.[25] The managerial identity of the CEO is flexible and can be adapted to different professional situations. Managers reshape their identities through their professional lives depending on the situation, social interaction, culture, and identity of their organizations.

What happens, therefore, is that the creation of the CEO brand identity suffers from a constant change in managerial and human identity, which is structured but can lead to the consequence of "role stress" for the

---

[24] Bendisch F., Larsen G., Trueman M., "Fame and fortune: a conceptual model of CEO brands", *European Journal of Marketing*, 47(3/4), 2013.

[25] Bendisch et al., op cit., page 601.

Figure 1.1   The model of Bendisch[26]

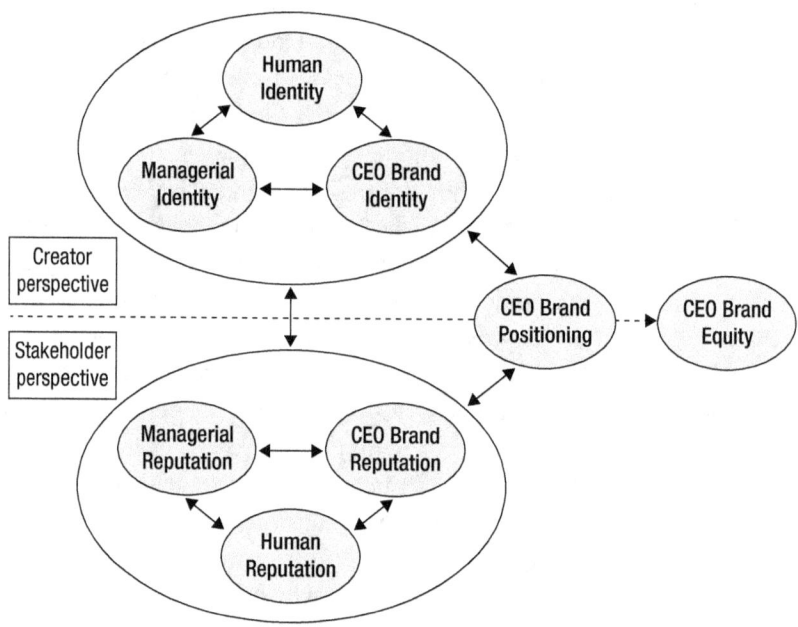

Source: Adapted from F. Bendisch, G. Larsen, M. Trueman, «Fame and and fortune: A conceptual model of CEO brands», *European Journal of Marketing*, 47, ¾, 2013.

CEO, especially if the expectations on building the CEO brand identity clash with the CEOs personal values: "This stress can certainly undermine the value the creator perceives about their brand, especially if put under pressure to hide their individuality or must conform it to their business's interest contrary to their own beliefs, exactly as happens to all of us when managing conflict with reality."[27] However, this potential conflict is specific to human brands and within CEO branding requires the adoption of a guided model not only for conflict management purposes but also for the full exploitation of a fundamental resource to trigger empathy and identification within stakeholders and to create and manage relationships with them.

---

[26] Bendisch et al., op cit., page 608.
[27] Bendisch et al., op cit., page 601.

1.5.2 CEO branding mix: the Fetscherin model

In a study of a few years ago which placed the foundations for a definitive theoretical framework of the subject in question,[28] Fetscherin identified the primary components that make up the "CEO branding mix." Indeed, he has accurately described the theme of theory combined with practice, trying to reach conclusions, thanks to this combination would allow us to understand what a brand CEO should do and represent in real life, starting from this practical question: "What do Mark Zuckerberg, Oprah Winfrey, Richard Branson, and Jeff Bezos have in common? They are not only CEOs and living icons of the brands they created, but they are themselves the brand. There are many reasons why nowadays a CEO has more attention than in the past. When the media is in search of a business story, they often turn to CEOs or founders. Some companies are larger than entire nations in terms of the number of citizens, employees, or turnover. Movie stars communicate and generate expectations about the success of an upcoming movie, while CEOs announce expectations about company performance to the market and more specifically to shareholders. Their personality influences their image and reputation, which are closely linked to the reputation of their companies".[29]

Fetscherin takes on the idea that the CEO brand is made up of two components: image and reputation: These are the perceptions formed within a stakeholder's mind on the CEO's identity, in the present moment regarding image, and over time in relation to reputation[30]. *The CEO brands are therefore complex and unique as the human and managerial profiles converge within the CEO and at the same time create and "feed" their own brand, without being possible to establish a boundary between private life and managerial position.*

The attempt of Fetscherin and his model of CEO branding mix is to create a tool that, which while evaluating and understanding the possible distance between the projection that the CEO makes of his identity in an image and reputation and the perception of stakeholders over time

---

[28] M. Fetscherin, "The CEO branding mix", cit.

[29] From Fetscherin Mark, "The CEO Branding Mix", *Journal of Business Strategy*, Vol. 36 NO. 6, 2015, page 22-28, Emerald Group Pub. Lim., page 22.

[30] J. Cornelissen *et al.*, "Corporate Communications: A Practice-based Theoretical Conceptualization", op cit.; F. Bendisch, G. Larsen, M. Trueman, "Fame and fortune: a conceptual model of CEO brands", op cit.

and space, is able to align the CEO brand with the corporate brand so that the CEO becomes the company's ambassador. The complexity of this management also stems from the fact that Fetscherin realizes that all these elements are interrelated, cyclical, and intertwined: It is this CEO branding mix that has an individual and collective impact on the company's performance and reputation. The model focuses on both the influence that the CEO brand may have on financial aspects (including profit and performance) as well as nonfinancial elements (such as reputation, trust, and attractive capacity for individuals).

In the CEO branding mix (Figure 1.2), two elements are connected to the image of CEO, the CEO person and the CEO personality, while CEO prestige and performance are references to the reputation of a CEO. These are the four "Ps" which represent the critical factors to manage to constantly increase the positive impact of the CEO brand.

The systematization of CEO branding mix aims to alert the management and property: Analysts and investors see the CEO as the embodiment of the company, even more so if they are its founder. Fetscherin also affirms that consumers see the CEO as an authentic brand ambassador. This is why the CEO brand must become part of the company brand whether the CEO or the company wants this or not, and it must be able to be built, measured, and managed, like all other aspects of corporate reputation. The 4Ps should constitute the management framework to evaluate and identify projected and perceived inconsistencies between the image and reputation of the CEO, and consequently decide what

Figure 1.2   The 4Ps of the CEO branding mix

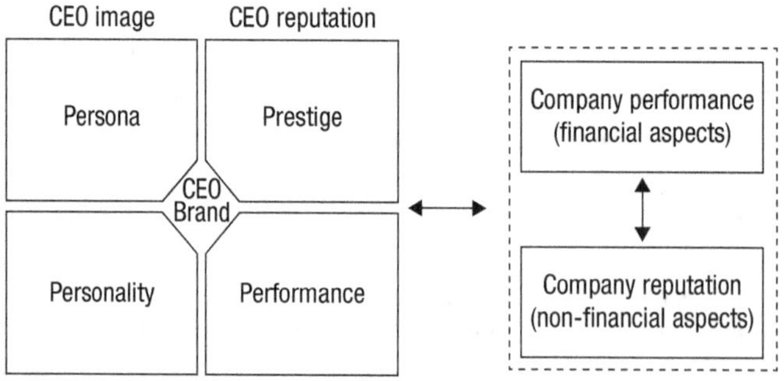

Source: Adapted from M. Fetscherin, «The CEO branding mix», *Journal of Business Strategy*, vol. 36, n. 6, 2015, pp. 22-28: p. 23.

actions and corrections to take. To be concise, it is worth understanding the specifics of some practical indications deriving from the Fetscherin model regarding the CEO person and personality. In the next paragraph, we will consider the theme of CEO prestige as a founding reputational component.

As for the person, Fetscherin refers to a cultural vision of the other, thus emphasizing that people not only formulate judgments based on physical characteristics, such as age, gender, and skin color but also on characteristics such as education, social status, appearance, and facial expressions. Another element of judgment concerning the CEO and their "power": Founders usually get more attention from the media, while in those who aren't founders, CEO duality (meaning that a CEO is also president of the board) and CEO tenure (years spent as a CEO) can both have a positive or negative impact. At the beginning of their term, CEOs tend to devote themselves more to the interests of their companies, but as they age, they tend to prioritize their personal interests. Physical appearance also has importance: There are studies[31] that show that there is a positive relationship between the attractiveness of the CEO and the company's performance. Attractive individuals are not only treated better but perceived as more intelligent and socially competent. However, Fetscherin also points out that within companies, people with childish features are more credible during a crisis, while during a typical routine, they are perceived as incompetent and weak. This brings to the conclusion that childish features could be an obstacle in a potential position of weakness.

Fetscherin distinguishes between the positive and negative traits of variable personality. Positives include honesty, humility, loyalty, faithfulness, charisma, and modesty and in a CEO are qualities loved by employees and the media. Carl Elsener, the owner of Victorinox, and Ingvar Kamprad, founder of IKEA, are examples of "humble" CEOs.[32]

---

[31] N.O. Rule, N. Ambady, "The face of success: Inferences from chief executive officers' appearance predict company profits", *Psychological Science*, 19(2), 2008, pp. 109–111.

[32] On humility as a competitive trait in the CEO-brand creation see: A.Y. Ou, A.S. Zsui, A.J. Kinicki, D.A. Waldman, Z. Xiao, L.J. Song, "Humble chief executive officers' connections to top team integration and middle managers' responses", *Administrative Science Quarterly*, vol. 59, no. 1, 2014, page 34–72. The study explores the concept of humility among CEOs and the process through

"The ladder of humanity goes from the highest extreme leading to poor self-esteem, to the lowest where the CEO appears arrogant, egotistical and self-referential. Finding the right balance is a struggle for every CEO," Fetscherin concludes.[33]

Furthermore, there are negative personality traits, such as Machiavellianism which provides abuse for others for lack of morality and personal interests, and narcissism which similar to humility can have both positive and negative effects depending on its level. If arrogance, lack of empathy, and inability to listen are signs of exaggerated narcissism and bring negative effects on a company, pride or great vision (which can be traits of some narcissists) can have positive implications. As Fetscherin states, George Soros and Jack Welch were not only "productive narcissists," but they were also charming people able to convince others.

1.6   CEO branding before anything else: the possible risks of an excellent reputation

The CEO's reputation alone is not sufficient to create positive value for the organization. It works as a catalyst only if CEO branding is aligned with corporate branding: Only in this way can the role of the CEO pursue the improvement of corporate reputation and bring value to the overall performance of the company.

If the CEO goes after his own performance in reputation without this being governed by the branding activity of its own company which it coordinates, the risk is different: the so-called "burden of celebrities"[34] can

---

which this is connected to integration of the answers of the top and to the answers of the middle management examining representants of 328 top and 645 middle managers of Chinese private companies. The study concludes that the humility of CEOs is positively related to the behaviors of leadership which is related to the organizational empowerment. If the CEO is humble, the top managers feel that their work achieves purpose, have more trust in themselves, and are more motivated to collaboration, share information, while middle managers feel to be more co-involved and show a higher commitment.

[33] M. Fetscherin, "The CEO branding mix", op cit.

[34] Segnalo tra gli altri da C.J. Fombrun, *Reputation: Realizing Value from the Corporate Image*, op. cit. e da J.B. Wade, J. Porac, T. Pollock, S. Gran, "The Burden of Celebrity: The Impact of CEO Certification Contests on CEO Pay and Performance", *Academy of Journal*, 49(4), 2006, pp. 64.

be one of the worst consequences. The expectations of stakeholders rise beyond measure and become more and more difficult to satisfy, forcing managers to adopt increasingly risky strategies or leading stakeholders to change their attitude toward the organization, which will negatively influence performance. Humility of the CEO is positively associated with the behavior of leadership oriented toward organizational empowerment. If the CEO is humble, top managers feel that their work acquires meaning, have more self-confidence, and are more motivated to collaborate and share information, while middle managers feel more engaged and are more involved. Second, a CEO with an excellent reputation that places a high degree of confidence in their abilities and actions to the point of considering themselves unfailing can bring this confidence to such an extreme that the resulting hubris could lead the CEO and their own company to reckless initiatives and to an uncertain future that again will negatively affect performance.

Last but not least, the cannibalization that award-winning and recognized CEOs undergo must be considered, which forces them to spend a lot of time in public and private occupations outside the company (such as writing books, giving interviews, or assuming responsible positions) which they instead would have spent on management: Again, this influences the process of decision-making and therefore performance.

The consideration of all these possibilities has led various studies to conclude that CEOs with a high reputation are inclined to be less efficient, while Fetscherin believes that the risk is presented with the inability of management between the 4Ps and the dimension of CEO prestige: "There are two schools of thought. The first: the 'efficient contrasting hypothesis' establishes that CEOs with a positive reputation are more inclined to act in the interest of their own company. The second: the 'rent extraction hypothesis' shows that top-rated CEOs place too much emphasis on their career progress and act more in their own interest than in that of their own company."[35]

Among the pioneers of reputational management, at a level of both prestige and performance, we cite Steve Jobs who brought the concept of CEO to a brand-new level: "His image and reputation as CEO were so positive that when he announced his resignation on August 24, 2011,

---

[35] See M. Fetscherin, "The CEO branding mix", *Journal of Business Strategy*, Vol. 36 NO 6, 2015, page 22- 28, Emerald Group Pub. Lim., page 23.

Apple shares lost almost 3% that day, for a corresponding ten billion dollars' worth of the company. The short-term effect of that sale immediately after Jobs announcement was driven by a lack of trust in the fact that Apple would continue to perform under his guidance. A negative example of a CEO brand is that of Daniel Vasella, CEO and president of Novartis. When he resigned on January 26th, 2010, shares gained 2%, and they gained another 3.5% when he resigned as president on January 23rd, 2013, based on the announcement of the change in leadership and strategy."[36]

1.7 Guidelines for setting strategy and management of the CEO brand

In conclusion, we can summarize what we have seen so far in an objective and guidelines to consider when addressing the creation of a strategic plan of CEO branding and how to manage it.

1.7.1 *Objective*

The CEO creates a brand of themselves and acts like a brand: will have to promote themselves with the aim of creating engagement with stakeholders, being pleasing to them, gaining approval, creating, maintaining, and improving their reputations.

1.7.2 *Guidelines*

1. Corporate branding and CEO branding must be aligned in a holistic and strategic vision of corporate communication: A soul-searching process is therefore necessary to be carried out by top managers and grounded by an evaluation process on effectiveness and efficiency of the projection of corporate identity in image and reputation. This allows an evaluation of how to maintain alignment and coherence or any pathological situations in the relationship between corporate branding and CEO branding.

---

[36] See M. Fetscherin , *The CEO branding mix*, cit, page 22.

2. Maintaining the achieved alignment and following a strategic plan requires knowledge and consideration of various factors, of which the positive or negative impacts on company performance must be constantly evaluated. It is therefore necessary to adopt a framework that is theoretical and solid.

3. The pressure of stakeholders and the media exposure that increase the volatility of intangible assets are at an all-time high: Therefore, constant and coordinated monitoring is essential in every activity of the CEO, both internal and external to the organization, as well as the possibility to resort to corrections to and implementations in a fluid and flexible way.

4. The demand for brand differentiation and the human factor that qualifies and makes every CEO unique are decisive elements for giving the CEO branding tool the value of its competitive advantage. Customization of CEO branding strategies related to the objectives deriving from the vision, values, culture, and corporate climate is therefore essential for each company. If it is decisive to learn about strategies, beliefs, and values that underpin the behavior of other CEOs, it is absolutely not recommended to not absolutize the behavior of corporate CEO competitors or partners for the benchmark.

Appendix. The CEO Branding Management and Company Reputation in the Digital Age

by Giorgio del Mare[37]

The concept of CEO branding, that is, the influence on the corporate characteristics of a top figure has undergone several changes in recent years. "Forced" digitization, which affected everyone without distinguishing between those who are enthusiastic or resistant to technological change, has led companies and top managers to reconsider their own business strategies and the range of tools used to follow them effectively. The strong willingness to continue to exist in the future leads cyclically to a review of one's own identity profile and of everything that comes as

---

[37] CEO ProperDelMare Consulting.

a corollary of this. Despite themselves, CEOs have sometimes had to react to the media revolution on the web and review through risks and opportunities, its external and internal communication, marking a new phase in the relationship between leadership and the reference market. In the first part of these reflections on the theme, I will analyze how the phenomenon has evolved in the direction of making inseparable the personal reputation of the leader from the corporate image and how this affects the audience of customers and consumers. We will then take a look at the current Plat Firm Age, a business model that requires constant interaction with the ecosystem and how the "social leader" is its beating heart. After a review of case studies on how visionary CEOs impacted the company's reputation, I will close the reflections with a passage on the evolution of the communication from top management in the near future.

A.1   *From corporate branding to CEO management*

In the past, often external communication of companies has dealt with creating a positive image, sometimes very distant from the reality of the organization toward the general public. This approach, with the evolution in various directions of the analytical capacity of all stakeholders, is now outdated, overtaken by some time by the exponential growth of attention to company reputation. The reputation, contrary to the "test-tube experiments," is clear not from well-executed cosmetic operations, but from the judgments given in a determined timeframe toward the actual work of the organization, through their members that are considered more representative: A reputation that is as positive as possible constitutes an asset of huge value, capable of significantly contributing to business success. If the consumer is, in fact, increasingly digital, on the other hand, it is increasingly more sensitive to the perception of the ethical sphere that connotes this brand, an aspect that comes to weigh in the choice of a product or service in a manner of similar quality to what is offered. In this, the involvement of the CEO in the development and implementation of communication strategies is strong, very strong, which sees them as increasingly relevant and proactive. They "are the company," when they speak it is the organization itself to express a thought, when they act it is its mark that moves with them, with continuously less distinctions (unfortunately) between the public/professional sphere and the private sphere. In light of this phenomenon, for several years even in Old Europe, the more enlightened leaders have left behind the figure of the distant and unreachable leader, locked up in dusty rooms, and completely impervious to the thought coming from the bottom of the pyramid, to adopt attitudes which could venture us to define ourselves more the USA style.

Even before the advent of the digital revolution in the American context, we were witnessing the use of what, paraphrasing a very popular definition, we could define flatline communication. A communication that rejects the old hierarchical model of top-down information transfer, with its inevitable distortions of the message level after level, instead of reaching the entire population at the same time all the corporate population—insightful, concise, and clear communication. A communication that is directed toward the outside often aims to create connections with the "man in the street," the average consumer of the product, like a market increasingly sensitive to empathy, involvement, and inspirational power. Sometimes, this can be done by emphasizing on their lack of academic training or past defeats rather than present successes, on the constant and inexhaustible need to continue learning especially from younger collaborators. A leader who talks with his employees and not at his employees, developing a leadership model that Groysner and Slind have defined as "organizational conversation.[38]" This model shuns any kind of one-way or fragmented communication (newsletters, open letters, etc.) preferring face to face wherever possible, as well as interactive digital tools such as forums and company chats, to generate an inclusive and constructive dialog with the entire population of the company. This conversational style, of great immediacy and effectiveness, when brought to a level of external communication, is the basis of what we can define as CEO branding or the "exploitation" and enhancement of communication skills of the media leader as a key factor for success. By acting, first of all, on one's own personal reputation toward the public, the CEO can give his company a competitive advantage by placing his figure, almost as if it were a product, by means of marketing mix logics in such a way that it is perceived as of "superior quality" and distinctive attractiveness due to its peculiarities. Fiat, in the Marchionne era, a person to whom I was

---

[38] B. Groysberg, M. Slind, «Leadership is a Conversation», *Harvard Business Review*, June 2012.

very close for human and professional reasons, benefited not only from his immense managerial skills but also from his personal brand, credible and respected throughout the world. For better or for worse, the CEO's brand is embraced by the brand of the company itself, and the fame of one influences the other, consequently significantly impacting not only the turnover rate but also the attractiveness for investors, positive media attention, and even employee retainment capabilities. How many executives today evaluate whether or not to accept an assignment in relation to the specific weight of the position of the CEO on the market?

Depending on each different case, the first is a consequence of the second, or the relationship is inverse. There is undoubtedly a relationship of direct proportionality between the goodness of the company's reputation and that of the CEO. The key role of the leader's external exposure in increasing the value of the market of your organization is confirmed by a research[39] that highlighted how for 50% of senior executives interviewed in the next few years, the CEO reputation will have an even greater weight than that of the company reputation. At the dawn of the new millennium, business leaders could reach the general public only through direct access to the traditional mass media and attendance during industry events; Internet 2.0 has gradually brought more and more notoriety to those who knew how to ride the tiger, acting as an incredible sounding board for the company's product.

A.2   *Evolution of influencing channels from radio to YouTube*

At the time of the first Greek philosophers, communication was mainly oral, then writing arrived, which Plato used while considering it inferior to dialog as an instrument of knowledge.

"In the hands of those who know how to use it, it is a terrible weapon" wrote Adolf Hitler in his famous book *Mein Kampf*, in reference to the radio and suggesting his idolatry toward the medium. Later came moving images and cinema (of which Triumph des Willens, Riefenstahl's undisputed masterpiece is the most shining example of how the artistic peaks can meet propaganda) became an effective card in the game of persuasion of the masses. To date, the image is the new dominant language

---

[39] «The CEO reputation premium: Gaining advantage in the engagement era», Weber Shandwick/KRC Research, 2015.

that seems to relegate the written word to the ancillary role, since people are more willing to watch rather than read.

A Canadian study[40] carried out by Microsoft on a sample of 2,000 interviews found that the modern obsession with multitasking at any cost reduced a man's average concentration time to just 8 seconds, comparable to the attention of a goldfish. It is, therefore, easy to think of social media with its multimedia as a main tool to survive within our society of images and distraction. Facebook, Twitter, LinkedIn, and newer platforms such as Pulse and Medium are just some of the new arrows that digitalization has given to the CEOs' bow to breakthrough to the heart of consumers.

Being social, however, does not automatically mean creating engagement around one's personal brand and social networks, like any other tool in human hands, it only makes sense if used consistently with the brand positioning strategy.

The medium is the message McLuhan stated in 1964, reminding us that the means we use to communicate is not neutral at all, but it does influence itself beyond the content that we are trying to get across. LinkedIn for its professional nature is probably the most used, but the sector in which CEOs operate heavily influences the methods and channels used for communication. The business-to-business (B2B) industry has very different needs than Public Relations or Apples business-to-customer (B2C). It is certain that a low-cost platform through which to story tell in front of a potentially infinite audience is an opportunity that many top managers have wanted to seize. CEOs transformed into Chief Story Tellers mix stories related to their work with those related to their private life to express their own vision and support managerial decisions that have been made and reveal points of strength and weaknesses by approaching their target audience. This is to impose their personal *Weltanschauung*. Consequently, we are able to connect to the brand whose narration has transformed into a structured value which we perceive in tune with our, with our way of looking at and experiencing our work, holidays, everyday life. Online, there are numerous examples of CEO bloggers with a strong influence on a very large audience.

Brain Chesky, who is in charge of Airbnb, the online platform which has revolutionized the world of hospitality, registers around 70,000 fol-

---

[40] C. Hooton, «Our attention span is now less than that of a goldfish, Microsoft study finds», www.independent.co.uk, 13th May 2015.

lowers on Medium, over 351,000 on Twitter, and 174,000 on LinkedIn. In all of his posts (of all kinds: stories, personal anecdotes, company life, etc.), he always inserts references to Airbnb's corporate culture or the travel theme addressed by various perspectives.[41]

The personal brand of Richard Branson, founder of Virgin, is even larger than his creation. He has more than 18 million followers on LinkedIn and is able to like few others in the world to add value to the range of company products, so much so that we ask ourselves what Virgin's value would be without its posts on agile work and well-being within the workplace environment. His career as a writer shows how much he is loved by the general public as an icon of his perspective on life as well as business.

These are just the first names that come to mind. Platforms such as Pulse and Medium are now full of "internal influencers" within the company who communicate with their users through personal stories, company insights, anecdotes, and much more, with personal and informal communication aimed at creating positive emotions around their image, strengthening the sense of empathy toward their behavior.

A.3   *Characteristics of the leading influencer*

What is fundamental among the characteristics of the influencer leader is in fact the sense of proximity to the customer, experiencing the brand or product not from the inside but from a very different perspective, perhaps more attentive to the needs of stakeholders while remaining in the shoes of the customer. The perfect knowledge of the Customer Experience that is being offered, step by step, is the extra weapon.

On average, 80% of CEOs are convinced they are offering a first-class customer experience, but only 8% of customers agree.[42]

"I never knew of any kid who grew without the Passat poster in their room," said Sergio Marchionne, demonstrating that he fully understood what kind of emotions arose from having the steering wheel of that particular model between their hands. Another essential feature is the understanding of the context, knowing how to "connect the dots," making correlations between things that are only apparently unrelated: clues that

---

[41] See https://medium.com/@bchesky.

[42] F.F. Reichheld, B. Hamilton, R. Markey, «Closing the delivery gap: How to achieve true customer-led growth», 5th October 2005, www.bain.com.

emerge from market research, specific market actions that we want to see connected in a unitary vision, elements which help us imagine a possible future, and a new product whose less known performance can be combined with the needs (clarified or not) of a specific type of customer.

Integrity and credibility instead form the ethos, which according to Aristotle, alongside logos and pathos composes the three "musketeers of persuasion." Ethos, the character assumed by the speaker to gain the trust of the audience, is an excellent persuasive tool but totally ineffective when not supported by these other two characteristics. Much of the ability to persuade in fact depends on the interlocutor, on their human and professional history and who they represent. This also depends on their ability to apologize and admit errors or omissions in the management activity. In the digital age, limiting the outputs of big bosses to applause and celebrations no longer pays. It is no coincidence that a certain Zuckerberg, a master of CEO branding, was forced to sign an open letter of apology regarding what happened in relation to the data processing of users who use his social platform.

Ambition, never being satisfied with the successes that have been achieved but walking fast toward future challenges, has great media effectiveness and easily captures the attention of both the customer and the best talent around, always on the hunt for new stimuli.

In 2014, Fortune magazine attributed some of Google's success to its own chief Larry Page, called "The most ambitious CEO in the world;[43]" it is impossible not to know Elon Musk precisely because he did not stop neither in front of the 22 million dollars received by Compaq for its City Guide publishing company nor to the 156 that EBay "paid out" for its PayPal. Instead, he launched his personal challenge to the stars of futuristic memory with SpaceX and convinced that he can bring man to Mars in 2019, something that as this is being written has not yet occurred. A case in which ambition is strong enough to wash his personal brand from the stains caused by unorthodox Twitter.[44]

---

[43] M. Helft, «Google's Larry Page: The Most Ambitious CEO in the Universe», https://fortune.com, 13th November 2014.

[44] Famous for his gaffes, Elon Musk has often sent out bizarre and inconsistent messages with his image. An emblematic example is the tweet regarding his intention to take the company off the American stock market, which cost him a $40 million fine from the SEC, the American regulatory authority, and the Chairmanship of Tesla.

Finally, I would mention the ability to persuade. In complex organizations, the CEO is the person ultimately responsible for the behavior consciously consistent with the corporate values and objectives of each individual belonging to the company: They are the figure who needs a widespread awareness within a more or less hierarchical structure made up of hundreds of people. It's clear that those who bring with them success stories in this field are often born influencers, who are able to bring others to their own positions without appealing to the hierarchical level.

What Jeff Bezos founded the Amazon empire on was his knowledge of persuasive communication: The algorithms of his creation, capable of instantly matching customers with the desired objects, nothing more than the digital version of the commercial skills of small shopkeepers who knowing their customers well are always able to convince them to buy by offering them goods similar to those already appreciated.

In summary the characteristics of the leading influencer are listed below.

1. Sense of proximity.
2. Understanding context.
3. Integrity and credibility.
4. Ambition.
5. Persuasion skills.

References

W. Arruda, «Brand connection», *Executive Excellence*, 21(4), 4, 2004.

A. Atalay, A.S. Yucel, «"CEO" applications in modern sports management», *International Journal of Academic Research*, Part B, 5(3), 2013, pp. 19-25.

F. Bendisch, G. Larsen, M. Trueman, «Fame and fortune: a conceptual model of CEO brands», *European Journal of Marketing*, 47, 3/4, 2013.

E.T. Brioschi, *Total business communication. Profiles and problems for the new century*, Milan, Vita e Pensiero, 2006.

H.-M. Chen, H.-M. Chung, «How to measure personal brand of a business CEO», *Journal of Human Resource and Sustainability Studies*, vol. 4, 2016, pp. 305-324.

H.-M. Chen, H.-M. Chung, «A scale for CEO personal brand measurement», *South African Journal of Business Management*, vol. 48, 2017.

L.T. Christensen, G. Cheney, «Articulating identity in an organizational age», in S.A. Deetz (ed.), *Communication Yearbook*, 17, Thousand Oaks, Sage, 1994.

J. Cornelissen, T. Bekkum, B. Ruler, «Corporate communications: A practice-based theoretical conceptualization», *Corporate Reputation Review*, 9, 2006.

M. Fetscherin, «The CEO branding mix», *Journal of Business Strategy*, vol. 36, n. 6, 2015, pp. 22-28.

C.J. Fombrun, «Reputation: Realizing value from the corporate Image», Harvard, *Harvard Business School Press*, 1996.

R.C. Gambetti, S.P. Quigley, *Managing corporate communication: A cross-cultural approach*, New York, Palgrave Macmillan, 2013.

M.B. Glick, «The role of chief executive officer», *Advances in Developing Human Resources*, 13(2), 2011, pp. 171-207, https://doi.org/10.1177/1523422311415642.

S. Gorbatov, S.N. Khapova, E.I. Lysova, «Personal branding: Interdisciplinary systematic review and research agenda», *Frontiers in Psychology*, vol. 9, 2018.

B. Groysberg, M. Slind, «Leadership is a Conversation», *Harvard Business Review*, June 2012.

J.E. Grunig, L.A. Grunig, K. Sriramesh, Y.H. Huang, A. Lyra, «Models of public relations in an international setting», *Journal of Public Relations Research*, 7, 1995.

D.C. Hambrick, G.D.S. Fukutomi, «The seasons of a CEO tenure», *Academy of Management Review*, 16, 1991, pp. 719-720.

S.L. Hart, R.E. Quinn, «Roles executives play: CEOs, behavioral complexity, and firm performance», *Human Relations*, 46(5), 1993, pp. 543-574.

M. Helft, «Google's Larry Page: The Most Ambitious CEO in the Universe», https://fortune.Üom, 13th November 2014.

C. Hooton, «Our attention span is now less than that of a goldfish, Microsoft study finds», www.independent.co.uk, 13th May 2015.

K.L. Keller, «Conceptualizing, Measuring, and managing customer-based brand equity», *Journal of Marketing*, vol. 57, n. 1, 1993, pp. 1-22.

P.J. Kitchen, D.E. Schultz. «A multi-country comparison of the drive for IMC», *Journal of Advertising Research*, vol. 39, n. 1, January 1999.

P. Kotler, *Marketing management*, Millenium Edition, Custom Edition for the University of Phoenix, Boston, Pearson Publishing, 2002.

P. Kotler, W. Pfoertsch, «Being known or being one of many: the need for brand management for business-to-business (B2B) companies», *Journal of Business Marketing*, vol. 22, n. 6, 2007.

H. Mintzberg, *The nature of managerial work*, New York, Harper & Row, 1973.

H. Mintzberg, «The manager's job: folklore and fact», *Harvard Business Review*, vol. 68, n. 2, 1990.

P. Montoya, *The Personal Branding Phenomenon*, Santa Ana, CA, Personal Branding Press, 2002.

A.Y. Ou, A.S. Tsui, A.J. Kinicki, D.A. Waldman, Z. Xiao, L.J. Song, «Humble chief executive officers' connections to top management team integration and middle managers' responses», *Administrative Science Quarterly*, vol. 59, n. 1, 2014, pp. 34-72.

T. Peters, «The brand called you», *Fast Company Magazine*, August 1997.

F.F. Reichheld, B. Hamilton, R. Markey, «Closing the delivery gap: How to achieve trueÜustomer-led growth», 5th October 2005, www.bain.com.

A. Ries, L. Ries, «The 22 Immutable Laws of Branding», *Symphonya. Emerging Issues in Management*, University of Milano-Bicocca, issue 1 Brand E., 2001.

N.O. Rule, N. Ambady, «The face of success: Inferences from chief executive officers' appearance predict company profits», *Psychological Science*, 19(2), 2008, pp. 109-111.

I. Salim, M.S. Malone, Y. van Geest, *Exponential organizations. Il futuro del business mondiale*, Venice, Marsilio, 2015.

N.N. Taleb, *The Black Swan: The impact of the highly improbable*, New York, Random House-Penguin Books, 2007.

N.N. Taleb, *Skin in the game: hidden asymmetries in daily life*, New York, Random House, 2018.

C.B.M. van Riel, J.M.T. Balmer, «Corporate identity: the concept, its measurement and management», *European Journal of Marketing*, vol. 31, n. 5/6, 1997, pp. 340-355.

J.B. Wade, J. Porac, T. Pollock, S. Gran, «The burden of celebrity: the impact of ceo certification contests on CEO pay and performance», *Academy of Management Journal*, 49(4), 2006, pp. 643-660.

Weber Shandwick/KRC Research, «The CEO reputation premium: Gaining advantage in the engagement era», 2015.

2 From Seducer to Pioneer: The Four Steps Toward the Post-pandemic

by Stefania M. Vitulli

"Communication: if not love, then advertising."

Enrico Ghezzi

2.1 The "Golden Age": the seductive CEO. From the 1950s to the 1980s

In the beginning, they were one unit. Company and stakeholders did not need to be distinguished from each other because it was unthinkable that one could live without the other. The mesmeric range of action of brand communication was like that of old photographs, which assume credibility for the mere act of existing, to have withstood time, to be a testimony to events. The company sent out the message with certainty that it would reach the right recipient at the right time, with the right balance between authority, involvement, and satisfaction. They also had a perfectly recognizable tone of voice and an explosive and durable blend of "push and seduce" which has made certain advertisements, press conferences, and speeches to the shareholders of these years (depending on the level of economic development of the countries involved between the 1950s to the first half of the 1980s) pure, unforgettable legend. Not just in memory.

In the "golden age" of the company–stakeholder relationship, the product is king, and the communication humbly holds the train of his clothes. Both the company and its stakeholders radically believe that once created, their relationship can only last forever. The mechanism communication or promotional mix is a vertical monolog in the image and likeness of the classic steps of romantic seduction. Remember the scene in *Titanic* where

Jack Dawson invites Rose DeWitt Bukater to take his hand and follow him to the bow of the ship? Rose follows him, to a point that seems dangerous, overlooking the waves. But this is not enough for Jack: He wants to lead her to another place where there are only the two of them, a world where the rules are established by him and accepted by her, with the result of unforgettable emotions. Rose closes her eyes and does as he says and rises higher poised on the handrail while the ships glide on the sea, the only point of balance is Jack behind her. "Do you trust me?" Jack whispers in her ear. Rose trusts him, and keeping her eyes closed, opens her arms. Now she can open her eyes. It is one of the most famous lines in cinematic history: "I'm flying Jack!" Jack has succeeded in bringing Rose to another world, where it is not necessary to have your eyes closed to believe in the wonderful reality that others have wished for you. A world made exclusively of desire, dreams, and a bright and unstoppable future.

This is the almost uninterrupted process of seduction that for decades, thanks to communication, companies have managed to achieve toward the stakeholder. Thanks to indispensable accomplices such as economic development, technological innovation, media progress, and of course the everlasting hope to forget the two World Wars, it really seemed like the brand would be forever, in a friendly, understandable, authoritative, and credible way, alongside the faithful public. Certainly, the CEOs of medium and large companies in those years had a representative role of the fundamental brand among all stakeholders, just like today. However, they benefited from the positive signs and stability of two factors which starting from the 1980s (in some cases, as early as the 1970s, during and after the energy crisis) would start to oscillate, continuously and inexorably, influenced by the definitive mutation of the external and internal environment of the company and to have an impact on communication which was perhaps manageable, but never more controllable: trust and influence.

"In the 1950s and 1960s, big companies didn't think it was essential to have a famous and charismatic leader: CEOs rarely appeared on the covers of business magazines, employees made careers within the same companies, and traits that were highlighted and promoted were those of playing as a team. The advice of the administration is therefore wiser now, or when they chose solid insiders to govern companies?[1]" This is

---

[1] P. Krugman, *The Conscience of a Liberal*, New York: W. W. Norton, 2009.

what economist Paul Krugman asks in 2007 in *The Conscience of a Liberal,* an essay preceding his Nobel Prize for Economics in which he encompasses almost a century of economic history in the United States. He narrates how a gap was formed between rich and poor in the 20th century, which after a decline in the mid-century has revived in the last two decades, expanding to the point where it reached from the early 1980s to the early 2000s, higher peaks than the last 1920s.

What is interesting about this reconstruction is that Krugman tries to understand how figures of leadership like that of the CEO have become "autonomous" with respect to the management and control of the company board, up to defining the company more than how the company could define them. Before CEOs became Rock Stars however, the situation seemed more "balanced," at least this is how Krugman describes it. "In the corporate world of the 1960s and 1970s, companies rarely paid star wages to managers considered superstars. High wages were seen as an attack on team spirit or a source of potential union problems. In this sort of environment, even a board of directors that truly believed hiring superstar managers was the right way to proceed, certainly did not need to offer exorbitant amounts to attract those same stars[2]." Beyond the opinions of each one, Krugman's reconstruction leads us to clearly identify in those "golden" years a "balance" between internal and external stakeholders, which tends to perpetuate itself as long as holistic and collective logics are preserved and can hardly stand protagonism and eclecticism and those who encourage it. "Assuming there is a market for corporate talent, who exactly would the buyers be?" Krugman asks himself. "Who determines how good a CEO is and how much must be paid to protect yourself from the risk that another company will steal the entrepreneurial know- how? The answer is that the board of directors rely on consultants in the field of salaries, almost always chosen by the CEO, to determine the CEOs value[3]."

Out of provocation, the question asked by Krugman will soon find at the end of this "golden age" between the company and stakeholders a progressive response: It will be the stakeholders themselves who will acquire relevance year after year, as well as on profits, but also on the intangible assets of the company, to the point that their impact on reputation

---

[2] Ibidem.
[3] Ibidem.

will dictate the rules for management of organizations (salary included[4]), and ultimately even for the choice of their top management. This impact immediately created a bond which is known as "outrage constraint," which gave rise to the first cry of stakeholder capitalism in very remote times. However, this is the present and we are still focused on the 1980s.

In the 1980s, there was a forerunner to the revolution that almost 10 years later in the most illuminated organizations impacted the CEOs at the level of brand management applied to one's own figure. This is the person that is linked by academics to what is called *transformational leadership*, beginning from the mid-1980s when the concept of leader is forever detached from that of a simple manager (and from that moment those who want to earn the title will have to work on land that is different and additional, although also complementary to those of management): A leadership that is activated when the one who embodies it is able to lead the organization not only to develop a vision of what it could become, but also to complete this vision and to make the necessary changes for this institution and that are therefore lasting over time.[5]

This man is Lee Iacocca, the CEO who knew how to reach the first objectives that no other leader of any company before then had ever even attempted. Researchers believe that "As a result of Iacocca's leadership Chrysler made record profits, employee morale is at an all-time high and Iacocca was able to generate in them a meaning for the work that they do."[6]

Iacocca had already saved Chrysler in the 1970s with superhuman strength: "Some days in Chrysler I wouldn't even get up in the morning if I could have imagined what would have happened," he recalls in an interview.[7] However, it took the 1980s before he could "expose himself"

---

[4] When the paper came out, he sued one situation in place since the 80s, a situation that denied in practice the theories credited to CEOs as reference figures for a board serving the interests of shareholders. According to the report, it was the CEOs themselves who actually established their economic value for the company, subject only to constraint of any indignation from external pressure groups—public opinion, politicians, at least the same shareholders, able if necessary to cause problems for the organization. A modality that actually led to a disconnect between remuneration and performance.

[5] N.M. Tichy and D.O. Ulrich, "The leadership challenge—A call for the transformational leader", *Sloan Management Review* 26(1), 1984.

[6] N.M. Tichy and D.O. Ulrich, "The leadership challenge", op. cit.

[7] Lee Iacocca, Alex Taylor, "Iacocca in his own words", *Fortune*, August 29, 1988.

and appear for example in advertising campaigns for Chrysler cars. His "Pride is back," with which he referred to the positive consequences of the profound restructuring of the company and was directed to consumers, his way of addressing them with one of the most famous advertising phrases of the 20th century: "If you can find a better car, buy it." This not only became a memorable slogan but a sign for the United States that something could change for the whole country and this occurred through the economy and business leaders even more than the medium of politics and its representatives.

The "Iacocca phenomenon" was something completely different than the familiar faces of corporate bosses that we had become accustomed to in Europe and the United States (two names in particular: Henry Ford and Enzo Ferrari) because it embodied for the first time a vision and style of leadership that had to be formalized and "recommended" as a model to other companies and even other nations. "Iacocca's high level of visibility and notoriety could constitute the fundamental missing element in contemporary management."[8] In the closed-to-total scarcity of models of transformative leadership in those years, in which sad, colorless, charisma-less managers reigned, Iacocca was the first to provide a modus operandi and a tone of voice that would have taken almost 30 years, and several relational crises between the company and stakeholder to become a must.

2.2 Unity cracks: the active-aggressive CEO. The 1990s

How do you go from the seductive whisper of Titanic's Di Caprio (which served us as a metaphor to narrate the start of a romantic and apparently indissoluble relationship between the company and stakeholders) to incitement unbridled by profit, incidentally embodied by the actor himself in *The Wolf of Wall Street* where an unscrupulous boss attacks his employees? "There is no nobility in poverty. I have been a rich man and I have been a poor man and I choose wealth for my entire life." Is this the model of the leader that top managers refer to since the 1980s? And what are the environmental accomplices that lead internal stakeholders and outsiders to listen to this narrative as if it were the only winner?[9]

---

[8] N.M. Tichy and D.O. Ulrich, "The leadership challenge", op. cit.

[9] To refer to another cinematic reference, which clearly delineates the aggres-

On a beautiful sunny day in 1982, more precisely on December 15, Steve Jobs is pictured in a shot that, in addition to becoming famous, proved prophetic: standing above the cube representing the logo of his company, Apple's bitten apple, which was then multicolored, with a confident and almost provocative gaze.

The unity of the principle, between the company and stakeholders, has already undergone very strong shocks. The tone of voice of branded seduction (which is a promise of a romantic story, reminding us of "forever" but not yet true eternal love) has given way to aggression: You don't have to follow me and trust me because we'll be together because I am different from others and I won't betray you, but you need to go out there and shout my name, represent me, and become a witness of my greatness. Exactly as what happens in romantic relationships, small cracks at first and then landslides and collapses have scratched and then irreparably damaged the golden surface of the company–stakeholder agreement. Segmentation and differentiation of markets and goods and services, fair and unfair competition, mismanagement of crisis, economic and financial instability, renewed media power, multiplication of the managerial and initial (but immediately strong) signals that stakeholders are aware of their role, not only on the development of the company's activities and profit, but in the acquisition and maintenance of reputation. The unit cracks because one of the two parties involved in the relationship becomes aware of itself and its own power, while the other in most cases caught off guard, reacts aggressively. In order for the relationship to at least continue by continuing to call itself such (or guaranteeing the company the loyalty and recognizability of its stakeholders), the top-down monolog must become a dialog. The stakeholder must evaluate whether to grant the trust that they used to simply give in exchange for the brand experience, and

---

sive path taken by corporate storytelling in those years, always inspired by the world of finance rather than entrepreneurship, we can mention the even more famous Gordon Gekko/ Michael Douglas speech to shareholders of Teldar Paper in Wall Street by Oliver Stone. "In the days of the free market, when the country was a maximum industrial power, it was made it safe because their money was at stake. Today the management risks nothing in the company." As we know, the ending encourages shareholders to end greed itself, which "would work" to boost profit, far more than in the past where it was balanced, but now reduced to a "bubble"—management. An imperative obligation to give an account to the shareholders. The Carnegies, the Mellons, the men who built this great industrial empire.

timidly start the process of appropriation of part of the influence that the brand previously exercised over him with overwhelming confidence.

What was happening to the CEOs in the meantime? What was the communicational question asked to answer in exercising the highest managerial position in the company of those years? To trying to understand this, let's go back to that wonderful winter day in Cupertino in 1982, when Apple was looking for a new CEO.[10] Steve Jobs was not yet ready to take care of his creation, but he is certain that he knows who would be able to do it: John Sculley. The man in question is an expert on marketing and integrated communication. He is the creator of the campaign that brings PepsiCo to defeat Coca-Cola and become the number one in the soft drink market, he is the gladiator of cola wars, one who certainly does not aim to seduce but to challenge, defeat, and move on to the next goal. Sculley is the perfect witness of the new course of the company–stakeholder relationship and the embodiment of the new CEO model that will establish itself until the 1990s: The marketing man who believes in strong entrepreneurship, in which there are always winners and losers and not at this point (or even ever) "noble causes," and even less "purpose" to oppose a profit/winner.

Steve Jobs knew that for the transition period that Apple awaits before it becomes a global powerhouse (which lasted 10 years) he needed a CEO like Sculley: a man who gave Apple the energy to combine revolutionary technology with an aggressive approach toward the Baby Boomers market. It was no longer a question of taking them by the hand and leading them to the bow of the ship, they couldn't close their eyes, but rather had to keep them wide open and aspire to have a life that made them "suitable" for that product. Steve Jobs was confident in his choice, it was Sculley who hesitated. He felt that Jobs had undeniable charisma, but his business model was hard to understand: "There in front of me were Steve Jobs and Bill Gates (two young boys under thirty) who spoke of their noble cause of enhancing knowledge of workers with tools for the mind, to make them incredibly productive and help them change the way things were done in the world before then, all while entirely new industries were being created in the process. I had never heard of anything similar... I had never heard anyone speak in terms of creating new industries. In my

---

[10] For this story and for what it concerns, see Isaacson, Walter, *Steve Jobs*, Simon&Schuster, 2011.

world it was always a matter of winning shares in the market of industries that already existed."[11] Sculley attends the presentation of Lisa, the new Apple computer, visits the headquarters on the West Coast and most importantly has the opportunity to explain to Jobs the reasons behind his success: With the Pepsi Generation campaign, he wasn't selling a product, but a lifestyle. It was exactly what was needed for the new Mac, a computer that had never been seen before that Jobs would soon debut to the market. It wasn't just to entice fanatics of electronics, but to create the "Apple Generation." However, unlike what would have happened in the "golden age" of communication, the relationship was not born on a seductive basis, but aggressive as Sculley based on shooting power: the investment in advertising would have grown from 15 to 100 million dollars. It took a few months before this could all begin, for two worlds to meet and instead of colliding, creating a buffer which allowed the true narrative revolution that Jobs would have created to establish itself in the future. This was the "Fortune 500" world of Sculley's CEO, Donald Kendall, a pure representative of the seductive "golden age," where a waiter in a white suit attended meetings ready to serve him Pepsi in crystal glasses on silver trays, while he enjoyed a Havana. The world of the Do-It-Yourself economy that would be revealed in its disruptive role between the late 90s and the new Millennium, where not only would the classic dress code stop dominating but eclecticism would become the watchword. Seen from this perspective, the famous phrase that Steve Jobs said to John Sculley and which apparently convinced him to join Apple acquires complexity and becomes a fundamental symbol to summarize not only this step in the evolution of communication in the company–stakeholder, but a key phase in the evolution of the role of the CEO: "Do you want to sell sugared water for the rest of your life or do you want to help me change the world?" The CEO is invested with ethical as well as economical purposes and must decide whether to embody it: The mercenary seducer and the aggressive boss, legacies that Sculley regardless will carry forward in Apple, are preparing to become discarded clothes. With that sentence, with that type of "collaboration offer," the seed of brand policy is planted (and therefore coherent and coordinated CEO branding) which must take into account the birth of the inclusive concept of stakeholders: not only con-

---

[11] Cfr. V. Shah Mbe, "A conversation with John Sculley", *Thought Economics*, June 1, 2017, https://thoughteconomics.com/john-sculley-interview.

tractual interests bind the company and its public, but also ethical values, on the basis of which stakeholders can influence each other and influence the market even without being linked to the company by any economic, financial, or ownership constraints.

Of course, in Job's offer, the type of product counts: Pepsi isn't a lifestyle or a new vision of the world, it is sugared water. However, the symbolic value attributable to the position of the CEO becomes for the first-time founding: if you participate in the life of this company, if you support the spread of this brand, share its ethical value, and carry forward its battle. Sculley's communication strategy (selling not just a product but a lifestyle) in Jobs offers results perfected and enhanced. Translated in these terms, the famous offer from Jobs to Sculley sounds like this: "No longer sell a product as if it were a lifestyle but participate in a project that 'by design' since its birth is regenerative for the future of the world."

2.3   Complexity management: the superstar CEO. The new millennium

It was a slow process at heart, but the trap of retrospective distortion (explained so well by Nassim Nicholas in his book *Black Swan)* makes it seem not only predictable, but overwhelming and pressing. In about 10 years (from the early Nineties to the first years of the new Millennium), the consumer was transformed so deeply that neither seduction nor aggression nor a mix of the two could convince him or guide his decisions. At the same time, the very concept of stakeholder had, as we said, expanded to the point that it was no longer possible to identify economic and market or contractual interests as the only ones to have an impact on the organization and its activities, but it was necessary to consider among the guiding principles of the stakeholders with a balance between corporate reputation or ethical values. The companies found themselves taking on social responsibilities, being aware that the motivations and the consequences of their actions had to generate not only profit but also an advantage for the community and not damage or exploit the territories in an unfair way.[12]

---

[12] The three most complete and used definitions of Corporate Social Responsibility in the managerial and global governance fields were born in those years:

The consumer demands a dialog and beyond: In this dialog, his position is not defined once and for all, but it changes in relation to the answers it receives not only from the company but also thanks to the comparison with other consumers or ethical stakeholders. Technology, for the first time in human history, allows consumers and soon all corporate stakeholders to be involved in real time in a communicative and narrative confrontation with the company and to be able to emanate a communicative flow that slowly but surely conquers real power in the reputational arena. Internet, firstly with Web 1.0, followed by online interaction in real time with Web 2.0 and what will follow from ranking to social networks to apps. These are all aspects that generate a complexity that for the time asks companies to be present 24 hours a day and 7 days out of 7 in the communication flow. Globalization will add to this complexity a further stratification which will reflect on the awareness and ability to manage cross-cultural opportunities and barriers, while communities of stakeholders are able to communicate on brands, products, and services connected to them independently of the times, methods, and tones of voice decided by the brands themselves.

In a short period of time, the ability of companies to communicate their identity to generate image catalogs that over time turn into positive reputations to be maintained as such must be accompanied by the ability to constantly monitor the generative and transformative activity of stakeholders online about image and reputation and find innovative ways to penetrate this activity in order to influence it. The risk that autonomy, awareness, and real communication power of stakeholders lead every second to a potential reputational attack counterpoints the extraordinary opportunity that stakeholders become, at a very low cost, unthinkable

---

"The commitment of business to contribute to sustainable economic development, working with employees, their families, the local community and society at large to improve their quality of life." World Business Council for Sustainable Development, 1999, and the following year, the same World Business Council for sustainable development extended and specified: «Corporate social responsibility is the continuing commitment by business to behave ethically and contribute to economic development while improving the quality of life of the workforce and their families as well as the local community and society at large»; «A concept whereby companies integrate social and environmental concerns in their business operations and in their interaction with their stakeholders on a voluntary basis», Commission of the European Communities, 2001.

and unexpected, the most credible ambassadors of corporate communication, whether it is this or brand management. New consumers are identified as co-creators of value,[13] or even prosumer, with a term coined by Alvin Toffler in 1980,[14] which then returned to the limelight almost a quarter of a century later, thanks to the real and digital possibility to continuously involve the consumer in the creation of the product.

Building mechanisms that induce him to express himself, concretely or in an aspirational way on how, when, and why a product should be born, change, evolve, or simply "put it to work" on that particular product—from getting gas online to opening an online bank account.[15]

It is inevitable that this Copernican revolution also involved the figure of the CEO: It is precisely the time between the late 90s and early 2000s, up to the crisis of 2008 which will mark a setback and together will have an accelerating power on this process where superstar CEOs are born and affirmed, and it is in these years that the seeds are planted for the approach we have called CEO branding, and which will fully develop in the decades with the models we described in Chapter 1.

Now, for the last example of this kind, let's focus on another film featuring Leonardo Di Caprio, which can be seen as a metaphor for this process of intensification of the level of complexity of the management of the company–stakeholder relationship. Think of the scene from *Inception,* where Dominic Cobb "the extractor," the man who made the theft of ideas a possible even if dangerous profession, illustrates to his pupil Arianna how worlds can be generated originating from other people's hearts, how to explore the unconscious in search of these same memories, and how to make them converge so that they lead the unconscious to suggest real decisions based on beliefs whose architecture is based on already artificial foundations. The film is from 2010 and certainly foreshadows

---

[13] Cfr. C.K. Prahalad, V. Ramaswamy, "Co-opting customer competence", *Harvard Business Review*, vol. 78, no. 1, 2000 and also C.K. Prahalad, V. Ramaswamy, "Co-creation experiences: The next practice in value creation", *Journal of Interactive Marketing*, vol. 18, n. 3, 2004. As well as R. Gambetti, G. Graffigna, S. Biraghi, "The grounded theory approach to consumer-brand engagement", *International Journal of Market Research*, vol. 54, no. 5, 2012.

[14] A. Toffler, "The Third Wave", *Morrow*, New York, 1980.

[15] See also G. Ritzer, N. Jurgenson, "Production, Consumption, Prosumption: The nature of capitalism in the age of the digital 'prosumer'", *Journal of Consumer Culture*, issue 10, 1, 2010.

the next decade that led us to the casual manipulation in the creation of images that present to the past, the present, or the possible future. However, the scene is the perfect representation of the complex mechanisms that already acted and heavily influenced the everyday of the previous decade: heavily rooted on the web, globalization, and the awareness of their roles. The multiple factors of stakeholder feedback toward companies definitely undermine every top-down process put in place, from companies to the stakeholders themselves.

Companies react effectively and efficiently to the transformation in progress, starting early or at least "on time" toward that historical moment and we will see, starting from the 2010s, that the social imprint that the company leaves becomes an integral part not only of the vision, but of the mission of the company itself. Or if not, that it is reluctant to abandon any "bossy" attitude toward stakeholders. It is certain that for the first time, the CEO figure not being "ashamed" can have possibilities for the tangible and intangible resources of the company, with an unprecedented, replicable, and even scalable impact. The basis for the Mark Zuckerberg, Jeff Bezos, Oprah Winfrey, Richard Branson, or Steve Jobs to ideally continue the storytelling undertaken following the path of John Sculley is ready. CEOs become brands in the moment where the level of complexity is so high that as soon as a possible simplification is within reach (for example for the media, the possibility of creating a unique and human catalyst for the whole corporate action, the CEO) the opportunity is seized and amplified.

On the other hand, which better strategic graft than the nascent, multifactorial, multifaceted CEO branding could embody the over-stratification of tactics to positively influence the corporate reputation that multiply starting from the new Millennium? To give an example, in a long article entitled "Rebuilding corporate reputations,"[16] the *McKinsey Quarterly* managed to rank in 2009 (the dark period immediately following the financial crisis) at least nine ways of building relationships with the media that went "beyond the classic models of public relations." "In this more complex world of influence strategy, no single kind of approach is likely to be sufficient to deal with fast-moving situations. Companies must instead initiate a multidisciplinary, cross-functional effort that can

---

[16] S. Bonini, D. Court, A. Marchi, "Rebuilding corporate reputations", *McKinsey Quarterly*, June 1, 2009.

quickly identify reputational issues and plant responses in broader strate-gy, operations, and communications. The groups involved might include regulatory affairs, the general counsel, PR or corporate communications, marketing, CSR, and investor relations."[17] They preached the consul-tancy formats of that article: from *war rooms* created to respond in real time to the bombardment of news with the desired objective of "Leaving no attack without a reaction, no reporter without an answer," to *surro-gates*, highly credible individuals hired or artfully placed in positions of power to reinforce strategic messages so that "people with star power could speak in favor of the company." Each of these tactics, beyond their intrinsic value, demonstrates that the indissoluble unity of the relation-ship between company and stakeholders during the Golden Age was first cracked, then shattered, or it has become "liquid" as Zygmunt Bauman has taught us, and it turns to such an irrecoverable point as to require extraordinary interventions.

To put into practice that multidisciplinary and cross-functional effort that McKinsey advised 12 years ago, companies had to multiply skills and investments in communication and create highly flexible models. It is now beyond doubt that a truly extraordinary contribution to rebuilding reputation during the post-financial crisis was provided by taking risk and the taking up of responsibility (even "inflated" to the point of being assimilated to the mechanisms of show business) by the celebrity CEOs on the new direction of the relationship between company and stake-holders. Indeed, in some cases, it is clear how the behavior of the beloved and hated CEOs (an article in the 2002 Harvard Business Review was headlined "The curse of the superstar CEO"[18]) provided inspirational models for the transformation of internal and external communication processes of the company.

Chris Malone, author of *The Human Brand*[19] called this "heat" or even "charisma" (as the HBR article cited above defined the quality that makes a CEO a guide) and cites the New Testament. In one passage, the apostle Paul lists the various charisms or gifts of the Holy Spirit,

---

[17] S. Bonini, D. Court, A. Marchi, op cit., 2009.

[18] R. Khurana, "The curse of the superstar CEO", *Harvard Business Review*, September 2002.

[19] C. Malone, S.C Friske., *The Human Brand. How We Relate to People, Prod-ucts, and Companies*, Jossey-Bass, 2013.

and good leaders are also dotted with these qualities. Among these, we find members of the Church with extraordinary powers such as speaking in different languages or working miracles. A few lines later, the same source cites Jeffrey Garten, rector of the Yale School of Management who in his essay *The Mind of the CEO* described his first meeting with Michael Armstrong, CEO of AT&T: "He radiated confidence, enthusiasm, and energy of an experienced politician. You got the feeling that if you found yourself shooting a move and asking for a CEO to the casting director, he would certainly have brought you Michael Armstrong."[20] Such powers however in the CEO arena were in short supplied until the end of the 20th century, so much so that if we had to indicate the supreme precursors of the superstar CEO we would definitely turn to Lee Iacocca and Steve Jobs, and other names would only appear when looking much lower. With the 2000s and the birth of new global corporations, it will become at first difficult and later impossible to separate the successes and failures of a brand from those of its CEO: The brand reputation embodied by the CEO will become in the best moments, the flagship to be exhibited on official communication channels and to be fed to the media in dark times, the treasure to rely on while the company tries to recover lost positions in the real and digital scoreboard of global reputation.

However, as we said, from Lee Iacocca onwards, the model will take almost 30 years to become essential, so much so that in the cases of crises mentioned in the corporate records of this century, we have to wait until the end of the 2010s, because to revive the intangible fortunes of a brand, we must draw on the branding of a relevant CEO. We think of the deep crisis of *Nike* between 2001 and 2008 and the repeated criticisms received for the exploitation of child labor in developing countries, with the authoritative attacks of Naomi Klein in *NoLogo*[21] and the documentaries of Michael Moore. We think of the Mattel products crisis, which in the summer of 2007 had to collect over 20 million copies of its own toys (including Barbie dolls) that were made in China due to brain damage caused by ingestion of toxic substances released on contact and containing lead paints. Let's think about what happened to Nestle in 2008,

---

[20] J. Garten, *The Mind of the CEO: The World's Business Leaders Talk About Leadership, Responsibility the Future of The Corporation, And What Keeps Them Up at Night*, New York, New York, Basic Books, 2001.

[21] N. Klein, *No Logo*, New York, Picador, 1999.

when tens of thousands of babies were poisoned by contaminated milk and powder that had been produced in China, and four of them died. Today it would be unthinkable that if scandals of this magnitude hit the brands themselves, CEOs wouldn't go into the public eye, and their reactions, utterances, apologies, expressions on social media wouldn't be monitored. Not to mention that the implacable absence of the right to forget, although regulated by law, "imposed" by the network would in fact cause a pillory perpetual to the CEOs involved.

Richard Branson, Elon Musk, Mark Zuckerberg, and Jeff Bezos have led the way so that anyone who comes after them or with them, from David Zaslav to Lisa Su, from Mary Barra to Jack Dorsey, will know that the superstar component in CEO branding may turn out to be a blessing or a curse, and it certainly needs to be tempered and customized as the result of a corporate strategy, as well as requiring from the CEO in addition to total engagement, a consolidated dose of responsibility and awareness of every action in their own personal life ("After Zuckerberg privacy no longer exists"), but is now *conditio sine qua non*. Each CEO then has his own blend of brand and personality, which does not always coincide with wanting to please everybody at all costs. Keeping this in mind, we mention two memorable cases: one of long-term success, the other a transformed communication crisis turned into an opportunity, both embodied with the unmistakable personalities of Michael O'Leary and Guido Barilla.

The linguistic style of the first is unforgettable, presented in speeches intended for all kinds of interlocutors, including the European commission. O'Leary, CEO of Ryanair from 1994, commonly viewed as the creator of low-cost flying, had the habit of addressing professionals in the sector with aggressive and authoritarian epithets which bordered on insult, for example against flight controllers, travel agents, and the European Commission itself. At the same time, he was certainly a "character," giving many other CEOs the opportunity to consider these moments as a game with a "war-like" promotional logic. This creates expectation and attention on the brand, although it risks sacrificing the approval of the more politically correct stakeholders. Instead, there is a specific date of September 25, 2013, for the media eruption caused by Guido Barilla, president of the multinational company of the same time. The particular sentence that caused the scandal was "We won't create advertisements with homosexuals, because we prefer the traditional family. If gays disagree, they can always eat another brand of pasta. Everyone is free to do what they want as long as they don't annoy others," pronounced to the microphones of the transmission *La Zanzara* of Radio24, as an answer to a question on why the brand had never created an advertisement campaign with homosexuals at the center of the narrative. Gay associations, deputies, consumer associations, celebrities, and cultural figures and influencers invite consumers online to boycott the brand at local and global levels, with the hashtag #boycottbarilla in different languages. The ascent to regain the reputation he had lost only in a few minutes (Harvard University removed Barilla from his canteen, one of the immediate consequences) begins the next day with Guida Barilla's apologies: "With reference to my statements made yesterday at *La Zanzara*, I apologize if my words have generated misunderstandings or controversy, if they have hurt the sensibilities of some people. In the interview I simply wanted to emphasize the centrality of the women within the family. For clarity I would like to point out that I have maximum respect for any person without any distinctions. I have the utmost respect for gays and for the freedom of expression of anyone. I have also said, and I repeat that I highly respect gay marriages. Barilla in its advertisements represents the family because it welcomes everyone and since the beginning identifies with our brand."

The next steps are memorable and identifiable with a flawless strategy to manage a crisis. Already in his message of apology, Barilla affirmed his desire to "meet the members of the group that revolutionized the evolution of the family in the best way, including those I have offended with my words." A week later, the meeting with the national leaders of the Italian LGBT associations takes place and Barilla welcomes the "concrete proposals" from the delegation to remedy the error. About two months later, on November 4, responsibility was passed on to CEO Guido Colzani who is committed at the forefront in communicating strategic steps post-crisis, supporting Guido Barilla, and the company announces that it wants to change its diversity policy: "Diversity, inclusion and equality have long been part of Barillas culture, values and code of ethics. These are reflected in the policies and benefits offered to all staff, regardless of age, disability, gender, race, religion or sexual orientation. At the same time our commitment is aimed to promote diversity because we firmly believe it is the right thing to do."

This was achieved step by step, from the diversity training aimed at 8,000 employees to the health coverage being extended to families and relatives of transgender employees, up to the involvement of gay activists as consultants for change.[22] However, what was most important was Guido Barilla's constant media exposure on the subject, relentlessly reaffirming the brands beliefs on inclusiveness. The company reaches complete rehabilitation in record time, just over year: In November 2014, it holds the perfect score from the Human Rights Foundation, the US association for gay rights, that every year calculates the Corporate Equality Index, a ranking based on internal and external corporate policies which are inclusive for gays, lesbians, and transgenders. Therefore, in 2015, the company could boast that they were the "Best Place to Work for LGBT equality."

For a single sentence, expressed by the top figure, an entire company structurally changes its internal policies and makes one of the most rapid and radical changes of the new Millennium in terms of adapting its ethics. This achievement isn't just one concrete indicator of how the power of CEOs has expanded, but of how their most memorable and effective strategies to solve issues are constantly changing. Stakeholder expectation no longer focuses on the superstar CEO or to the limit of the service of the company and brand on which it exercises governance. The expectations— the satisfaction of which, in addition to maintaining and increasing reputation, is rewarded with the recognition of influence and granting of trust—begin to build on the birth and growth of a new breed of CEO, which the pandemic helped outline in record time with extreme clarity, which we see shortly.

2.4   Post-pandemic leadership: the pioneer CEO. The 2020s

We have an ingrained and understandable tendency to continue to rely on what we know, even though we know it's killing us.[23]

Bill Gates

At what point are we? Hard to say, unless we stop the world and observe our planet from space. For the first time in the history of mankind, due

---

[22] David Mixner, LGBT activist, writer and Barilla consultant on November 19th, 2014, explained in an interview with *the Washington Post* that what he was witnessing: "The most thorough effort to remedy the gaffe I have ever taken part."

[23] B. Gates, *How to Avoid a Climate Disaster*, The Knopf Doubleday Group, 2021 | *Climate: How to avoid a disaster. Today's solutions tomorrow's challenges*, Milan, La Nave de Teseo, 2021.

to the pandemic, megatrends in global levels have undergone an exponential acceleration whose consequences do not seem predictable. Climate emergency, artificial intelligence, digital connection, food sustainability, migration trends, revolution in the balance between workplace and private life, posthumanism, postpolitical, post-truth: These are the main transformative flows that have pushed themselves forward and deprived of the reference points necessary to understand the trajectory and location in the international chessboard, in the agendas of government and organizations, in the daily life of every individual, citizen, or consumer. The first pandemic crisis of the new Millennium, and in fact in the history of man, is the first planetary crisis that sees all nations across the world on the front line against the same enemy.

"On April 2nd, 2020, almost half of the world's inhabitants, nearly four billion, were either forced or invited by their governments to stay at home. The measures to contain Covid-19 are isolation, quarantine and in some cases curfew. Here, therefore, in all its ambivalence, is the choice between confinement and digital control. Different cultures have a decisive influence. In Asian countries, the collection of personal data, the complete filing of citizens, sometimes even the evaluation is common practice. In European countries all of this would be unthinkable. The critical sense, especially on these issues, is very high. The virus has an enlightening power and focuses on the complicated relationship with digital devices. On one hand we could not do without, because we would be deprived of virtual contact, no longer be informed and essentially leave the real world. On the other hand, we would not want to become a continuous source to be followed everywhere, spied on in our intimacy, monitored or even judged in health practices."[24] The essay by philosopher Donatella Di Cesare, dedicated to the political and economic stance of the Coronavirus emergency and the deep connections between the virus and globalization, paints one of the many pictures of the situation, but shares a few common instances with those of global analysts: The pandemic that exploded in 2020 stopped growth that for some time had been hard to find a measure and an end, but which, at the same time like every crisis, offered an opportunity for redemption and change. Now, the main question that should resonate in the minds and programs of global lead-

---

[24] D. Di Cesare, *Virus sovrano? L'asfissia capitalistica*, Milan, Bollati Boringhieri, 2020.

ership is one: "How to take this opportunity? What are the guidelines for redemption and transformation that the world asks of leaders?"

In unconventional medicine, called Ayurveda, there is a world that indicates with astonishing precision what many privileged observers report is happening to the human race, and not for the first time. *Prajna-Aparadha*, or the "error of intellect": It is one of the fundamental causes of imbalance for Ayurveda and is reflected in the constant repetition of actions and attitudes which, while we know are intrinsically wrong, we perpetuate in the name of material drives that prevail over rationalization. In short, the awareness of error or the discovery of System 1 or System 2 of Daniel Kahneman[25] are no longer enough, that would allow the error due to automatisms, but they would offer our species a possible way out in the moment when we really stop to reflect on the consequence of our decisions for future generations. This seems too late for both slow and fast thinking: The habit of making mistakes and the urge to continue to furrow deeper and deeper is so ingrained in our daily actions, that not even evidence has any transformative power. At one time, this would have been called Destiny. But we are in the 21st century and we must be able to think that culture, access to information, intellectual evolution, and growth in spirituality can bring awareness back to roles of guiding action. We must think of this in terms of salvation of the planet and nature, but of the human race and what we have founded and created over the centuries which is good, progressive, and just.

The references to the fundamental challenges we have mentioned—climate change, artificial intelligence, management of territories, migration and ethnic and cultural conflicts, distribution of resources, demographic shifts, attacks on global security at a political and technological level and of course, the pandemic—are therefore obvious. What is less obvious is the breadth of vision that a CEO who wants to be the protagonist of communication of its own brand must possess in this complex situation. Whoever leads a company today knows perfectly well what the company needs: the ability to find data, information, research, and comparing them is almost endless. Therefore, it becomes decisive not so much to "know" but to know "how" and "what" to know, since informa-

---

[25] Thinking fast and thinking slow, the two state dependent decision-making processes of our mental processes of our mental system developed by the 2002 Nobel Prize in Economics.

tion today is not power only if you are able to make the most effective decision with it, but if you take it as quickly as possible, with an impact on as many people as possible and with a positive reputational impact. However, the more information, the better the quality and sources to absorb, the more deciding becomes multifactorial, systematic, and making effective decisions depends on the ability to see opportunities and risks in an interconnected and interdependent way. However, decisions structured in this way appear so elusive as to seem impossible, and the hypothesis of acting by inserting new creative management methods into the processes is simply discarded in favor of stereotypes of which their probable failure they are fully aware. In 1979, *The Washington Post* published an article that has entered the myth of management: "The Cupboards of Ideas is Bare," where Bernard Nossiter questioned sociologists, political scientists, economists, urban planners, and philosophers about the main problems facing their contemporaries, from the Cold War to Vietnam, from liberalism to social democracy, from the seduction of new technologies to what J.K Galbraith called the "Belmont Syndrome," where economists commute between their beautiful homes in residential areas to office computers, while their real engagement in the world boils down to a territory that barely includes their families. According to all the interviewees, the intellectuals' cupboard was empty: Everyone agreed that the flow of thought (which was copious and profitable at one time) as a contribution to progress had been exhausted. So much so that one of them, the neo-conservative Irvine Kristol, announces in the article his official retirement from the professorship at New York University: "I don't have anything to say anymore. I don't think anybody does. When a problem becomes too difficult, you lose interest."[26] We do not believe we are exaggerating in saying that in the post-pandemic era, we are again very close to that situation: Governments and academia and more and more often even NGOs have run out not only of ideas, but also the offer of solid, lasting, and coherent references. Communities, movements, and individuals are instead on the sporadic search of precisely these ideas, combined with the ability to see, decide, and manage programs, but above all to the openness and willingness to communicate it clearly and continuously, risking in first person. If CEOs could be among the leaders

---

[26] B.D. Nossiter, "The Cupboard of Ideas Is Bare", *The Washington Post*, May 20, 1979.

who take it upon themselves to embody the answer to this question, it is time to introduce a next-generation CEO model.

2.4.1   *The transformative relationship with the post-pandemic stakeholder*

CEOs could be among the subjects that take in their hands not only the destiny of the company they are called to lead, but also a broader governance, if only in intent and personal exposure. In short, CEOs may now be required to know how to identify, manage, and understand (at a level of identity image and reputation of itself as a brand and itself as a brand coordinated with the corporate brand) post-pandemic stakeholders who express a new-generation complexity that we have just called postmodern. The subjects who can have an impact on and that can be influenced by the activity of the company find themselves bewildered and threatened at the same time by the loss of certainties and promises that were characterized during the preceding centuries. This is not a crisis that concerns the choice of objectives and strategies to be pursued, but the very choice to act, since its linearity starting from a certain act leads to a certain result. The interconnected and interdependent stratifications of economies, territories, societies, and at the same time ideas and political and intellectual systems are no longer controllable nor manageable in the modern way we were once used to. Each individual is absolute, and each culture is absolute, pushing the social communication of this free absolutism to extremes, thanks to the possibilities offered by digital and technological interconnections in a broad sense: recognizing a "universal truth" becomes practically impossible, unless you want to "export" it from one culture to another (be it national, religious, or branded culture) in what would now be seen as an exercise in hyper-colonialism to be stigmatized and rejected, with incalculable reputational damage for the organization that generated it.

Therefore in the contemporary world: Stakeholders follow post-hierarchical and post-bureaucratic forms of aggregation, created by thousands of communities, alliances, associations, digitally connected groups on a global level, and ready (once a "critical measure of awareness" has been reached on a given ethical endorsement) to connect, giving proof of knowing how to move with actions such as procott/boycott in the real world and in real time and/or with the creation/support of political "parties" in a transnational and cross- cultural way, they could include environmentalists, feminists, consumers, and workers in various titles, ethnic, sexual, religious minorities, etc.

How then can a CEO brand embody a decision, an action if we cannot know the outcome of this action in advance, given the level of complexity that distinguishes us? How can a CEO communicate in order to obtain positive images and reputational results, if the authority conferred on him by his role is not recognized in a post-hierarchical and post-bureaucratic system, who sees, and not always, in their peers a temporary mirror of ethical reflection, thanks to the comparison and comfort of the media? How can a brand CEO communicate itself as a model of governance if it is the credibility of the concept of governance itself to have entered a structural crisis, since it is now clear to everyone how the algorithmic management of the main systems and processes, hyper connection, and the possibility of manipulating big data have created a communication "bubble" in which it has become impossible to discern in real time, true, and fake? Here we are specifically talking about a "CEO brand," we repeat that: their decisions "are" his brand identity as much as how much his personality and communication of these decisions and this personality (in formal and content coordination with corporate communication strategy) is transformed into its image and reputation.

An attempt is worth the effort, a proposal is possible: The post-pandemic stakeholder awaits, as much as before, an interpretation of the reality, economic, social, and political. However, this can no longer be understood either as univocal or as definitive, or as "controllable" in its own effects and results. The promise (to be expressed in a communicative strategy) of the brand CEO will therefore no longer cling to any analytical monopoly, to any information management, to any incarnation of subjective "power." Instead, it will be the victory of the ethical gesture, possible on the utilitarian forecast, also expired because it is impracticable. The record responsibility, constant presence, and awareness (thanks to which human relations and communication would be strengthened in their essence) of "functionality" have also expired, as it is linked to a modern idea of need and necessity as primary driving stimuli of the human[27].

---

[27] See also in this regard, the contemporary revaluation, for example with the mindfulness movement or the theories of ecological action of Viktor Frankl's thought, Man in search of meaning, Franco Angeli, 2017, toward that among

Here is where the needs of the post-pandemic stakeholder could find in the human factor of the CEO brand (equally complex, holistic, responsive, and ready to evolve) a strength that would give strategic corporate communication models constant renewable energy. As the transformation accelerates, even organizations that are more flexible and far-sighted struggle to keep up; while the cabinet of ideas empties more and more, dominant culture, even if outdated, struggles to give up its leading role to new cultural experiences.

Therefore, it would be sensible to formulate a corporate communication strategy that provides the CEO a catalytic role of conceptual power. A CEO branding strategy that should be structured according to objectives ready to beat fruitful paths in the global debate precisely as generators of an unacceptable conflictual multiplicity, which was stable until a few years ago. The brand CEO would then no longer have one pre-written recipe to be followed and accepted by its stakeholders, but most would like to propose:

1. As a communicational spearhead that affects behavior physiologically resistant to change by internal and external stakeholders of the company.
2. As an ethical investor, defusing the potential for conflicts and obstacles to sustainability.
3. As an incubator of social, economic, and political instances with high representative potential, which thank the possibility of the media exposure of the CEO himself, from niche becomes mainstream.

The latest generation CEO is a pioneer who does not act "from" their world other than his own stakeholders and then communicates in order to reach them, but a subject completely immersed in complexity, to the point of admitting that they do not know in advance the results of their actions, just as happens to the stakeholders, but instead to know how to provide ethical reasons. The pioneering CEO has the necessary ethical spirit to "firstly" take a decision-making path (a specific action in a specific situation) "for" the common good, in consonance with a collec-

---

others of Abraham Maslow.

tive feeling, in order to foster that massive transformative purpose which could if not resolve, at least provide "meaning" to events.

2.4.2 *The keywords of the "human factor": authenticity, simplicity, and sharing*

The post-pandemic era was unimaginable until February 2020 and as we have said so far, this epical change could not fail to have definitive consequences on the global vision of leadership. Change is destined to be perpetual, constant, pervasive, multiplicative, unstoppable, and exponential: Calling it the "new normal" is an understatement to "that" normality that we will never have back. Although the theories on this subject have been constantly burdened into an "instant thought" that has only increased the level of performance anxiety of international management, the imperative needs of stakeholders in the face of the present challenge can be condensed in a few lines:

1. *Authenticity* as opposed to the unstoppable loss of credibility of the traditional institutions, media intermediaries, and most recently the "expert knowledge."[28]

---

[28] On the "crisis of expert knowledge" experience massively after the loss of credibility of the scientific community following the media contribution of virologists and infectious disease specialists during the Covid-19 pandemic, see C. Sorrentino, "Scientists and the pitfalls of the media", the magazine of Il Mulino, 12 January, 2021: "The digital environment has only produced a further acceleration to this process, because it becomes access to information is even easier. The so-called disintermediation potentially allows anyone to read, listen to or observe information on any social phenomenon or event that has occurred. The digital environment has only produced a further acceleration to this process, because access to information becomes even easier.

Reputation online has arised from sharing. Often having little information directed to the broadcaster, you have to count on those who appreciate it. And here we are now in the era of likes and shares; as well as platforms such as TripAdviser which help us choose the best restaurants. But if we pass from food onto validations which are much more complex, such as the effectiveness of the vaccine or medical treatment, it can be well understood how everything becomes much more difficult. For this reason, we have welcomed with pleasure and enormous expectation the appearance of virologists and scientists on our screens. First bewilderments were recorded in front of the different positions they assumed. However, that's just how science works: expressing doubts, trying and trying again, failing and starting

2. *Simplification of the narrative,* as opposed to increasing the level of complexity in the trust attribution process.
3. *Absolute protagonism of ethical value,* as opposed to profit and capitalist development as the only catalyst for historical attention.

It clearly emerges that the human factor, the "human touch," that we so strongly missed during the time of isolation due to the global lockdown, plays the game as captain in the heart of all stakeholder teams because it is the only one able to guarantee that *authenticity* which we previously mentioned. The CEO, the highest expression of corporate leadership, therefore has its path marked: not only by exhibiting themselves in the media to announce a world as it should be and not to satisfy individual desires, but by *exposing themselves that they will do it first to be at the service of the community.*

This is because they have the wisdom and humility necessary to take action in everyone's names and indicate the way to go: not in the face of ambitions linked to control and management, but to compassion and care. To try to define, in a sort of cultural micro-map of a CEO at a qualitative level, we reflect on the cultural indexes created by Geert Hofstede, which reveal themselves to be particularly illuminating.

1. *Adheres mainly to feminine values:* compassion, care, harmony, quality of life, and modesty that favor a system of management focused on consent, intuition, and equal opportunities.
2. *They are more collectivist* than individualist.
3. Requires a low level of power distance, therefore a strong propensity for *delegation* and
4. For *democratic participation.*
5. Has a *long-term orientation* and a low rate of avoiding uncertainty, therefore is *tolerant* and *open to change* and in contemporary situations of extreme complexity will be less anxious and predisposed to stress, as it faces ambiguity and risky situations without multiplying the rules, but as a physiological dimension.

---

again. It was therefore normal that faced with a new virus many hypotheses were put forward, even divergent ones. But then something happened which tells us about the insidious and attractive strength of the media logic. From experts they have turned into characters of comedy which has been the talk of the pandemic."

He is the pioneer who is no longer enough to lead, but who finds himself wanting to "share": He learns not only from his own mistakes, but from the mistakes of his own interlocutors, with whom he is in constant communion of purpose. In fact, it shares with the "human" spirit, therefore imperfect in an evident, vulnerable, and exposed way. Only through this constant sharing (spiritual, digital, public, private, and away from the public) do they obtain confirmation of the delegation from internal and external stakeholders, in a seamless osmosis, made possible only in these times and through connections. Once the influence is earned, the mathematical ability is demonstrated by measurable KPIs at any time and on each "follower," the CEO will have trust, only providing that he shows himself totally authentic as a "gift," which now has something similar to secular faith.

However, to maintain the influence we were talking about and transform it into trust, the pioneering CEOs' media strategy requires concrete and deeply partisan language, a constant alignment in reaction to global events that trigger a conflict that admits no margins of ambiguity, and where the message starts from the brand, an elementary, cross-cultural, foundational storytelling. Every word, gesture, and image can become icons or memes: A symbol of an iron contract between CEO and follower or an inexorable sentence of leaving the reputational market.

In conveying the message, the superconductor is the *ethical value*. Whether this is about climate change, gender gap, cancel culture, neo-feminism, surveillance capitalism, artificial intelligence, mental health within the workplace, social dilemma, right to health, or any of the battles that follow one in another in the real and in the digital, stakeholder capitalism which will increasingly be represented by the activism of the generation Z requires companies to embody their political vision in a Greek sense: Whether we call it citizenship, corporate activism, or sustainability, it must convey a message which, with complete mastery of a global overview, is a balanced expression of corporate objectives, individual beliefs, and adherence to social demands.

The model of the pioneering CEO is the one that on paper seems to have more probability, and clearly more margin of risk, to catalyze global attention. However, it is difficult if not impossible with these premises to profit as the only survival of a brand: It is perhaps the pioneering CEOs, women and men at the top of the scale of their individual priorities put instead purpose, equal rights, opportunities, and representatives of minorities, defense of the concrete future of the next generation, to have to imagine not only transformative brands, but transformative stakes.

We go back to the center, to the focus, the direction to be given and taken. It could be the right time because the original pact between company and stakeholders (born in that "golden age" with which we began the reconstruction of this chapter) is recreated. Again "one unit" as in the beginning: Ideal generative ground for an osmotic and holistic branding strategy, which would allow the pioneering CEO to leave a common footprint which is no longer "serial," no longer "contingent," but aimed at a duration in the time of an authentic relationship as the primary objective of the relationship itself.

References

L. Bebchuk, J. Fried, D. Walker, «Executive compensation in America: Optimal contracting or extraction of rents?», *National Bureau of Economic Research*, Working Paper 8661, 12/2001.

S. Bonini, D. Court, A. Marchi, «Rebuilding corporate reputations», *McKinsey Quarterly*, 1st June 2009.

E.T. Brioschi, *International communication. A spatial projection of total business communication*, Milan, Vita e Pensiero, 2015.

D. Di Cesare, *Virus sovrano? L'asfissia capitalistica*, Milan, Bollati Boringhieri, 2020.

V. Frankl, *L'uomo in cerca di senso*, Milan, Franco Angeli, 2017.

R.C. Gambetti, G. Graffigna, S. Biraghi, «The grounded theory approach to consumer-brand engagement», *International Journal of Market Research*, vol. 54, n. 5, 2012.

J. Garten, *The mind of the CEO: The world's business leaders talk about leadership, responsibility the future of the corporation, and what keeps them up at night*, New York, Basic Books, 2001.

B. Gates, *How to avoid a climate disaster*, The Knopf Doubleday Group, 2021.

G. Hofstede, «Dimensionalizing Cultures: The Hofstede Model in Context», *Online Readings in Psychology and Culture*, 2(1), 2011. https://doi.org/10.9707/2307-0919.1014

L. Iacocca, A. Taylor, «Iacocca in his own words», *Fortune*, 29 August 1988.

W. Isaacson, *Steve Jobs*, New York, Simon&Schuster, 2011.

D. Kahneman, *Thinking, fast and slow*, New York, Farrar, Straus and Giroux, 2011.

R. Khurana, «The curse of the superstar CEO», *Harvard Business Review*, September 2002.

N. Klein, *No Logo*, New York, Picador, 1999.

P. Krugman, *The conscience of a liberal*, London-New York, W.W. Norton, 2009.

C. Malone, S.C. Fiske, *The human brand. how we relate to people*, Products, and Companies, Jossey-Bass, 2013.

B.D. Nossiter, «The cupboard of ideas is bare», *The Washington Post*, 20th May 1979.

K. Prahalad, V. Ramaswamy, «Co-creation experiences: The next practice in value creation», *Journal of Interactive Marketing*, vol. 18, n. 3, 2004.

C.K. Prahalad, V. Ramaswamy, «Co-opting customer competence», *Harvard Business Review*, vol. 78, n. 1, 2000.

G. Ritzer, N. Jurgenson, «Production, consumption, prosumption: The nature of capitalism in the age of the digital 'prosumer'», *Journal of Consumer Culture*, 10 issue, 1, 2010.

Vikas Shah Mbe, «A conversation with John Sculley», *Thought Economics*, 1st June 2017.

C. Sorrentino, «Gli scienziati e le insidie dei media», *la rivista de Il Mulino*, 12th January 2021.

N.M. Tichy, D.O. Ulrich, «The leadership challenge – A call for the transformational leader», *Sloan Management Review*, 26(1), 1984.

A. Toffler, *The third wave*, New York, Morrow, 1980.

World Business Council for Sustainable Development, 1999, 2000, 2001.

3 Lectures from CEOs. From Theory to Practice

by Gabriele Ghini, Stefania M. Vitulli

Throughout the course of the book, we have explored the theoretical basis of construction reputation. In order not to limit ourselves to an academic discussion, we have wanted to test these theories and verify their real application through a selected group of Italian company leaders, or in the case of Bob Kunze-Concewitz, Italians by adoption. These are 15 CEOs with personal stories and very different professions. We are sure we have collected opinions from managers which have enriched our discussion, both for the commitment recorded in the use of multiple company channels, including social media, as well as for the quality of actions of visibility in producing a multiplier of corporate reputation.

The top managers interviewed represent excellence in the panorama of companies operating in Italy both as Headquarters and as branches of multinationals, with the significant participation of Luca de Meo, CEO of Renault Group World, in terms of branding and communication strategies, ability to transmit values, and identification and bonding with the company they lead.

We had the honor of collecting the contribution from the CEO and entrepreneurs who are really playing the role of "intangible asset" of their company in building brand, equity, value, credibility, uniqueness, and solidity to their business.

In our interviews, we were able to verify the weight that each individual CEO attribute to the seven factors that characterize the RepTrak model, that is, Performance, Products and Services, Innovation, Workplace, Governance, Citizenship and Leadership.

Practical indications have emerged that constitute a real grounding of the theoretical model with a series of practical behaviors of great relevance.

The following paragraphs take up and develop the most significant and impactful statements of the various CEOs.

3.1   The Italian approach to CEO branding

CEOs: Alberto Calcagno (Fastweb); Federico Casini (Aon); Paola Corna Pellegrini (Allianz Partner Italy); Brunello Cucinelli (Brunello Cucinelli); Stefano Cuzzilla (Federmanager); Ugo De Carolis (Rome Airports); Luca de Meo (Renault Group); Daniele Ferrari (Versalis); Alessandro Foti (Fineco); Isabella Fumagalli (BNP Paribas Cardif); Riccardo Illy (Polo Del Gusto, Illy Group); Robert Kunze-Concewitz (Campari Group); Gian Maria Mossa (Banca Generali): Fabio Pompei (Deloitte Italia); Giulio Ranzo (Avio)

3.1.1   *Credibility in the management of Environmental, Social and Corporate Governance (ESG)*

The paradigm shift in corporate strategies from an exclusive focus on profit to the inclusion of social responsibility is the main theme raised by all the conversations with the CEOs, nothing in particular, the refusal of a generic and rhetorical attention to the environment for a credible ESG management proposition in line with the company mission. It is an important evolution that gives depth to the corporate brand and the image of the head of the company, who is personally involved in this change.

Paola Corna Pellegrini (Allianz Partners)
"I live the role of CEO both as a guide and as accelerator. I think about my people at 360 degrees, not only as collaborators and therefore ensuring their well-being within the company, but paying attention and creating the most appropriate conditions, even in improving their work–life balance, which allows them to take care of their families and loved ones, and their general needs beyond company life.

This commitment of ours is greatly recognized, an attention that also leads to Diversity and Inclusion initiatives which aim to enhance the different genders, abilities, ethnicities, and sexual orientations, a recognition that reflects positively on one the best indicators of our corporate climate analysis.

Diversity—which in various areas continues to need attention and sometimes protection, which is why in our company we create the conditions for it to be always guaranteed, first of all by setting an example.

In fact, I believe that in order to promote change, including cultural change, it is necessary to take the first step and confirm it every day.

The Valeria Solesin prize is a concrete example. When I first read of the girl who died in Bataclan in 2015, I wanted to learn more about her, pushed and shocked at the same time, perhaps because she was the same age as my daughter. A research that allowed me to discover that she was a professor at the Institute de démographie de l'université Paris-1-Panthéon-Sorbonne and worked precisely on the themes of Diversity and Inclusion, in particular on the balance between work and personal life. Valeria started a path that I believe had a great social value and a legacy that could not be lost, a reflection that I had as a woman, a mother and citizen, but also as a professional at the lead of my company, which I immediately thought could be the promoter of the Valeria Solosin award.

I therefore set up a university competition inspired by both the studies of Valeria who deepen the theme of the dual role women have, divided between family and work, and other contemporary research which highlights the positive effects of a balanced female presence within companies. A prize in her memory, to enhance and reward the research theses that address the analysis of the labor market from a socio-economic, demographic-statistical, and legal perspective on "Female talent as a determining factor for development of the economy, ethics and meritocracy in our country."

The involvement of Valerias mother certainly couldn't be missed, so much so that from the day I received the families' endorsements we are now friend, from the first moment I involved the Forum of Meritocracy of which today I am Vice-President, an association that certified its methodological rigor by sharing its values, and the Winning Women's Institute, the first Italian Gender Equality Certification. Since our first year, we have had between 10 and 14 prizes for a total prize pool of between 30,000 and 40,000 euros at each edition, offered by as many leading companies, as well as the involvement of over 35 Italian Universities. Having managed to bring together institutions, private companies, associations, and the academic world represents in itself an important result, a best practice on which it is important to reflect and capitalize upon.

This is what we are still doing today with InclusioneDonna, the alliance of more than 60 associations and many ambassadors committed to the issues of equal opportunities, a continuous work that aims to deeply influence political choices to contribute to a significant cultural change that profoundly influences the world of work and our society".

Brunello Cucinelli (Cucinelli)
"Until some time ago, you presented the product, now you have to present the company. It is clear that when presenting the company, you must also have a product that lives up to its expectations. So, never underestimate the product, but the company must come first! This is because before buying I inquired: who are you, how do you produce, how do you behave with humanity? How many profits do you make? Do you make the right profits or are they too high? Would you buy something from someone with a high profit? You are selling a product, did you respect its creation? Have you given the right wages to those who work? This is totally different than it was 15 years ago, because now there is the possibility of documenting the consistency between what you say and what you do. If you make me work in an unhealthy environment, I can photograph it, publish it and say 'Look at what place I work'. Who is the entrepreneur who says: 'I try to carry the respect and moral and economic dignity of the human being?'. It is a big change in humanity. When we were farmers, my grandfather gave the first bale of wheat to the community, not the last. Hence the balance between profit and gift. Do you have the right profit? How do you behave? Is there a part of this profit that goes as a gift to humanity? Do you remember 14 to 15 years ago when we began talking about ethics? Aristotle considered ethics the highest aspect of philosophy. This is why I believe that first of all you must be credible and act accordingly.

We have had thirty years of what I call 'Crisis of Civilization', now we have noticed something very important which I believe started through the eyes of a child, Greta Thunberg. My granddaughter says to me 'Grandpa, let's go to the demonstration to see Greta'. We went to the demonstration together and then you are there, and you see the bright eyes of a child that makes you change your mind. They aren't the eyes of an adult, because their eyes do not hurt you, but the eyes of a suffering child are a lot stronger, aren't they? For the first time on our website we have written 'Human sustainability' and 'living in harmony with creation', because I call sustainability living in harmony with creation and I feel the guardian of protecting creation."

Stefano Cuzzilla (Federmanager)
"Today, a company that is not attentive to the environment, risks not only to not be competitive, but also to not be attractive in the eyes of investors. Cash flows in the coming years will reward companies that are attentive to processes, to the environment and territory that surrounds them. Whoever runs a business cannot afford to remain isolated in their own line of business and not consider the territory, because every business lives in its territory. This implies that the company is reconsidered as a key figure in the community in which it operates, not just as an economic player, but also social and value.

Opening up to the outside means building relationships and therefore reputation. It also applies internally of course. Employees must recognize that the company they work for operates with consistency, attention and with many tangible effects. This is fundamental not only for the competitiveness of the service/product but above all for the commitment of the staff.

I'll make an example. Everyone remembers when in '94 Ferrero significantly felt the effects of the climate crisis: due to a disastrous flood the factory suffered extensive damage. However, the people of Asti worked day and night to help put the factory back on its feet, because they felt its effects, they lived there and knew they had to help. They managed. What was called the 'Ferrero Miracle' explains the meaning of the term reputation: the whole world is willing to help you because it recognizes your value, that you are a precious economic resource and it is necessary to react in a compact manner to crises. And if you have a reputation as a company that is attentive to its territory, the environment, the social sector, even when complex interventions of an institutional or financial nature need to be carried out, everyone knows that they are betting on a winning horse, because by helping you, they also improve your reputation. In doing so, a virtuous circle and a chain reaction are fueled in which political, financial staff, customers and institutions warn that attentions to the social determines positive effects on the business and reputation.

We, as Federmanger, stand by our companies and help them in institutional offices to make their commitment perceived and valued on environmental, social and governance issues, promoting meetings for discussion, knowledge and training, acting as antennas on the market and as a sounding board for the political world, to make their business more effective and contribute to the cultural evolution of our members. We have 180.000 members, the country's ruling class, able to change the way companies are led. Now ESG issues have become one of the pillars of business and communication effective at the market."

Daniele Ferrari (Versalis)
"I am convinced that being passionate about one's activities, developed honestly through commitment, trust and above all consistency with one's values, contributes in a fundamental way to building a positive personal and corporate reputation.

Holding various roles, CEO of Versalis, president of Cefic (European Chemical Industry Council) and member of the boards of directors of two listed companies, I have to pay close attention when exposing myself on issues relevant to the sector I represent. The chemical industry is the basis of almost all industrial supply chains: have you ever considered how there is chemistry in everything? As a 'technology provider', the chemical industry can only be among the main players in a transition to the circular economy. In this context, the reputation aspect is very interesting. On plastic for example, I took several firm and unconventional positions. The phenomenon in plastic in oceans, the so called 'marine- littering' has exploded within the media, and has led to the negativeness of the material, when instead this phenomenon is the consequence of the mismanagement of the end of life of plastic products.

As CEO of a company that produces polymers, both at corporate and association level and in collaboration with other manufacturers, I have promoted many initiatives to try to combat this negative image that is now associated with plastic.

When someone says that plastic pollutes and should be replaced and banned, I feel compelled to take a stand and reiterate that a full cycle assessment of the life of the products is required and take into consideration all the impacts on an economic, environmental and social level. When I hear slogans like 'plastic-free' I think we miss the opportunity to spread the concept that waste, especially plastic waste, is a great resource and the only solution to prevent it ending up in our seas, is to educate on separate collection and promote and invest in reusing, recovering and recycling. The reactions to these positions are generally positive.

I want to tell you about some concrete initiatives that we carry out in Versalis. The development of technologies for the recycling of polymers is one of the pillars of Versalis's strategy for the circular economy and we have already industrialized mechanical recycling processes of end-of-life plastics by launching Versalis Revive, the first range of polymer based products containing recycled plastic. For example, we produce expandable polystyrene using raw material from the recycling of domestic waste collection products such as polystyrene glasses, trays and yogurt cups. The finished product can be made into insulation boards for saving energy or the protective packaging of household appliances and furniture. We also recover urban post-consumer polyethylene to transform it into new products for the agricultural sector and packaging. The most ambitious project we are pursuing is the development, with a partner, of a chemical recycling technology, a virtuous project that allows the recycling of plastic technically to infinity and allows to obtain new plastics identical to the original ones, able to satisfy all applications.

I cite these examples because my goal is not to limit myself to a little 'Greenwashing', but to develop concrete solutions: I want to ally myself with whom has the technologies to convert and recycle, with the entire supply chain of plastics to stop pollution in rivers and seas, recover waste, work them and reuse them for something useful. I think this is a lot more serious than simply declaring 'No plastic!'. The whole company is focused on this direction, starting from top management. It is no coincidence that our image is so strong that many young people want to come and work for us."

Alessandro Foti (Fineco)
"In our conception of business, social mission is of a fundamental relevance. I want to be very concrete: we carry out our social function if we manage our customers money well, we do it in a way which helps them achieve their goals and foster a process of financial knowledge, characterizing everything with fair pricing and transparency. In Italy we have a financial wealth of 4.4 trillion; by eliminating approximately 800 billion euros of financial investments from entrepreneurs and 1000 billion euros of severance pay, we arrive at a total wealth of 2600 billion. If Italians

invested in a more modern, and therefore efficient way, and intermediaries were a little more careful by recovering 1% more per year than overall return, we would be talking about a wealth effect of 26 billion euros for the Italian system. It becomes clear that ours can be defined as an extraordinary social mission. The more the company is committed to a business that has a socially relevant impact, the more focus on the core business and its more or less virtuous behavior becomes important.

At the same time, this mission also represents a corporate interest, as better management of financial assets increases the client's wealth, and consequently that of the company. In short, we are faced by two phenomena that exclude themselves, indeed a company that works in this way is more likely to remain on the market a long time.

By applying these principles, in addition to the shareholder, another stakeholder is also favored, namely those who work in the company. In other countries, the concept of governance is much more evolved than ours and recognizes the employee stakeholder role. I can use the example of Germany, where I had the experience of managing a bank and where a third of the workers are present on the supervisory board: attention to the fact that the company is managed sustainably over time is very strong."

Isabella Fumagalli (BNP Paribas Cardif)
"For a group like BNP Paribas it is very important to have a social role and contribute to building a sustainable future, an issue that is of particular interest to our young Generation Z customers. For them, it is a serious priority that who has the financial means to make a difference, becomes a character of change and an enabler of the sustainability of the planet. It is a more innovative and inclusive connotation of CSR, but it begins to make sense and have significance when it is brought to the top level, therefore it is my direct responsibility. My typical working day is divided by one third in Business, one third in Management, and a third in CSR. Making my commitment meaningful means first of all spending myself personally so that CSR does not remain behind and brings back the old concept of 'something will be done because I put X on the budget, and I need to spend it.

The real difference I can make as CEO is internalization of the concept of social responsibility and making ours integral to our offer: it is true, we have created a policy which was born from listening, is modular, follows customers, does what it promises, is transparent, but this is not enough as it must also have a social impact. By leveraging a concept of very strong leadership, I have to make sure that people, my clients and employees, become protagonists of the sustainable components themselves, passing from spectators to actors.

To the customers I will say: 'Dear customer, instead of protecting only your health, why don't you also think of the health of others? If you want to add 1 euro for Telethon which concentrates itself on scientific research, feel free to do so'. At that point, Telethon sends an update to the customer of what has been done with their contribution, and the person feels important. Likewise, I have to engage employees by leading them to act for a common cause, that of business, but not only. It means saying to people, 'I need you. Help me convey the values of my brand and what it means for us to be socially responsible'.

When employees feel important and are engaged, they bring strong, innovative and concrete ideas. You have no idea how much creativity we have released thanks to the engagement of our collaborators on this issue. Let's not forget about how many people work within BNP Paribas, globally we are about 200.000. Imagine what it means to have managers who truly believe in it, and people who take action together. We managers are just the multiplier. But we have to be there and take action in the first person. For this, leadership is important.

The good thing is that our people have a natural willingness to help, to the social aspect, to values, but sometimes there is a little resistance, which can be cultural or generational. We talk a lot about the interest and inspiration Generation Z gives us, because aside from being digital natives there are CSR natives, but despite this there are not many of them within the group.

Therefore, the task of managers is also to act on resistance and transform Generation X or Baby Boomers, because the values of the new generation is what it takes to make our planet sustainable, we don't need anything else."

Riccardo Illy (Illy)
"Our essential values have always been economic, social and environmental sustainability. Economic, in a broad sense, therefore not just for us. Economic sustainability also means commitment to pay our suppliers at a price that makes their business economical, so that they are suppliers

today, tomorrow and throughout the next years, if they will be good at updating themselves and maintaining the requested standards.

Social sustainability toward the territories from which our materials come: coffee, tea, chocolate, mostly developing countries where there is still child labor, where conditions are often penalizing and where there is no economic bargaining power.

We pay our suppliers in those countries a price which covers all their costs, leaves a margin and also a bonus when the quality exceeds our minimum requirements. As for illycaffé, we have formalized this aspect with a certification issued by Det Norske Veritas, which verifies the sustainability of the illycaffé supply chain from suppliers. As you can see, our efforts in terms of sustainability are very concrete and focused on our business, in order to contribute positively on our planet."

Robert Kunze-Concewitz (Campari)
"We work in a sector, that of economic beverages, which is exposed to many criticisms, from the World Health Organization to various governments of the world, therefore we want to address only the responsible and positive side of people.

We work hard with associations by category to promote the 'Mediterranean way of consuming alcohol', and we have a very intense and structured internal program to train our people and promote a responsible consumption of our products.

We are members of 30 trade associations and Social Aspect Organization in 19 countries, and in some of them Group Executives hold key roles. Our group is also a member of Spirits Europe, the European association of producers of alcoholic beverages in which 31 national associations from 24 countries and 8 main players from the spirit sector are represented. Our commitment is to help promote responsible behaviors and lifestyles.

Our motto 'Toasting Life Together' comes from the mission of our brand. We are first in line on social themes thanks to our Campari Foundation, of which I am Vice-President. The foundation has a mission for working on education and we do beautiful things, not only in Italy but all over the world. Furthermore, we have other foundations in other countries that are not all known as Campari. Campari Group's sustainability path has been active since 2011 and sustainability is one of the levers in choosing and defining company policies. Our sustainability strategy is based on five areas: our people, marketing that promotes responsible consumption, quality and the environment, responsible distribution, and commitment to communities where we are present.

I'll give you a very concrete example, Negroni Week: an international initiative that aims to raise funds for charities and NGOs. Bars, restaurants and retailers in the 60 participating countries donate to the charity part of the profit made from the sale of Negroni. More than 7700 exhibitors participated, collecting over half a million dollars. In this way, our social role is deeply intertwined with our business model."

Gian Maria Mossa (Banca Generali)
"Personally, I believe that 'sustainability' must be interpreted in a deeper way than the abstractness and rhetoric that characterize the debate around this concept.

The interpretation of sustainability that I advocate provides the best and fastest possible incorporation of the economic and social dynamics that characterize the specific ecosystem in which a company operates, engaging in structural changes. This has immediate implications on the role exercised by the management which must discover a more innovative concept of action or control, of awareness, proximity to business and accessibility. At Banca Generali we are working very intensely on the inclusion of economic and social dynamics. The concept of sustainability leads us to think from a design perspective rather than a hierarchical one, where everyone must take responsibility for their actions on the defined value basis and must not be put up for discussion. I think this is one of the most relevant aspects of leadership.

This is an approach in which we strongly believe, which we also share with Parent Company, Assicurazioni Generali. The mission indicated from our CEO group for all societies of Generali Groups (and which I strongly share) is in fact based on three pillars: People Strategy, Brand Reputation and Sustainability.

The concrete interpretation of sustainability that we have given at Banca Generali is based on creating a sustainable business over time, and therefore, not only aimed at generating profits over a short period but giving strong signals about our efforts for the future generations. In line with these objectives, we promote sustainable investments and support our clients in the construction of accounts that take into question different sensitivities regarding sustainability. For this reason, we have developed a project which associates the solution of ESG investments to an approach based on 17 'Objectives for Sustainable Development' promoted by the United Nations. With the contribution of Main-Street- Partners (London based investment society specialized in sustainable investments with a social and environmental impact) we have implemented our proprietary platform for building accounts with a quantitative method, which measures contributions on ESG issues, adding this new dimension of value to the investment.

Alongside this, for a few years now we sponsorize initiatives dedicated to the promotion of culture, music, art and sport of the youth: I think this is a sign of closeness to the history of our country and an important contribution dedicated to the future development of our young people.

Therefore, creating value through growth and sustainable growth is our best business card."

Fabio Pompei (Deloitte)
"As Deloitte, we have been placing at the center of our strategic objectives not only economic results, but a broader ambition, summed up clearly by our motto 'Make an impact that matters'. A purpose that unites us in belonging to Deloitte and which means wanting to leave a positive and concrete sign not only to our clients, but all stakeholders associated with us, primarily our people and the communities within which we operate. This is both at a local level, but also globally. Our people are our principal 'asset' and we are aware, due to the 50% of them under 30 years old, that each one of them has a decisively different sensibility of those of past generations, especially on themes tied to climate change and sustainability intended in the most extended manner. For this reason also, we annually conduct an in depth and detailed analysis on a global level on Millennials and Generation Z, in order to fully understand their needs.

However, theory is not enough. As Deloitte we bring forward various projects to improve work-life balance, historically a theme which is very much felt within professions of consulting. On the well-being side we have also launched concrete solutions that concern nutrition and psycho-physical balance. Initiatives which have an objective of social impact and demonstrate to young people that there is an active attention towards their needs and the needs of the community in which we operate also have a fundamental role.

I believe that young people are very sensitive and attentive to these two aspects. We see it in the responses we had when we launched these initiatives. Even with the Deloitte Foundation, born in 2016, we have various ongoing projects, the result amongst other things of direct reporting from our people. It is thanks to the foundation that this year we have activated for the first time in Italy, Volunteer Hub: the first volunteering program within our company which we have experimented with. An enthusiastic novelty in which our people can put their skills at service of associations that deal with education, culture, solidarity and care of more fragile people.

In general, and even more specifically with the launch of Volunteer Hub, the positive response of our youth continues to surprise me. Despite the significant effort required by their work, they find the time to carry forward projects of solidarity, to propose them to us internally, sustain them, and make sure that they are enriched with contributions and support: this is a clear demonstration that if you do something real and concrete, young people always welcome this with great enthusiasm.

We make sure that our values on which we base our operations are very clear and the coherence in our actions in regard to these values. Undoubtedly, today more than yesterday, there is also a theme of communication and therefore the efforts which we are making from this point of view is also to have a more effective communication, more aligned with the expectations and ways of interacting with the youth."

Giulio Ranzo (Avio)
"With a view of the growing business in the long term we started to seriously confront the ESG (Environmental, Social and Corporate Governance) beginning from our business capability, that is, our expertise in doing our job well.

When the market becomes aware that you know how to manage your business and that you are credible and have stabilized a track record, then they will take your declarations of becoming more sustainable seriously. I believe it is necessary not declaring yourself an expert of ESG to follow trends, but this effort must be clearly connected to your sector and your skills. It is not enough to declare an effort in the ESG sector, but it is necessary to undertake ESG initiatives related to their own business sector.

We operate in space, and in space there are two large themes, one on space waste and the other on communication with countries without the dedicated infrastructure. The first because we are already risking to fill space with waste and this could cause significant damage. The second, in collaboration with the United Nations, to speed up the growth of countries, many of them African, which risk to remain excluded from the progress. These are important themes, and of long-term value, but which are taking a lot of effort, and which will contribute to building a strong reputation, both of business capability and corporate character.

Taking clear positions on aspects you are aware of has sense and is in line with a concrete approach to business, therefore we remain concentrated on our sector, and we want to contribute in an area that we master and in which we can make a difference. Only in this way can we guarantee credibility to our efforts, otherwise we risk losing this credibility and impacting negatively upon our reputation."

3.1.2 Social responsibility of proximity

Some companies exercise a significant impact on the territory in which they operate, and we have appreciated important lessons from the managers interviewed. Furthermore, in the case of Illy we have wanted to explore the reasons of his lasting political efforts at a local and national level.

Ugo De Carolis (Aeroporti di Roma)
"Today we position ourselves as Europe's best airport both for the quality of services to the passengers but for the large attention to quality in general, and sustainability. The airport is considered the classic no-zone. You're in Rome and need to travel to New York, the time spent in the airport is something that if you could forget about, if you could cancel it to reduce it to the minimum you would do it, because it is not even wasted time, it is 'no-time'. It isn't wasted, because you need to do it, but it is something you would like to avoid. Instead, I am trying to make it even more of a 'location', so that your experience within the airport is an integral part of your travels.

Leaving on holiday? You start to have fun here, you start to eat well, you can start shopping, you can watch a show, you start to feel good. Leaving for business? You can start work here, go to meetings, you can find a place where you can send emails etc. This is in order that time can prolong itself in some cases and you start to hear the client say: 'Wait, I'll arrive early, because if I can buy, attend meetings etc'. This approach is making Fiumicino a special place because if you are able to transmit this message the behavior of everyone will be influenced, from your employees to your collaborators, directly and indirectly. We have created an archaeological part that we keep open and bring schools to visit etc.

We are also working on an important project which will allow to optimize the energetic impact on the community of Fiumicino. We want to be able to give a concrete contribution to the population living near the airport by integrating the airport structure with the local community and thus bringing positive and significant impacts."

Riccardo Illy (Illy)
"When talking about the producers of raw material, there is also a social aspect linked to the territory. Thus, some initiatives of illycaffè aim to satisfy the needs of the territory, typically of sponsorization, support on onus and through this we have created the foundation of Ernesto Illy which has precisely this objective. Then, there is environmental sustainability which sees us engaging in reducing our carbon footprint in all forms: from the correct use in saving energy, to the use of recyclable material, therefore the creation of all products in a way that limits its impacts on the territory. My brother Andrea recently developed a model of virtuous agriculture which has brought us to stabilize some very ambitious objectives for the next few years, to arrive to a point where zero impacts are made in terms of emissions of carbon dioxide for the entire productive cycle.

In '93 they asked my availability applying for being the mayor of Trieste. I had no political experience; we had a family meeting and I said 'They are asking me to do this'. There was a precedent, as a grandfather of my mother had been a deputy in Vienna, he was from Rovigno, therefore he had a political role which could have been important in that era. We discussed this for a long time, on one side saying that there was a social role to carry out, the local society asks you for a person to govern the city and the response must be therefore positive; we would see, but also a risk to our reputation. I would be going into a career I had no knowledge about, I would need to learn fast, and it brought some risks as the scandal of Tangentopoli had just erupted. Therefore, the risk of making a mistake, to be compromised, could have brought about heavy relapses on our company. In the end, we voted, my sister voted against to protect me from the evil of politics and my wife because she would have lost her private life for the next few years; but the majority voted yes, so I decided to accept the role.

I will cite a specific case where I was forced to defend my values and reputation: it was a matter of appointing an important administrator of another entity working in the area, where the municipality and therefore the mayor also had a say. They presented to me the name of the person and their curriculum, and I accepted it to the President of the Region at the time. After a few days, I learnt that there were some negative elements, not from the ethical, professional or reputational point of view, but of political ties of which I had no awareness. But at this point I had given my word, and I had to keep it. In 15 years of political efforts, I ran a lot of risks. I remember that after a year of being mayor they called me court to answer for a resolution we had hired.

There was a hypothesis of a crime of completion, a term I imagine you have not heard of, which means 'to bring unfair benefit to a third party', of a consultant we had hired to resolve heavy entrepreneurial situations with a few thousand employees involved, and I thus asked: 'How come they never sent me a warranty information, nothing...' and my lawyer responded that at the beginning of investigations the warranty information is not sent, but only the registration in the register of suspects is made. So, I asked him to check the register to see if there was another inscription. After a few days he phones me and says 'Are you sat down?' and then 'I checked, you were registered twenty five times'. Only a year had passed, and I was already registered twenty-five times in the register of suspects. I never had a trial.

I suffered the only conviction from the court of auditors confirmed in appeal and also in cassation unfortunately, but there were three identical cases: two have been merged, the third went to the part, I was acquitted on appeal, and I believe that for fifteen years of political commitment this is a record, but I was always aware of the risk of compromising my company due to my political commitments."

Robert Kunze-Concewitz (Campari)
"We put a lot of effort into working on the educational aspect of populations in our local reality. Often, our establishments are in areas where there is still a lot of poverty, people who don't know how to read or write, such as in South America, Jamaica etc. We fund employee education projects and we give scholarships to children to contribute to the development of the territory. We have established a strong sense of family spirit, we define ourselves 'camparisti' and belong to the local community by

demonstrating through facts the reality of Campari as a familiar public company.

We defined a Supply Code and from 2017 the Global Procurement function has expanded the number of providers under its area of competence, up to the point of rebuying the Non-Product Related Suppliers, thus, the suppliers of materials typically not attributable to the product with a consequent increase in the subscribers of the code. The ethical values included within the code and which are applied to the suppliers and their employees, and the same principles which inspire the activity of Campari Group are the following:

1. Correctness, loyalty, honesty.
2. Impartiality and immediate communication of real or even potential conflicts of interest.
3. Confidentiality.
4. Transparency and completeness of information.
5. Refusal and condemnation of any form of discrimination.
6. Prohibition of forced or juvenile labor.
7. Health and safety on the workplace.
8. Respect of the legislation in environmental aspects and ecological standards.
9. Prevention and reduction of global warming.
10. Prohibition of unfair competition.
11. Adherence to the Code of Ethics and the Policy Quality, Health, Safety and Environment of Campari Group.

We do not compromise on these values. If you want to be part of the Campari Group you must accept them and live these values as an integral part of your operation."

Fabio Pompei (Deloitte)
"A year ago we launched a project called 'Impact for Italy'. It is a manifest in which we created objectives to contribute to the growth and development of our country. Not only and not simply as a provider of services for our clients, but also as interlocutors of institutions and administrations to to try and provide our contributions to face the challenges our country faces with initiatives that are in our DNA, therefore with concreteness and not simple declarations of our intentions. We expect a demanding

task, but we can rely on a solid network (of over 8300 people and 8000 clients) and we can act as privileged interlocutors of various stakeholders across the whole system of the country: business community, institutions, third sector, research institutions and universities, up to citizens. Deloitte is a global network, but it has a significant presence across the entire national territory. Thanks to these characteristics we are able to offer a tangible contribute in supporting institutions and clients, favoring a co-operation between the public and private and contributing with a center of studies dedicated to realizing periodic researches related to different sectors and areas of competence. During the first year of 'Impact for Italy' we have aimed at pillars such as innovation, sustainability and internationalism: our objective remains that of offering innovative proposals and solutions in terms of the challenges and most current needs.

Guiding change, and not suffering from it, is the key challenge of our time to train and lead our talent toward the future."

3.1.3   *The credibility of expertise for a clear vision*

A unifying and qualifying factor which has emerged throughout the course of all our interviews has been the emphasis placed on our interlocutors on personal credibility which springs from their profound knowledge of the business they manage. Far away are the times where mediocre CEOs affirmed to be able to manage any type of business simply because they were able to read financial statements and guide a team. Our panel of interlocutors, all leaders of successful companies have highlighted, all with a different focus, the necessary imperative of managing every aspect of their industrial sector, of knowing all the smallest details, of being a point of reference for all stakeholders to give necessary safety in mastering the volatility of the market. In this chapter we have inserted the most significant and indicative affirmations on this subject.

Ugo de Carolis (Aeroporti di Roma)
"Business capabilities are the first and essential factor in constructing a brand, in the sense that the first thing in building reputation is the quality of your product or service. In 2015, Aeroporti di Roma arrived at the minimum of our reputation in terms of offered and perceived quality. My priority therefore was that of studying the peculiarities of the airport business, identifying all aspects which impact customer experience, revisiting and readdressing them. A bad reputation is extremely compli-

cated to change, as you need to face, image, revolutionize processes and approaches to clients and businesses.

Today we have arrived at almost the end of the third year as the best in Europe in terms of quality. Now that we have reached the level of desired quality, we spend a lot of time communicating social responsibility. Therefore, we have prioritized communicating that we are the best in quality and now we can afford to communicate that we are those who consume less water in the world per passenger, we are those who have constructed sustainable buildings etc. However, this message is credible because we are able to offer an excellent quality; if you communicate that you consume little water, but it rains inside the airport, how

is that credible? So first, you must have the product, after that it is fundamental to say what you do for sustainability, and you can have a role in society and help your environment collectively."

Luca De Meo (Renault Group)
"Throughout the course of my experience I have defined a model of how to manage an automotive company. The model is based on four levels.

The first is the definition of KPI, thus attributing a weight and numeric value to any aspect. You define some objectives, you track advancement and the company is managed and organized with precise numeric values.

The second level is defining processes which are so perfect and can be independent from the quality of the people who operate them, and this requires a complete mastery of all the functions of the mechanism of the company.

The third level is stimulating to the maximum the creativity of all company aspects, so putting people in the condition of expressing to 110% their intellectual and creative skills. This implicates both guaranteeing freedom of thought as well as expressing opinions without the fear of being criticized in case of being wrong. But it is also clear that without a set of guidelines the company can descend into anarchy, and therefore my role is that of continuously guiding our route and communicating it clearly.

The fourth level is that of giving purpose to the organization in order for them to go further than the classic sense, so money, bringing profit to shareholders, controlling cash flow or fixed costs. It means motivating people towards the positive impact their work will bring to society, giving meaning to daily work.

This is my role which comes from the credibility of my experience in this sector, in the trust people have in my regard because they are aware of my ability to read the market and define the guidelines of my company."

Alessandro Foti (Fineco)
"We have clearly identified our stakeholders: actionists, clients, dependents, and consultants of Fineco. Our objective is to guarantee these groups of stakeholders and excellent experience in the short, medium and long term. I suspect of financial activities which are exclusive in creating a charismatic image of management, because this bluff will eventually be understood. As far as we are concerned, our company constantly maintains a very high reputation in investigations regarding our clients.

I expect some sort of transitive property to occur, in the sense that a company with an excellent reputation by definition needs to have competent management, so I would say that our attention is 99.9% focused on this direction. Some delegated administrators have staff of dozens of people exclusively dedicated to curing the image of CEO on the market; we prefer that these people are concentrated on managing business, improving customer experience to give excellent returns to the market, sustainable with time, and have customers who are satisfied, but within an atmosphere of quality. In these years we could have realized definitely higher profits taking advantage in an aggressive manner of the not equal information which there is in regard to the clients on the financial market, but we decided to not go down that road.

The first reason is the recognition by the investors of the added value created by a sustainable management of my business. Secondly, by doing this I manage to protect the economic dimension of the context in which I work: I create the conditions for a better environment, adapted to increase my business in the future.

This is not a question of being a good Samaritan, we don't see ourselves as a charity as our aim is fundamentally to earn. But we want to do this in a way that is sustainable over time. The market recognizes this approach, because the value of a business is not due to the earnings in the moment, but from the flow of profit over time. Being in harmony with your context and making sustainable business becomes an excellent deal. The three pillars on which we constructed Fineco have always been the same: a huge operative efficiency (doing things better than others while spending less), innovation (anticipating the change in the structure of the market), total transparency and respect of clients: I repeat, we are not a charity, but being essentially good people is an excellent deal.

Over the course of the years each company generates in its internal a culture that tends to be homogeneous. If a company is managed structurally in a perspective of profit in the short term, inevitably management and people who work internally will tend to also progress in this direction. A sort of autoselection occurs, thus who is not aligned on the same philosophy will leave the company. In the case of Fineco the management has remained the same from the moment of its foundation, which is a unique history for this sector.

Once I heard a CEO affirm that the most important thing was to make a good budget; after that results would follow. My suggestion instead, is to have a very humble approach, because the creation of this type of result which then brings to reputation, is a result of daily activities and efforts. I refer to a maniacal attention to many small details, which are those that allow us to reach our final objectives.

Many CEOs don't enjoy concentrating on 'dirty' work, that of refining details day after day. They believe that this consists of an activity that gives them little visibility, as nobody sees all those hours, the days spent on the smallest details. But it is precisely that type of work which makes the difference between services that work well and those who don't. A constant approach is needed, as well as a meticulous reinterpretation of all the mechanisms of function: even a process that works well needs to be rerouted, as it could lead to it working better."

Fabio Pompei (Deloitte)
"Today channels of communication are innumerable and compared to the past they provoke an incomparable propagation effect. I believe this fact allows leadership to take up an even more important role, with the CEO that needs to lead certain directions and behaviors and needs to be able to communicate both internally and externally, otherwise there is the risk that certain activities and initiatives, if not adequately communicated, will lose part of their efficiency or could be interpreted wrong.

Even the choice of elements on which to expose leadership is fundamental. In my case you must consider that I lead a very particular context because ours is a services network, with many different types of businesses, and therefore very different areas of skill in order to be exposed mediatically.

In such a context, leadership has a role that goes over the exposure on technical and business aspects, balancing itself more on themes of ethics, social responsibility, diversion and inclusion. The exposure of leadership on these themes has an ability of reinforcing the brand and positions which society and that brand assume. Thus, it could have an ulterior competitive advantage to the business. The ability of having a global vision which goes further than business and its strategic objectives is certainly an aspect, which compared to the past has a higher level of relevance. This is also valid for themes of responsibility, integrity and ethics of the CEO. Reaching results in an ethical and responsible manner is an element which is awarded, and which Deloitte has assumed in its mission, externally but also towards its own people. Maintaining full control of the internal narration of an organization is fundamental to guarantee transparency to instill confidence towards its people, clients, institutions and all referenced stakeholders."

3.1.4 *I'm not ashamed (even in crisis situations)*

All the interviewed CEOs, each with different accents, have highlighted an essential part of their role, which is that of being responsible for taking important decisions. Everyone was aware of the uselessness, if not the damage attitudes of 'superstar' can have and being able to take charge of problems in the business as a point of reference internally and externally is one of the fundamental roles of CEOs.

Brunello Cucinelli (Cucinelli)
"At the eruption of the crisis in 2008 our company had 1450 retail clients. I wrote 1450 letters for each of them: 'Dear Client, it is 25 years that we work together, I don't know what is happening, but know that I will stay by your side'. If I bring testimonies of some letters, you would find them emotional, because if I am by your side, I know you will be by mine, and it is a way to face the crisis together. It was a situation where nobody knew how and if the market would recuperate. On September 16, I reunited all dependents and I said: 'I don't know what is happening, the company has finished its money until the 31st of December 2009. So, you won't lose your jobs until 2009, and we will see what happens after that, but I ask you to treat your human relationships even more, especially, with more creativity and geniality'. We made the most beautiful collection in the

world in January 2009 and delivered the best year. Why? I don't know, this is the answer to the question, you are loyal and frank.

Coming back to our current times, with Covid-19, firstly, we never touched the salaries of our employees. The company employs 2000 people, 1000 here at Solomeo and another 1000 in other countries: I immediately told everyone to not panic. This is a solid brand, which has grown almost uninterruptedly for forty years (the revenue of 2019 was 607.8 million euros, almost 10% more than 2018), therefore it can afford to pause for a year, without having a dramatic effect on those who work for it. We are confident, and in this way, we can face the future, not necessarily lightheartedly, but certainly with some positivity. Also, for these reasons I met 'virtually' with our shareholders to fully explain our decision to not distribute dividends this year and instead reinvest them in the future. Everyone understood.

2020 has now happened, it is useless to wish it hadn't. Now we need to not be distracted by the shortcuts that leave what they found. Also, for this reason I decided to not participate in the next edition of Pitti Immagine Uomo, programmed for the start of September: at that point we will already be way forward, it would be a setback that we cannot afford. However, 2 days ago I confirmed I would join the edition next January; I repeat, it is a temporary situation from which we will come out. With my collaborators I discuss the window decorations for Christmas, those of January, how to charm our consumers in these next few months. Planning for before then- May, June, July- does not seem to me a safe option.

I was one of the first to understand the danger of the situation because I grew up with my Grandfather who would tell me stories of the Spanish Flu Epidemic of 1918, and my Father with his memories of the Influenza pandemic in 1957; rather, we still talk about this a lot now: he is 98, lives next door to me, and every morning, face masks on of course, we talk from a distance. Furthermore, one of my idols, Pericle, was killed by the plague. Keeping all these examples in mind, when our Chinese employees began to talk about Covid-19 at the end of January 2020, and how things were rapidly precipitating, I honestly began to feel scared and I immediately understood that necessary actions were to be made, from smart working to the closure of structures.

Seeing how things went this was the right choice, but there were certainly some dark times: especially in mid-March, when the pandemic seriously exploded in Italy. I then showed the workers in our company the videos I was receiving from China, where in the meantime life was slowly starting again: I didn't know what to tell them, if not showing them we would also go back to normality, if not slowly. Us Italians find ourselves in a complicated position as the epidemic outpost in the West, without terms of comparison to understand how to act: I tried to reassure them in this way, and I did the same when the pandemic exploded in the United States. Over there in my opinion, they are in a worse situation as firing employees in this situation is the norm, they do not think about it twice. Fortunately, our mindset is completely different: for this I state, and I repeat that my priority was guaranteeing the salary of who works with me. They are the company, they are essential now more than ever. For profits, dividends and good company there is time.

This is not the first crisis that our company faces and will not be the last. We experienced some horrible moments after 9/11 in 2001, and in 2008 where we were overcome by a financial crisis of frightening dimension, worse than even this, which can be considered more intense but also circumscribed. We got out of it, and we did it well. I think we should treasure what we are experiencing, choosing every move well and moving forward."

Stefano Cuzzilla (Federmanager)
"I have clearly invested a lot in my person, both in training and in continuous updates in order to be able to best represent my company. When you have this responsibility, you are constantly involved with institutions, and if you want to have a positive impact upon society you need to be constantly updated and credible. We touch upon topics which aim at investing in the future lives of people, so social security and pensions, and we can be efficient only if, as head of this organization, I expose myself in first person and am able to earn the trust of institutions. In comparison to the past, when managers who would retire after forty years of service in the same company were highly rewarded and admired, the labor market is nowadays characterized by a constant volatility and we need to do all we can to protect our associates, supporting them in facing moments of change and discontinuity; our social role has increased out of proportion and we can only obtain results without being ashamed and showing our faces constantly in a qualified manner."

Ugo De Carolis (Aeroporti di Roma)
"The role of CEO in the management of reputation is that of showing face, not being ashamed. First of all, in a company, in good or bad, the CEO is the one who synthesizes and gives an image to the company. So, the strategic approach of the positioning of the company in the perspective of reputation has to be totally coherent with the CEO.

I'll explain myself better: if I didn't believe that recycling my waste was truly important for the world, if I personally didn't believe that what I was doing was right in the moment in which I communicate, you would easily see the difference between the person and the company, with disastrous results. The CEO is the face that you show in positive moments and also negative moments. When you have a difficulty in the airport you need to go and talk about what is happening, but what is fundamental is what Americans call 'Walk the talk', doing what you say and saying what you do. I don't believe we are in a situation anymore in which leaders of companies cannot appear, especially companies which have a large impact on the public. People tend to identify more and more the product with the person and it goes more and more in the direction in which what counts is service.

I come from the world of automotives and if you talk to the dealers, they will tell you that it is almost 15 years that a client asks them to open the hood of the car. Before they all felt like Formula 1 drivers and they wanted to see the motor, besides the fact that now you can't even see the motor, you open it and cannot see anything, only a box. If you watch automobile adverts people will ask you how much they are connected and thus it is all linked to service. So service is a lot less hard and a lot more soft, and as it is more soft it is more efficient when linking it to a face or soul.

This doesn't mean that 40 million people passengers who come here need to know my face, it needs to be clear that I am not Tim Cook, I don't have a product as retail as Apple, just as I don't think that the market recognizes the face of the stylist of Gucci. However, the moment you talk about the business community you need to show your face, and especially, the face of your employees because it is them who will transmit to the passenger a certain way of working. Leadership is who guides, gives driver, direction and the unique style of a company."

Daniele Ferrari (Versalis)

"If your name is on the door of CEO this means you need to invest in business as if it were your own. And you need to understand that everything you do is an example in the center of the company and is testimony of your external reputation, defining your values, which need to coincide with those of the company. You can acquire installations or other societies, but you can't buy fidelity and trust of people, which instead you need to earn through example. The first thing I did when I arrived in Versalis was visit all the establishments, present myself to all staff and see with my own eyes the business reality of the territories. I then reunited all the senior executives, over 200 managers, and I told them we would face together the difficult situation we were living in, that it wouldn't be easy, but I would present them with a plan to come out and be winners together.

Change under any aspect was the key theme: I remember drawing a simple image, a triangle divided horizontally in three parts, to explain the change to attitude where in its apex there were those who 'don't want change', explaining that if for the rest of the company there was availability and support (for those 'who had never done it' or who 'didn't know how to face it'), for this category there were no solutions.

We have made a radical change, presenting to our stakeholders the new company, even changing its name from Polimeri Europa to Versalis: 'the new face of Chemicals'. Since we are here talking about 'faces', it was necessary that there should be a new 'face' created for our new identity. We began to reposition ourselves in those external channels in which we previously weren't present, such as media, associative sectors, conferences and international round tables, and we managed to communicate our business turnaround in a distinctive way, as it deserved.

Thanks to this new position I had the opportunity to represent the company to the maximum levels of the sector, recovering a central and strategic position for business. To relaunch the company, it was also necessary to close and reconvert some establishments, and I was always personally at the center of these operations to give credibility to the company. We currently organize our monthly meetings of our Leadership Team in a different establishment to be ever present for the entire company, involving and updating colleagues about the various company developments. Furthermore, every year after the approval of the multi-year plan of investments and the presentation to analysts, we stream to over 5000 people of the company and explain our strategic planning. The key word in this project is 'engage' and impacts the organization upon every level.

Today we find ourselves in the era of circular economy with mediatic attack upon plastic, we have largely invested in initiatives which safeguard the environment, both as Versalis as well as a participation with global alliances which involve the whole supply chain, such as 'Alliance to End Plastics Waste' or the 'Circular Plastic Alliance'. Personally, I am very busy communicating these initiatives to protect our reputation and that of plastic materials, which thanks to their versatility are an integral part of our daily lives and are of primary importance. You can simply think of the emergency scenario we faced caused by the diffusion of Covid-19 during which plastic products used in medical practice, such as medical equipment and food packaging showed with force that they were essential goods, exactly as the whole plastics supply chain demonstrated how it was strategic even at a national level.'

Alessandro Foti (Fineco)
"Fineco is a public company, the investors are its owners and as a consequence are directly interested in understanding how a company evolves. This situation puts me in front of an alternative: I can choose a comfortable route, explaining well to the financial director and the investor relation what they need to say and do while I sit peacefully in the office and complete my strategies. Or, as I truly do, I constantly meet dozens of investors during roadshows and live or virtual conferences, letting investors directly speak to someone who shows their true face to expose their activities. By doing this, I am working for the company instead of the construction of my personal brand: this is an important assumption of responsibility, and it is clearly greatly appreciated.

The decisive aspect is that once a position has been established, you need to guarantee consistency with the choices you apply. If you tell investors a story which will not be realized you will lose credibility, and we cannot afford this. Being in constant communication with investors and being consistent with delivery guarantees a continuous maintaining and enforcing of reputation. You only run a risk the moment you betray expectations, when you present yourself in front of your community of reference without maintaining promises.

Having a transparent relationship with your investors means exposing yourself, explaining the strong points of your company and also its weaknesses, giving a clear picture. I'll give a strong example: when the decline in the interest rate curve occurred, we chose the route of transparency, exposing with precision in what way the decline would impact us in terms of the reduction of our interest margin. Contemporarily, we presented the list of all the actions we would take to have a clear image and provide all the elements from which they can draw the consequences of the case.

If I present myself to the market saying, 'I believe the company is underrated, it should be valued much more', from my perspective I am not maintaining a serious approach. Instead, approaching investors and saying, 'This is our company, these are its strong points, these are the points which need attention, these are all the metrics, this is the way in which you can set your modelling to understand how the company works', you are being serious and professional, which gives credibility of behavior to the leader of the company."

Isabella Fumagalli (BNP Cardif)
"That reputation is now not only a corporate theme is something that I experience every day firsthand. The expectations towards our group impact greatly upon my management, because it is not enough to say: 'I am BNP Paribas', 'Yes Isabella, you are BNP Paribas, so I will listen to you, but I want to see you as a person, as a manager, how do you interpret the fact of being BNP Paribas? How do you truly practice your group's values?'.

This happens because the client is no longer looking for the difference between what is true or false, I notice this because young clients especially want to understand if I truly believe in what I am saying, and if I don't believe in it, it is better to simply not say it because this comes an unstoppable boomerang through social communications. What is to be attributed to us is that the company has chosen specific values, its manager embodies them and they are therefore true. Otherwise, it will not work. But the only way to make them an integral part of the sustainable model in time and inseparable from BNP Paribas is leadership. This means assigning managers the responsibility of embodying them and activating all their people. It is the most difficult job, whilst it would be much easier giving money to social cooperatives which makes a circular economy, something which however does not generate true sustainable change.

This is, in my opinion, the new revolution of the concept of reputation, which has certainly always been more fundamental, but now more than ever also has a strong individual component tied to single managers. A personal and professional business card that with socials has acquired a level of transparency and visibility which is completely different from the past, where as a CEO you are required to expose yourself as people, both towards the market and towards employees which in you need to recognize the image of the company."

Robert Kunze-Concewitz (Campari)
"We have various antennas to manage reputational risks. There is research we carry out, both internally and externally, because reputation begins at home, and therefore for us, being the best place to work is extremely important. There is also some research that we carry out abroad, and last but not least we have a constant monitoring of the media. We also have a recovery plan to manage situations of crisis, and as CEO I am also leader of the Crisis Management Team, supported by various functional directors, from our director regional managers and from the part of all my communication team. It is my responsibility to be first in line for all themes which directly involve my company and it would be absolutely incorrect to send somebody else.

My exposure is also directed to help understand the values, purpose and mission of my company and give a taste of our culture. My role in this regard is to be the spokesperson to transmit an entrepreneurial approach and be down to action. Our business style is what I like to call 'humble and hungry'. And I need to be the first to embody this."

Giulio Ranzo (Avio)
(In August 2019 a Vega rocket exploded a few minutes after takeoff. It was the first incident after 15 rockets launched perfectly. Avio had an immediate collapse in the stock market. In a short period of time the company recovered its position and reputation. In our conversation with Giulio Ranzo we couldn't not talk about this argument to hear more about his experience in regard).

"In case of crisis we have ready in the company a procedure which foresees a series of moves. In the following hours of the accident, we registered a video in which I explained, in an extremely transparent and frank manner what had happened, without any filter. I think this approach paid off. After explaining the events I anticipated that another five weeks would be needed for another update. After exactly five weeks we made another video exposing what we had understood up to that moment, until we were no longer able to explain the dynamic of the facts. Operating in this way, with honesty and transparency, we managed to calm the market.

On the internal front instead, I immediately gathered all my employees, I explained the events and encouraged them to move forward and remain united. The result was that people no longer wanted to leave, working until 2 in the morning every night, to give their contribution. Therefore, this constant dialogue with engineers and employees was extremely productive. It was not the first time they saw me in the factory, dialogue with them is constant, I constantly visit production facilities, I know our colleagues one by one, and closeness was an important element to give credibility to our affirmations, showing commitment and coherence."

3.1.5 *The storytelling of strong choices*

'What people remember is how you made them feel'. Entering the emotional dimension of people through strong storytelling of your own company and product is a winning choice by the CEOs of success. The characteristics of this storytelling are: involvement, participation, a story rich with significance and ability to leave situations of crisis even more strongly.

Federico Casini (Aon)
"Up to a few years ago, when we phoned a potential client and presented ourselves as Aon, very often they would ask us who we were and what we did. So we would have to potentially explain our activity and what services we offered, whilst today everyone knows us. In fact, when we sponsored Manchester United, we acquired an international visibility which now reports all the activities which Aon offers to its clients. The objective was dual: on one side make the brand and reality of Aon known, and from the other start a path which has allowed us to tell our story, a company which has made hundreds of acquisitions worldwide and that now enhances the concept of 'united', creating the biggest society of management and brokerage of risk.

This path has been supported by a strong internal and external communication to tell the stories and values of our company based on the concept of uniqueness and collaboration. In fact, Aon in Gaelic means unity, uniqueness, and this message has become a must for us all. Now that we have reached this objective, our communication will be directed towards our main contacts/clients, to tell the value proposition of Aon, strong in skill and professionalism made available to risk management, risks that are ever more complex, determined by strong situations of crisis triggered by world events (see Covid-19) which have profoundly modified our way of living."

Brunello Cucinelli (Cucinelli)
"When I came out on the cover of *Forbes*, my father who is 98 told me 'I am not interested, as long as you are a good person'. What he would tell me as a 12-year-old, he tells me now. Maybe he tells me with damp eyes. I also had damp eyes when he told me 'You are a good person'.

The truth is that you need to be real and transmit this to the world. I have my office in a tower of the 1300s. Who created this worked on it over 700 years ago? When I am there, I ask myself how many people died and lived here, how many made love, how many were fascinated by this place. When we restored it we found a dead body, we blessed him and left him here.

We are the keepers of our world. Dante says: 'And the way still offends me', and I say 'And the way you still honor me by telling me one thing.'. So, change has occurred, then there will be those who believe in it, those who believe a little less, those who don't believe but regardless have to take action, because they are part of my role as keeper. This is our culture. My mother had no idea how much her employer earnt, because he only knew the true profit. Now, do you think there is someone who doesn't know my profits?

Have you ever watched the Dead *Poets Society?* The way the professor acted? 'Tear the page, my captain, oh my captain'. He was an idealist, so he had ideals: gentleness, firmness, 'Benedectine firmness', because Saint Benedict doesn't joke around, but always tells you to be lovable, rigorous and sweet. The world needs idealists and fairness. You need to know where you work, and you need to know if your work brings damage to humanity or not."

Robert Kunze-Concewitz (Campari)

"We defined our message which is prevalent and reaches the core of our business: 'Toasting like together'. It synthesizes the mission and story of our brand. It is the base for an emotional storytelling which is strong and immediate. We work in a sector, that of alcoholic beverages, which is subject to strong criticism, therefore we want to address ourselves only to the positive and responsible side and we put a lot of focus on the mature and aware way to consume our products, which is the 'Mediterranean way' as we like to put it. This means in a social environment, also associated with the consumption of food. We also work a lot with other associations of category to promote this 'Mediterranean way of consuming alcohol' and we work a lot in our interior to raise awareness, educate and training our people, following a precise and amply experimented code.

To give a concrete example: we constructed the Aperol brand with our consumers. Our method is to go to bars where we educate barmen and let them try our cocktail, the perfect serve, one consumer at a time. We go and then come back, we organize events and parties. We have amphibious vehicles which go to beaches, snow cats in mountains, we organize concerts and then the consumer becomes our ambassador, in fact, the drink which has featured more on Instagram in the world is the Aperol Spritz.

I can give you an example of a crisis we had in 2019. The *New York Times* published an article called 'Why Aperol Spritz is a bad drink'. It is the biggest brand in our market. What happened is that we were activating the unity of the crisis and before we could intervene the consumers did. Thousands of customers went on the site of the *New York Times* and got very angry: 'How do you dare; I am now suspending my subscription.'; 'This is fake news.'. Incredible comments, of such anger: 'Aperol Spritz is fabulous.'; 'I adore Aperol Spritz.'. In only 48 hours we had a billion impressions and the potential crisis turned into opportunity. As soon as we saw this situation we decided to not intervene and let the customers have their say. Even the media began to attack the *New York Times,* from the *Washington Post* to the *New York Magazine*. On CNN there was a debate discussing whether they believed Aperol Spritz was good or bad. From Martha Stewart who declared it to be her favorite drink, to an impressionable number of other commentators who expressed positive judgements. Then we come to the middle of the article, where the comment of the journalist is fairly stupid because she states that 'if you use bad prosecco, it becomes a bas Aperol Spritz'. It's as if I used Diesel in a Ferrari and later complained that it doesn't work. We even found out that this is a journalist based in Paris that wrote a book about French aperitifs last year, sponsored by one of our rivals. In a few days we had an imposing growth in our value on the market."

3.1.6   *CEO or hero? Humanizing the CEO figure*

Stakeholder capitalism is bringing a humanization of the figure of company and CEO. The pandemic has accelerated this necessity. No longer the super manager sat at a monumental desk in the corner office, but a person with their abilities and weaknesses who embodies the company and transmits its message.

Alberto Calcagno (Fastweb)
"Personally, I have always had a very direct management style where contact with the organization at every level is crucial. Discussing in merit a wide range of themes, from strategic to operative, using a 'hands on' approach, typical of an entrepreneurial reality is from my perspective a competitive advantage.

If we make a sports comparison, I have in mind for my role an analogous figure to that of the player captain. In this direct comparison it is clearly fundamental to be coherent and authentic. Many time the CEO has a tendency of showing only aspects of security and invincibility, in reality remaining a human being, I think it is also normal to not hide any fears or weaknesses, because they are able to establish a relationship of inclusion and identification with all employees.

There is a big difference between communicating the message 'We are stronger than everyone and everything', and 'We face a difficult situation, but I am sure that together we will be able to manage it'. To cut short distances and recover this relationship, it is important to show face, and for example, explain our decisions in an exhaustive manner, what has brought us to carry out that specific action, what is rational of that agreement or strategy.

Furthermore, direct and personal exposure with a video, even only 15 minutes, can have a very strong impact compared to a cold press conference, both for my people and the market in general."

Federico Casini (Aon)

"In every company, but generally in all moments of life, I believe the theme of example is fundamental. People, beyond their role or profession, watch you, judge your behaviors, observe your transparency and coherency between what you say and what you do. I deeply live within the reality of my organization, and I need to lead by example and be the reference of company rules. From now, following Covid-19 and the increasing use of smart working, I no longer have an office and I live my professional life alongside my colleagues, side by side, with no barriers, with the objective of sharing principles, objectives, strategies, enthusiasm and participation. If I didn't have flawless behavior, I would not be able to look them in the eyes, and I could not represent the values and principles of Aon.

As a company we also have a procedure thanks to which employees can denounce in an anonymous and protected manner if someone or something steps out of the ethical rules of the group, and the first in line in management needs to guarantee adherence to company codes, starting from myself."

Paola Corna Pellegrini (Allianz Partners)

"As CEOs we have the responsibility to enhance diversity giving everyone the possibility of expressing their own talent. The humanization of the CEO is an indispensable passage. Empathizing with your own collaborators and becoming for them a point of reference is fundamental also in terms of reputation, both to attract and maintain talent, now more and more careful in terms of inclusion and social responsibility when choosing to work for a particular company. Our example is inevitable, our actions necessarily have an impact on our reputation, but inevitably, and of immediate reflection, also on the reputation of the company we lead and represent.

It is for this reason that I continue to expose myself in the first person, bringing my testimony and promoting themes that I can consider fundamental for our society. For this reason I also recently accepted the role of President of AICEO, because I believe us CEOS can and must play an ever more significant role in helping our country find the ability to grow sustainably, to offer good jobs which adapt to everyone's personal preparation, in particular for our youth, to free creativity transforming it into innovation for our businesses and public administration, to be inclusive towards all diversities and maintain our talent.

This is even more necessary in a moment like this, where the Coronavirus pandemic has highlighted even further our fragilities, but at the same time has given us a leap in skills and culture which usually would have taken many years. We must capitalize on these advances because, as Churchill said, great crises must not be wasted and Italy must put in common factor its best abilities and skills to position itself, talking about reputation as it deserves."

Luca De Meo (Renault Group)
"The transparency of information and the necessity of consumers to identify a brand with a person, the public image of the CEO has become essential. I would not be able to obtain any result if I didn't have an excellent team, starting from the workers of the factory, but I am aware that in my role I must give the image of the company. So, when I arrived in Barcelona as CEO of Seat, I immediately integrated into the city, learning the language and living its context.

I was surprised by the shows of affection that I received, also because it was the first time we saw a CEO so involved in the relaunch of a national brand. It is certain that I see elements of great danger in the heroization of the role of CEO, but I believe that my task in to stay on the frontline, alongside everybody to give my people the courage to face the future, to help them understand in a simple way where the market is heading.

The most important role a CEO can have is the ability to read the future aloud, to write it, explain it and be close to their people. The results have been superior to expectations. They perceived me as one of them, both inside the company and in Spain, and I aroused an attachment to the company which has brought important results to all levels.'

Gian Maria Mossa (Banca Generali)
'I believe that the company image which the CEO manages to share has a fundamental role in determining the force with which the business is carried forward by the whole team. Banca Generali is a business made up of people: my team is built on 2000 entrepreneurs which are not employed by the bank and are courted everyday by competition with figures that make no sense, because we are those which on average have the largest wallet. My colleagues travel around Italy and receive work proposals every day.

To remain with us they need to define themselves in top management which clearly has a strategic priority: the one that puts them in the condition to work better with their colleagues, which is the only asset they can count on besides their professionalism. This deals with men and women who when looking up, need to identify themselves with the manager. If they don't see reflected in the top manager the values which they propose to clients every day, then they will lose trust in the company.

Personally, I know of very strong brands which have not been able to enhance their heritage because leadership was missing, both as a presence and as an example. My priority is that my people identify themselves in the values that top management, myself in particular, represent every day."

Giulio Ranzo (Avio)

"I believe humanizing communication today is important, because people understand how we are also risking our own funds. We are not simple employees who at the end of the month receive a stable salary, but we risk our savings and are therefore aligned in interests. In my opinion, this aspect of humanization is central to my role and that of everyone in the first lines of management. I speak about everything to my collaborators: technological novelties, new contracts, agreements with third parties, relationships with various authorities and relationships with the media.

It is important to make it clear that in your work you have to move a certain number of levers, with a team that operates on its priorities. I see that this personal and transparent approach has a great comeback on the trust towards the company, in creating an equal community and aligning everyone towards the same objectives, at this point known and shared."

3.1.7 Walk the talk: honesty and transparency in business

Coherency between affirmations and behavior united to an awareness that is indispensable to be transparent and always tell the truth to all stakeholders emerge as central aspects from conversations with all CEOs. We have reported the following significant passages.

Alberto Calcagno (Fastweb)

"It is indicative of a phenomenon which however comes upstream: if you work in the services industry you need to have a natural desire to take care of people. When I say people, I mean: clients, employees, providers, I mean all of those who somehow have a relationship with your company.

What does taking care of mean? It means going further than the economic relationship, which in the case of the clients is simply a financial industrial indicator to reach determined objectives, or that employees are an industrial number which you need to reach your objectives.

Taking care means going beyond a commercial relationship, trying to undertake a deeper relationship. We will make a simple example because in the end we need to be practical: the theme of transparency is a reputational theme; for us reputation is essentially to be as transparent as possible, to be clear. The decision of transparency can seem one of the simple, and indeed most obvious decisions to take for a company of service which relies on its clients.

The client should be the only real owner of the company as it is them who pays your salary. In reality, especially in the world of telecommunication, it is one of most battled territories, indeed I believe it is a sector which is considered the dullest. Why this? For two reasons: one, because the world of the over-the-top such as Facebook, Google, Amazon and Netflix have completely changed the way of interacting with clients, starting from their expectations. Before the over-the-top, relationships with the client were completely unbalanced in favor of the company, therefore they could afford to do whatever they wanted, to make you sign a 250-page contract, and abuse their position. Then what happened: the over-the-top arrived, and in a very simple manner they tell you they offer one of the best services in the world for free. Facebook and Google arrive, and they essentially offer you simple and usable services where everything works, and if there is a problem, they solve it at a fast pace.

Then the clients begin to say: 'I expect this level of service'. All of these services are free, and successively people begin to believe that everything related to this world, including the Internet and telephony must also be free. Therefore: 'Why does Facebook cost me nothing, but my telephone operator expects 30 euros a month from me?'. Obviously, what they don't know, or pretend not to know is that all of these over-the-top make hundreds of millions of dollars using information about you, but the message which is communicated is composed by two aspects, that the service is usable and simple, and it is free.

Obviously I need to take the positive from these events. I cannot clearly provide free service, but I can work on the rest. The rest is not transparency in general, but transparency of service. Therefore, getting rid of the barriers which only generate distance between the client and company. Today clients have an enormous power through socials. So my objective is to separate myself from all the negative connotations which the telecommunications industry has earned. My ambition is to let Fastweb reenter the few companies which are considered part of the family.

There are some companies which have managed, through the quality of their products and the management of their employees to earn their place between families. My objective is to get to that point. Obviously, this is an objective, and it takes time. First step: let's get rid of what doesn't work, a dull conversation and incomprehensible offers. We also have a strategy called 'Nothing is as it was' to create a relationship which goes beyond business which becomes unequivocally personal and deeply transparent."

Federico Casini (Aon)

"We construct our credibility and support our brand through a continuous positive relationship with clients and insurance companies. Each one of us, including top management, has the responsibility of a certain number of clients which they need to visit with high frequency firstly to verify and secondly guarantee satisfaction towards our services.

We have a program called Aon Client Promise, dedicated to our first 700 clients, which imposes us to always be available and constantly present to expand our services, immediately knowing eventual problems or necessities of the client and consequently detect the more effectual and efficient solutions, avoiding damages to reputation. The results of these programs are extraordinary and tangible in the degree of satisfaction measured towards clients also in comparison to competitors.

The same type of attention is dedicated to the relationship with insurance companies. Because reputation is built with direct action, but even more so through good references from clients and spreading of words, working in this way lets us grow even further on the market. I also add that this reputation attracts the interest of the media who are curious to know us better, and therefore we have activated a virtuous circle."

Brunello Cucinelli (Cucinelli)

"You need to always be real. You are in difficulty, sad, joyous, it goes well, or it doesn't, you're in a worst mood in a certain moment because that is what life is like. You need to be real. It is clear that this is the reputation of a company: real. Real is not the same as transparency. Also, transparency, but being real is something different. Because you can be transparent, but not real. Real means that I need to understand the state of mind of that human, that company.

Bad moods accompany us from birth, sometimes they are strong and sometimes they degenerate. You are real when things go well, go badly, you need to truly represent how things stand. I said to one of my Chinese clients: 'Confucius says: I am not here to invent, I only want to transmit'.

However, with the Internet, the reputation has totally changed because twenty years ago when we read something in the newspaper, we were able to bin it in the evening. Where would you go to find it again? There needed to be someone who carried out a specific search, who knew how to find this news. Not today. On YouTube I can find what I said 10 years ago, the jokes that I can no longer say. Therefore, it is incredibly important to pay much more attention to what is said, and truth has a major weight on the reputation of my company."

Isabella Fumagalli (BNP Paribas Cardif)
"From a few years thanks to the Internet, our relationship with clients and their awareness of what they purchase has changed radically. We therefore have the possibility to personalize the service on specific needs united to the necessity of transparency and honesty in the relationship.

We cannot present ourselves to the market and say 'Dear Client, I make the right product for you, I put it on the market, make it fit.' Rather, our approach is: 'Dear Client, let me understand what you need, and I evaluate the product which better fits your needs.'.

Co-creation started thanks to listen. In BNP Paribas Cardif we recently launched a beauty product, but we first had some focus groups with various clusters of clients, including generational. Because an aspect that today has been ulteriorly accentuated is that each generation purchases in a different manner, so we have had to create twelve clusters for age, generation, women, men, region and provenance. Only in this way we were able to realize a modular product, which tries to cover all needs which we have understood. This gives the client the keys to decide what they want to activate.

It's not about: 'You get this product, and then when something happens, we will talk about it'. Rather: 'Try to understand what your need is and the risk you are willing to take and entrust to me'. In this way with co creation I go and give the client further education, which consents them to address their awareness on risk taking. In function of this I can make an offer which lets me represent the client in the best way possible, who can then individually decide to activate or deactivate some parameters so that products become modular and modifiable with time depending on their lifestyle and their needs.

There is another important aspect. Clients trust who have sold them the product, but it is important to mention that the brand is not enough, it is hard to differentiate the brand from who is in front of you, on the telephone or online. For the client these become one single entity: the brand, and you who phoned me. We come back to a personalization of the relationship, which can be done through modern technology, but this does not deny that a personal relationship is needed: we are human, we are social beings and this must be preserved, otherwise it won't work.

The relationship of trust has transformed. Before the client was less aware and informed, they needed to entrust themselves to the brand, now you can trust who is in front of you. In this way the relationship becomes frank and you can afford to make some errors. The error is excused if you recognize it in a transparent way and are ready to remedy it."

Fabio Pompei (Deloitte)
"My perception is that today the theme of reputation is a lot more complex than it was in the past. In general, the central aspect on which it was based was that of the quality of services. Today this aspect is no less: there is still an essential component of reputation, but to this many other components have acquired a strategic importance, such as sustainability, transparency, integrity, attention towards your people, social effort and therefore of the CSR. This does not deal only with the reputation of companies, but it implies a daily transformation of our way of acting.

I'll give an example: the theme of environmental sustainability is now essential for any company which is up to date with the modern era. Once upon a time vague affirmations prevailed (greenwashing), now acting concretely to reduce one's own environmental impact is an imperative which cannot be subtracted. I will tell you more: it is our own young people who ask to adopt internal policies which are increasingly attentive to the theme of the environment. Every year we employ almost 2000 people so becoming recognizable from young graduates on themes of their interest such as sustainability, social effort and transparency has become fundamental. Furthermore, declined in a more advanced vision, the theme of sustainability has become an international question, which crosses borders and does not apply only to young Italians. It represents our number one challenge of these years and for this reason we are the first who try to be a model of business sustainability: we help businesses to develop sustainable revenues, who are virtuous in the processes, production chain, management of staff, interaction with territory and collectivity. Even the protection of people, from both the physical and psychological perspective represents a primary aspect of importance in the political world of Deloitte, inside and outside the work environment. Transparency and coherence between affirmations of principal and action: by now we know that these values are essential. What benefits from this is both the quality of human capital which we manage to attract, and the reputation of our brand towards potential clients."

3.1.8 'The Tinkerbell Effect'

Tinkerbell is a fairy invented for the film Peter Pan of 1953. A busy fairy born before the laughter of children. In the Disney version, Tinkerbell has magical powers. She can fly with her fairy wings which make her light when in the air. She is able to launch magical energy, spread her fairy dust which makes people also extremely light and able to fly. Using her powers, she has telekinetic abilities and can mildly control people's minds. We wanted to report this image suggested to us by Doctor Fumagalli, of BNP Paribas Cardif, because with only two words she expresses in a very efficient way an original and interesting aspect and behavior of modern leadership.

Isabella Fumagalli (BNP Paribas Cardif)
"The problem is: How do I act toward internal resistance? Here as we have said, leadership comes to play with the example of concretely bringing forward business values, saying to people: 'Do you feel in your place, do you feel like producing, bringing about results for the common cause?'.

However, this is not only about teaching employees to act towards one objective, it also means relighting everything which over the years has gone out in their ambition. It means making them feel considered and a part of the company. These people, who are producing 50% of their potential, the next day bring 110%, and of this 20% is dedicated to social causes. I will give you a concrete example. We had a theme of major involvement with the women in the company. It was six years that we used the Cal14ideas for startups through a project called Open F@b, never a woman, or at least very few. Perfect, we said to ourselves, we will launch a project dedicated to digital female talent, so we can easily find female entrepreneurs. This is how 'MIA-Miss In Action" was born, the first accelerator in Italy for startups and innovative female PMIs, promoted by BNP Paribas Cardif and Digital Magics, which has now become a fixed appointment. We have already made two call4ideas and we are launching a third edition: we evaluated almost 300 innovative projects and declared seven as the winners which we have used to influence our products.

The female client interests me particularly because she tends to be more suspicious, she is less easily convinced, but when she is convinced, she truly is. In general, she is more demanding and if you think about consumption, especially in our regard, it is the women in families who decide what must be bought. Obtaining women's trust means sustainable business because if you earn their trust as a responsible person, they will surely purchase my products. So, it is also very important to include the female thought within the company through fresh ideas, but also enhancing internal talent.

For this reason, I organized a few breakfasts with a few of my collaborators, in small groups. From 9 to 9.30 with the CEOs. We started this in an unserious manner to then discover that it led to some excellent ideas. Through the use of the female internal lever, I received many ideas on the possible needs of the market, and I came into agreement with many of my colleagues, of other societies of the group as well, responding to many unanswered questions."

3.1.9 *Speeding up when in curve*

We are all good at driving in a straight line, it is important to simply hold steady the steering wheel. The difference between pilots can be seen in the ability to manage the car in the curve. This metaphor could not be missed in the interview with one of the most expert and brilliant CEOs in the world of automotives.

Luca De Meo (Renault Group)

"The role of CEO is that of guaranteeing a vision on the future to the people of a company and to external stakeholders. It is as if we were in a circuit, in a descending curve. In the people who drive cars there are two categories: those which in a similar situation accelerate because they picture where the curve will bring them, and those who press the brake because they are scared of what they will find at the end of the curve. My role is to understand what there will be after the curve, where we will find ourselves after this phase of striking change, and to lead the company and team with their feet on the accelerator. I also expect this approach from my collaborators.

I do not need people who press the brake when in a curve, but managers who are able to accelerate without fear. The phase in which we find ourselves will be remembered in a similar way to the Renaissance period, or the discovery of America. We will find a new and unexplored world. We cannot afford to be slowed down from the fear of the future, of what comes after the curve. We need to know how to accelerate without leaving the road, but also without letting our fears paralyze us in imagining and creating our future."

3.1.10 *The strength of surnames*

In Italy, family businesses play an essential role in the economy. The interview with Riccardo Illy has allowed us to deepen on a few specific themes which are related to the reputational approach of a company which carries the surname of its founders and managers.

Riccardo Illy (Illy)

"The reputation of a company is amplified in a positive or negative sense when we talk about a family business whose managers often have the same name as the company. When I entered illycaffé in 1977, it invoiced 10 billion lire and sold 1000 tons of coffee a year. In 2019 we invoiced over 500 million euros with over 20.000 tons of coffee, and in addition to this we have a company of tea, chocolate, viticulture etc.

Our reputation has been fundamental, on one side to acquire clients and thus to sell, but on the other hand to buy services, starting from financial ones. When I entered the company the debt in comparison to its net assets was 7:1, therefore if there hadn't been an elevated reputation of my father who was president at the time, no bank would have given us a loan. Loans at the time were unsecured, so they were based completely on the trust for a person, also because there were no goods to be given as a guarantee.

We base our reputation on business culture, whose fundamental factor is the system of values which are written and shared. Reputation pays in the long term; if one only has quarterly objectives they probably don't concentrate on the reputational field because in three months there will be little profit. However, if a business such as Family businesses work with a generational finish line, reputation becomes fundamental of the product as well as organizational and social aspects.

In line with our company values, our reputation is based on the promise of guaranteeing quality. In the 80s we began to produce our first 100% Arabic blend and after a while we found dozens of competitors who said they used a 100% Arabic blend as well. So, we had a few samples analyzed and discovered that this was not at all true. We did not report them, but we preferred to obtain the first certificate of quality of product, released from Qualité France. I remind you that I am talking about the first half of the 80s, when the first certificate of quality was not yet famous. Therefore, we truly created quality, but we needed a third party to certify this. The market consequently recognized our seriousness and quality. From then we have continued, and we will continue to request a certification from an external organization for all our products in line with our behavior we have now maintained for ninety years.

Reputation must be built day after day, with actions which must be coherent and that often brings in the short term the necessity to sacrifice some things. In 1977, my first year at illycaffé, I had a good example of what defending reputation meant. There had just been a frost in Brazil which had destroyed several thousand coffee plantations which had led to prices rising sharply, from just over 100 cents per pound to over 300. We had three possibilities: maintain quality by increasing the price, reducing quality to let prices stay the same or maintain our promise to the market. All the other competitors had reduced quality increasing the percentage of Robusta which cost 30/40% less in comparison to the Arabic blend, thus not needing to increase their prices. We went for the third option: 100% Arabic with a small increase in price, thus a drastic reduction of the margins. We lost money and we closed the balance sheet at a loss, for the first and last time at illycaffé. Our image and reputation however remained intact without lowering ourselves to compromises. I believe this is thinking in generational and reputational terms, instead of earning in the short term. Surely the industry which has an elevated reputation earns more. The consumer is more willing to pay a superior price because they know they can trust, they know they will effectively obtain a superior quality.

Many companies are excellent in marketing and less in production: they communicate well, they promise well, but then when someone has paid a superior price and tries the product, they discover that the quality is that of others which cost 20% less. Meanwhile, a company which has a reputation based on effective quality manages to overcome the resistance of an elevated price and consolidate a relationship. Furthermore, in regard to banks, an elevated reputation allows you to get lower rates, beyond the rating which algorithms calculate, or even better, reputation becomes an important part of the algorithm."

3.1.11 *The player captain*

The image of the CEO as a player in a team has emerged a few times in the course of our interviews. The strong awareness of being an example to your own team is one of the most important elements in the expression of one's own business leadership.

Alberto Calcagno (Fastweb)
"For me the CEO is an absolutely empty expression, instead I am much closer to the sporting concept of the player-captain. What is the difference? That unfortunately, the CEO sometimes pursues personal interests which can also, not necessarily conflict with, but can be a weakening aspect of company performance. Instead, if the player-captain wins they will get a bit of merit as the others, but if they lose, they will lose more than others. This means that for me it is much more important to work on substance and make sure the organization focuses on vision and behavioral values.

I search for coherence and especially the cancellation of distance between the company and people in general. Between the company and clients, the company and employees, thus the company is not an abstract entity but it is the result of our daily behavior with our employees and our clients. This is the most important thing to me which I dedicate all my attention to. I think I am the CEO who does more vision meetings, who involves more people, who speaks to everyone, who communicates in a factual way with people internal to the organization, because together we discuss what it is we need most.

Obviously brand communication is fundamental, but I believe that true branding is done in the way a Fastweb agent across Italy behaves the way I would behave. To do this, I need to constantly put effort in a work of profound cultural transformation, but we are heading in that direction. Having a sportive mentality, I am always searching for something more because the first law of sport is this: 'As strong as you can be, there will always be someone stronger than you'. So, you can never be content with the results you have reached, but you need to constantly improve yourself."

Stefano Cuzzilla (Federmanger)
"As soon as I took up the position of the CEO, I promoted two diligences to the interior of my organization and related societies. I wanted to understand if and in what measure each team was aligned in regard to principal objectives, and at the same time create a feeling of team, of belonging and shared values of mission. The message which I gave was very clear: there can be no competition in our interior, we are all tiles of the same mosaic. I let them understand that the entire system depends on the strongest brand, therefore the Federmanger brand, and if this brand went into crisis, everything would collapse.

I explained this to the people who led the other companies of the Group, and to all the staff, therefore I had to dedicate much time to realize many encounters at all levels. In this way I managed to make people appreciate the reasons behind the profound transformations I introduced within the Group. I am convinced that any person who has the task of guiding, who intends to exercise true leadership, is obligated to be on the front line so that they represent the final terminal of what people feel, so they need to give indications, mediate between different positions, favor teamwork. During my first two years I travelled across the national territory, without worrying if my destination was main headquarters or a small local branch.

Earning everyone's trust means investing much time in constructing a relationship with people, because another thing leaders need to do to earn the required consent to favor great change is listening to various points of view, be present and making sure that direct collaborators feel understood within their necessities.

Obviously, this approach also carries some risks. The first is the personal type: the risk of being absorbed by everything, to live in first person the problems of others, to take on too much, to be constantly called to solve particular questions. I will not hide that this often brings you to not dream as big and prevents you from concentrating on other projects. Precious time is subtracted when you fly high. The second risk is about the company. If a leader does not know how to guide behavior well, if they are not able to surround themselves by able people which they can delegate tasks to, the rest crumbles. You need to transmit real change to the DNA of the organization, otherwise a simple distraction or distance for another task can contribute to the collapse of the system. There is also a third risk, which is always possible and must always be kept to mind, that is failure. I am referring to the fact that change must be realized within set times, because otherwise it will not happen.

When the objective is innovation of processes or the organization, the management of time is fundamental. This is why, as I said, people need to be strongly engaged in the project and who is governing needs to constantly verify in the first person their effort in reaching objectives. Therefore, when we talk about leadership, we need to recognize that direct participation is the first relationship of the boss."

Isabella Fumagalli (BNP Paribas Cardif)
"Something I greatly reflected on during lockdown, which has seen 700 people passing from one day to another to smart working, is how management, delegation and responsibility have been managed very well from my employees who ask me to maintain this level in value of sharing and participating. For us managers this means giving up completely your comfort zone, it means test and learn. The boss will become even more equal, charismatic to the right level to give direction, but not instructions.

Our future business will be evermore characterized from the creation of centers of skills, from the activation of people's creativity, from a check focused more on collegiality, from the authorization of error and a major flexibility on hours and locations in which to carry out business, thus: 'Work in an agile manner but give me your idea and your contribution to the collective function'. A decisively different approach from the traditional one we were used to.

This is because if I say to my employees: 'I need you as a person, non-only as a technical, as a professional. I need you as a person. I leave you the freedom to create because I am interested in your creativity, not only your power of performance'. In the end, every single role can express a creative component. This approach expects you to behave as a very different boss, but this is also how we attract young talent. No Generation Z comes to us only because we are BNP Paribas Cardif.

They say 'If you are BNP Paribas Cardif, you have more chance of doing well, but if you don't show it then it does not interest me' because they measure the coherence of bosses. It is in this way that over the last few years I have matured a further awareness of the social aspect of my leadership and how this can have a wider role in attracting talent. From this I thought it was right to invest more on my communication.

There are people who read my articles on social media and write to me: 'I read this, it interested me, it convinced me. Help me understand why I should come to work with you'. Up to five years ago the message was: 'I want a fixed place, a solid insurance company'. Now it is no longer like this. If we want to attract young talent, those who will be the future of the company because they understand what the consumers of tomorrow will want, the only way to convince them is through the fact that we are good at what we do and allow them to express their full potential.

Therefore, it is very difficult to be a boss, think of the revolution in the way of operating in senior people such as myself. This means to completely requisition yourself, also because aside from not thinking in terms of power and role, today the boss is a lot more visible and accessible online. The relationship of sound has never been more equal. I trust my employees, but my employees must trust me, and need to consider me real, consistent and active in their regards. Therefore, just to begin, the boss is online, and this is another sport in regard to the boss who arrived in the morning, made a few institutional reports and dictated laws.

The moment in which a manager is online there are two aspects. The negative is that one is always on the radar and this is a lot of effort. You need to always be ready, transmit content, and therefore study and know how to change and keep up to date with times. The positive aspect however is that opportunities are generated which are strong and unexpected, because if I start from the idea that the boss is a responsible person, it is clear that their abilities of influencing become much stronger and must be used. Jokingly, I often say: 'Five years ago I was happy to be CEO of a great insurance company, whilst now I am an influencer'. I am on social media despite being a very reserved person.

What remains very important to me is transmitting the message: 'Dear employees, dear clients, thanks for helping us reinforce our brand, because in reality without you our brand makes no sense."

Gian Maria Mossa (Banca Generali)
"The model of modern leadership which I believe is right to embody is that of being in the front line and therefore showing my face for the institution service which I represent. I believe it is incredibly important to experiment in the first person, communicate in the first person, be present in the first person and accessible in the first person. Today more than ever the hierarchical concept must be abandoned, and we must go towards a logic of planned leadership which means starting from the assumption that at the base of everything there are people. There are values which must be shared, and this does not depend on the classification, salary, seniority. The boss of the company must always be a witness. The saying 'Sometimes you must compromise' for me does not exist.

Today more than ever the face is one, and it must be the same both in your role at work and in your private life. You need to always be at the front and therefore the risk of being judged and evaluated increases exponentially. The beauty of all of this is if you are able to keep your humanity, demonstrating that you, as all people who work, also need confrontation and support. Differently from others within the organization, you have the final responsibility, and you must take this.

Hiding yourself behind institutions to not give a response is in my opinion the first absence of leadership. A manager of this type may also lead effectively, but they are not a leader. The concept of leadership is therefore based on the ability to carry responsibility for your actions, starting from values which are not put into discussion, and which are the constant example. In a world that is changing constantly it is no longer possible to have everything under control. You need to be able to live in a constant situation of experimentation. This generates stress by definition, because to innovate you always need to take risks.

However, I try to operate in the logic of risk management, understanding and examining the areas of danger and thus trying to create the right debate and confrontation to mitigate risk. My objective is that of taking decisions with my team, but assuming in the first person the responsibility."

3.1.12 *From work–life balance to well-being*

Companies are making up for the decline in welfare benefits in an increasingly important way. The attention and interest of a great number of employees is moving to a balanced management between working time and free time, to health benefits, support loans to families and other benefits which enable them to lead peaceful lives. These new necessities could not pass unobserved from our company leaders. The same argument is strongly connected to the management of ESG (Environmental, Social and corporate Governance) which we found in paragraph 4.1.

Alberto Calcagno (Fastweb)

"We are the company with the most extended and complete health insurance for everyone: for our senior executives, but also our employees. We have the most advanced smart working of all Italian and European companies, and we motivate our people to take part in smart working. This organization of work increases productivity and efficiency, therefore we encourage it. Recently the chapter of education of children has been opened and coming from a small village on the Ligurian coast this is a significant topic for me.

If I hadn't come to Milan, and later had never gone to London, I think the possibility of making a career for myself would have been greatly reduced and I believe there are many people who don't arrive and are not able to make the most of their potential. We have put in place an education program which gives important opportunities to the children of employees who obviously pass a selection process. For example, in the summer we pay for English language courses in the UK, or specific courses at university, or sometimes we grant scholarships. With these initiatives we are changing for the better the destiny of young people, but also of their families and our country. This attention on young people also positively impacts upon my company.

In my role you realize you can act upon specific levers of importance, so you must take advantage of this fact. This is my concept of taking care of people. So, I want to fill with ideas of this concept of welfare, because I am convinced it is not only a return of investment of the employees, but for our company and community.

From the feedback which I have on these initiatives I am aware that I am contributing to changing for the better the life of many people. The impact on reputation is certainly positive, but it is not as much this that pushes me to operate in this way as much as the awareness that if I can take care of someone, I will. My words of order are courage, sustainability and taking care. The last is the most important.

It is evident that the experience of Covid-19 has amplified this necessity. We were the first company to start smart-working way before the lockdown and we were also the first to extend it until October 2020. Our first preoccupation was putting in safety our employees and their families. This was our first objective, before any economical result. We tried to maintain a sense of closeness and inclusion thanks to our business internet which has become our place of digital conversation. We created a daily dialogue in which alongside themes of business we deepened on cultural, medical and sometimes even themes of leisures. In the dark months of March and April having the possibility to maintain a strong link with your own company was fundamental. I started posting videos twice a week to keep spirits up and sustain a sense of belonging.

Not only has this experience made us stronger but it has indicated an organizational style of work based on authenticity which will also help us in the future."

Riccardo Illy (Illy)
"For many years we have decided to implement company policies to compensate, in our small way, to the low birth rate in Italy. As we know, for some time now we are the second last country in the world for new births. Worse than us there is only Japan, and we believe the main cause is the absence of nurseries, which by the way, penalize another fundamental social indicator which is busy women. This is trivial: if a woman works, she says: 'I can't have children because then I would have to leave my job or I wouldn't know who would look after them'. With a single move two factors which are fundamental for the economy are penalized: the birth rate and the employment rate. The birth rate shows a decline in the number of inhabitants, which in Italy was of 400.000 people in the last year. We also lost a large number of immigrants, therefore the migratory balance is negative because more people left than those who arrived. It is difficult for a declining economy to raise its PIL if the population is falling. Therefore, we have organized a company nursery in external agreement with a structure.

Furthermore, to continue to illustrate our business culture regarding our employees, I remember than when I was young, my mother would tell me that when an employee of illycaffé got married, had to buy a house etc, the business would give them a mortgage and this was a typical thing. Before the law expected this and without trade union agreements, we would give TFR advances to employees to help them buy a house or deal with other expenses. This is our business style, to contribute to the welfare of the local population and it is our tangible demonstration of our attachment to the city of Trieste."

3.2   The International approach to CEO branding

During 2022 and 2023, we interviewed several CEOs in different countries to get their opinion about the impact of the CEO Brand on their company's Reputation.

We decided to cluster the conversations so to highlight the main topics related to reputation that each CEO decided to reveal and to sum up, for each interview, in a memorable motto the core of the CEO strategic approach related to reputational challenges.

CEOs: Cosimo de Carlo (Edag Group AG), Jérôme Debreu (Kiekert), Arnd Franz (Mahle Group), Britta Giesen (Pfeirrer-Vacuum Ag), Norman Goldberg (Tesa SE), Mitchel Golledge (Tyres), Rainer Hüttenberger (Sto), Ole Kristian Jødahl (Alimak Group), José Luis Ramon Moreno (Neolith), Joerg Pohlman (Lohmann Gmbh & Co. Kg), Michael Radke (Hörmann Group), Andreas Ronken (Ritter Sport), Nawal Ouzren (Sensorian Pharma), Andrew Westacott (Australian Grand Prix Corporation)

3.2.1   *"Reinvent mobility, reinvent yourself"*

Mr. Cosimo de Carlo—Chairman of the Group Executive Management and CEO of EDAG Group AG (CDC)
www.edag.com—Global Mobility Engineering Expert
Turnover 2022: about 800 million euros.
Employees 2022: above 8.000 people
And
Prof. Dr. Gabriele Ghini—TRANSEARCH International Partners (GG)

GG: What do you think is your role as CEO in constructing a strong brand?

CDC: I believe reputation plays an important role in building new business relationships. Naturally this can be built through the quality of products and services and especially through the fact that already existing clients promote EDAG . For example, they can say that they have always been working with EDAG and that it proved to be an incredibly important association.

Therefore, reputation is key if you want to access new clients and support them in developing their products and accelerating their time to market.

GG: What do you think is your role as CEO in constructing a strong brand?

CDC: My role as CEO is essential, in terms of both my observations and beliefs. In the past few years, we have assisted to what I define as the "personification of a company with its CEO." This means that clients and employees associate more and more the company with the values and personality of its CEO.

It is almost no longer possible to separate a company's brand from its CEO. Consequently, my communication via social media and internal communications channels has become more and more important to me. The company I manage is not as big as others (we have about 8,000 employees), but within my sector, it continues to remain an important point of reference for competitors and customers.

I am constantly present on social media to foster a strong brand. This is what my employees are expecting from me. I dedicate about an hour of my time each day to social media and communications. This is how I spend the first hour every day after waking up at around 5:30 am.

GG: Is this something that you do personally, or do you have a dedicated team which supports you in these actions?

CDC: I have a support team which follows a communication plan which we define at the beginning of each year. We also try to synchronize our communication with the main events of the year. We involve as many employees as possible to increase our audience and spread out as much as possible our values and our unique selling prepositions. This also has a multiplicator effect for the recruitment of the talent in our extremely competitive job market.

Furthermore, I always give kudos and emphasize our achievements by reposting many messages of our employees. They are proud to be directly valued by their CEO, and this increases the value of EDAG as employer and as market leader.

When I get in touch with people of my network, I realize that they are really well informed about our achievements and our values. This includes not only employees, applicants, competitors, and partners but also actual and new potential customers. This is proof that the time invested in communication really pays off. Nowadays the buying process has changed: thanks to social media, a potential customer is much more informed than before. One knows already a lot about you as a company before contacting you.

Again, this confirms that it is highly important to share our strategy, our values, and our achievements within the virtual world. I have been working as CEO of EDAG since 2018 and from the beginning my number one priority has been to define with clarity our vision, mission, and long-term strategy and most importantly to create our own employer value proposition. In a nutshell: "WHY EDAG?" and not only "WHAT DO WE DO AT EDAG?"

GG: Here you mix internal and external communication. You have spoken about both aspects as a combination, correct?

CDC: Yes, of course, it is a combination. Nowadays, the barriers between external and internal communication are blurred, much more than they would have been 10 years ago. When we communicate externally, the message immediately spreads internally. We live in a world where more and more information are shared.

The moment in which I use a communication network such as LinkedIn, for example, to announce that I have enjoyed this interview, many employees will know. This means that good external communication has nowadays a positive impact on the quality of internal communications.

GG: This is very interesting. When you made these decisions, were they shared and accepted by the board or was it mainly your own personal initiative and feeling in creating such a program?

CDC: This is the way I interpret the role as CEO. I strongly believe a company must have a clear vision and mission and this needs to be very transparent for every stakeholder: employer, applicant, partner, and customer.

As CEO or generally as manager, we serve as figureheads. Every day, we represent our values, we inspire our employees and our customers. Why EDAG and not another company? Not only because we develop some of the most beautiful automobiles in the world, but also because we have a clear vision: "to shape the future of mobility together. Efficiently. Safely. Sustainably." Like Georg Bernard Shaw says: "Progress is impossible without change; and those who cannot change their minds cannot change anything." In a similar way, we say at EDAG: "Reinvent mobility, reinvent yourself."

GG: Do you believe in the maximum transformation of mobility?

CDC: Yes, I am convinced that we either transform and influence our future or we endure it. As CEOs, we have the clear responsibility in front of our employees and shareholders to make sure that our company will be successful in the next years. We want to be at the front line of the transformation of mobility. Viktor Hugo says: "The future has many names: For the weak, it means the unattainable. For the fearful, it means the unknown. For the courageous, it means opportunity."

GG: What are the three main challenges that you will face in the next few years?

CDC: First of all, to transform our company from a pure automotive player to a mobility and technology player. Sixty percent of added value of a vehicle in the future will be due to software, therefore establishing major skills in this sector will be our priority. As I always say: "Tech or dead."

Second, I want to continue the process of internationalization of our company. Europe is losing its centrality while China and the US are fighting for the technological leadership, not only in the automotive sector. We need to be able to create more and more global solutions for our customers worldwide while considering the local specificities.

Third, the use of artificial intelligence and automation to further increase our efficiency and quality, to better support our customers in reducing their time to market.

GG: What risks do you see from your personal perspective?

CDC: I always prefer talking about challenges and not risks, since I like challenges. The main challenge is to make sure that people trust you. I do not want to be a prophet, but an implementer. A strategy process is not only top down, but also bottom up. You need the involvement and the commitment from everyone in the hierarchy of the company. Otherwise, a vision remains a vision and does not become reality.

The second challenge is linked to what you said at the beginning of our interview: brand and reputation. Walk the talk, we need to make sure to deliver what we promise. And not only me as CEO, but every talent in our organization. We also need to be open to feedbacks and ask our employees and customers if we meet their expectations. Today, we can make use of platforms where people can rate a company and its CEO. If you are open to this, you can constantly improve in "the Age of Access."

GG: Do you also have any other means to measure reputation?

CDC: In my past, I worked a lot with the net-promoting score, to better understand our promoters and detractors at customer level. At EDAG, we recently implemented a new Human Experience Management (HXM) tool to better value our talent and better accompany them in their career development. This year we will introduce a new Customer Relationship Management (CRM) system to lever not only efficiency but also transparency in the so-called customer journey.

GG: How satisfied are you with the quality of our managers?

CDC: I am an optimist by nature, so I always try to look on the positive side of the members of my team. As Peter Drucker said, "concentrate on your strengths instead of your weaknesses." My role as a leader is to make sure that every member of my team is motivated and develops not only as a manager but also as a person. I foster an open-feedback culture and I try to regularly praise my colleagues to make them feel appreciated for their performance. In the meantime, I learn everyday, thanks to my team.

Recently, a manager in my team described my leadership with three characteristics: trust in people, freedom to act, and continuous challenge.

It fits quite well with my style!

GG: In your company, does the phenomenon of the "Great Resignation" exist? Can you feel it and experience it? In the United States after the Covid Pandemic, there was a major issue with people leaving their everyday jobs as they had re-discovered values of their lives that beforehand, they had not experienced, which are not focused on commitment to work.

CDC: Certainly, Covid has accelerated a process which I believe was already in effect before. Beforehand, work–life balance was already an important topic of conversation. Now, we rather talk about work–life blending. With online meetings, we have discovered how to manage our time more efficiently. However, I am convinced that nothing can replace the interoperation between people and the added value that a team of people can generate when they work together in the same physical place. This is the reason why we still invest a lot in our facilities: to create the right environment and to foster innovation and team spirit. When it comes to repetitive tasks, these can be completed at home in front of our computers, but it is by exchanging our ideas in the same room that we generate the added value and the innovative solutions that our customers are expecting from us. I also believe that with my physical presence in front of our employees or customers all over the world, I can better transmit my values and my commitment as CEO. That is the reason why I travel almost daily.

3.2.2 *"If you trust me, I will deliver"*

Mr. Jérôme Debreu—CEO KIEKERT (JD)
www.keikert.com—Technology Leader in Automotive access systems
Turnover 2022: above 800 million €
Employees: above 5.000
and
Prof. Dr. Gabriele Ghini—TRANSEARCH International Partners (GG)

GG: How important do you think is the reputation in B2B, and how do you build a strong reputation in this industry?

JD: I think when you study my CV, you can understand my background a bit better. I am probably like you, I stick to the original foundations of European culture. I speak English, French, German, and a bit of Chinese. First of all, I have worked in 65 countries in the world. I have worked in Congo, Mozambique, Argentina, Chile, and Brazil. I have been based in Vietnam, Japan, and for eight years in China. Today, to make a shortcut, I probably spend about 2 hours a day maintaining my network, for marketing information, tax information, you name it. I am pretty convinced that you need values wherever you go. I met a German CEO and despite the differences with French culture, there was somehow a very strong connection. Nobody knew me, because I was in the shadow. Diversity and inclusion are also very important. I have Chinese and English colleagues and other nationalities from all across the world. You need to be proud of your routes. Roots, communication, and thirdly, being a mentor in the industry. In the Communication department, I was suffering not being myself and not being completely honest and open. Again, branding, education, roots, and values are important in the industry. I think to be successful as I am today in a very difficult environment. It is a challenging environment, but I stick to my values. This is a 165 years old company. During WW2, the company was already the world leader within electronics. This is a secret between you and I, we were running the German rockets to the UK. You cannot change the DNA of the company or of a nationality. This is a very local German company with German customs. If you were to change the DNA or blood of these people, they will be confused, and the company will die. I stick to my roots, my values, and my network. It has to be German run, but Chinese owned. That is okay, but ownership and operation is completely different. If you trust me, I will deliver. I use my network in Germany, my network in China even. I am related to board members in the Bank of China. This tells you a lot about the branding and where it comes from. The biggest disruption can be American concepts, which can be diversity, inclusion, and climate change. Everyone is for this, it is just overemphasized and made to take control somehow. This is to try and change our roots, and I will always stick to the original roots of the company. Taking over the CEO position, I have always wanted to stick to the German plants. We need the right price for the right product, and this is a different mindset. When it comes to issues such as the War in Ukraine, I believe that setting up companies there could be risky.

It is important to view the war from different perspectives, in terms of Zelenksy for example, but also for example viewing that sanctioning innocent people in Russia is wrong. I have 200 people there, and I have promised them that I will pay them until the end of the war. This war is a war between Russia and the West, why should I punish people in the middle of nowhere because I follow American rules? I don't follow political rules, I don't deliver weaponry or tanks, I have nothing to do with this, I am only delivering commercial products. When I say we restore the DNA, this is about the true diversion and inclusion, and I don't care about American politics and sanctions. I have worked in 65 countries in the world, including countries such as Andorra and Rwanda, so I know enough about diversity and inclusion. Everywhere I have been, I have always been a foreigner. I was sent to Asia to run a business from nothing to develop it greatly. These are my values. I respect what I do, whether it is always politically correct. I know my environment, and I know that in some cases it is stupid to expose oneself too much. But on the phone with you for example, I can communicate openly. But to achieve this, you need intercultural knowledge, I believe I know politics a little bit more than Biden, who is a typical American, or Maccron, who has only lived in France.

GG: Do you have tools to measure your reputation in the mind of your clients?

JD: This is the first time I will be directly exposed to customers, but I can tell you where my previous customers or suppliers are. These are the banks for example. I have had issues with companies due to cultural reasons, for example often the Chinese do not understand what they sign. Long story short, I arrived and called my friends in the banks and announced that this was a great company. The biggest way to measure your reputation is trust. I have 10 million in my name because the banks believe that what I say I will do. I had to replace a German bank with a Chinese bank, and again having trust is important.

GG: I saw that you are investing a lot on your people, on the internal brand and reputation, so making your people feel part of the company. This is an effort you are making specifically for them.

JD: Absolutely. When you look at my executives today on the internet, I have six people, four of them are ex-colleagues. When I am on the stage, for example, I go on the stage with my people, and they all talk. I promote them a lot and behave like the father of the company. I consider that this is my company and I behave in this manner. I project myself for the long term. I have an obligation toward the company, its employers, and their families. My main focus is rescuing and doing the best for the company, and then I think about myself.

GG: Do you think that your reputation is useful for you to attract the best talent in the market?

JD: Yes, definitely. As of today, I have been classified as a powerful CEO, for example of the 15 most attractive employers in the region. This was a big surprise to me. The company just before me in the rankings is Anker, and the top one is a big German company called Argo.

Because of the new generations, new mindsets, and the disruptions affecting the world, hiring good people is becoming increasingly difficult and demanding. The market is for the company and not the employer. You need to have a brand where the people feel at home and comfortable; I think they need a father figure, they need values, sustainability, and reliability, but true guidance, not only on paper but in person. I don't disturb people, but they know that when they need, they can send something, and we will always be available to help and support. Then we come back to our values and our branding. You can be a CEO and say that you focus on the company during the week and take time off on Saturday and Sundays, or you are always available when needed. Personally, I am always available, and of course this is a life choice.

GG: Are you using social media, are you appearing frequently on this? How do you develop your own brand?

JD: What I do with my business partner, a supplier, is customize the bank's interests to fit our employees, I am aware of local politics and current events in the city. I do more on one on one, but this is an example of B2B.

GG: What do you think are the most important challenges about your brand and reputation in the next few years?

JD: I am very confident that I will continue to promote the company in the best way. This is not arrogance, but hard work. The biggest challenge will be the political European environment. As much as it's important to have strong leaders in the industry, in politics there can be bad mentors who negatively affect the economy and business. I do not like Europe at the moment, including Macron who does not do the best politics. For myself, I try to maintain my network. How come, when you are French president and President of the European commission with so many people working for you, you do not know what's going on? Even today, Biden is coming to Poland as if he were the President of the European commission, he is saying what is right, what is wrong. This is unbelievable. This is Europe, we have our own internal network, and we need to fix it on our own. If you stay with a British or American company, the risk of sanctions hitting you will be even stronger. When banks such as Deutsche Bank were hit by American sanctions a few years ago, declared by America, this was highly questionable, because we must ask ourselves why a German company must pay a fine to America who has a different concept in understanding business. This means that these companies can no longer work alongside Blacklisted companies. I have to fight with the stupidity of the politicians, and I don't feel like the European commission is protecting the entrepreneurs.

3.2.3 *"Trust and confidence for a reliable performance"*

Mr. ARND FRANZ—CEO LKQ EUROPE—NOW CEO OF MAHLE GROUP (AF)
www.lkqeurope.com Europe's largest vehicle parts and services offering
Turnover 2022: above 6 billion

Employees 2022: more than 26.000
and
Prof. Dr. GABRIELE GHINI—TRANSEARCH International Partners (GG)

GG: I studied your business. I think we can define your business as a B2B and B2B2C business due to the strategy you wrote on your website. The brand building of your company is much more complicated than a B2B or a B2C. There is also a B2B or B2C component which in my opinion makes your strategy for building a brand a bit more complicated. I would like to get your idea, how important is brand building in your strategy?

AF: Thank you for interviewing me. This is of course a very complex material we are discussing. In the end, whether it is B2B or B2C, what is important is keeping your promises. Whenever creating customer expectation through communication, you must deliver as a company. For some very strong brands, it even goes beyond the promise and in other cases, it may be the other way round. In the end, it is all about building and defending the reliability, the credibility, and the trust between a company and its customers and other stakeholders. With over 80 acquisitions in Europe in the past 10 years, LKQ has inherited strong brands which are well known in the B2B market, whether in Germany, the Netherlands, Italy, or Eastern Europe. Therefore, we are in a period of integration. But in the end, all our brands represent a promise which we gave our customers, across Europe, while we build LKQ as a reliable brand across Europe.

GG: What about your role? As the CEO, how do you play your role in building the brand of yourself and then of your company?

AF: Our business is mostly serving local customers locally, so we also need strong representatives of the company in the local market. We still need to send a consistent message to all markets that we are the most universal, most present, and most reliable partner for businesses across Europe. In some cases, the only partner with a full parts and service portfolio. I work with my leadership team to support this communication. The other big message that we have is: *LKQ is fit for the future.* In a time of transformation and change, we make sure that our customers and our business partners in the market related to us understand that we are not nourishing our company from the achievements of the past, but we are investing into the future to support further growth opportunities for our customers and our investors. LKQ's initiatives in digitalization and electrification in the automotive sector are two very important themes in almost every form of communication that I am involved in, whether this is in conferences, discussions, or social media.

GG: So, digitization and electrification are the two pillars you are building your communication strategy on. What kind of media do you use? Are you present in the digital media, on social media, are you mainly present in specific conferences, specialized conferences?

AF: Traditional press coverage bridges into social media and vice versa. We start with our key messages, differentiating the communication channels by stakeholders, such as investors, business partners, or the public. Our communication to governments is very much European and is similar to what we communicate to the public because we believe public opinion influences policymaking in Brussels and member states and vice versa. Building on our themes, messages, and stakeholders, we derive the channel strategies. Social media, of course, have become a very strong part of this channel strategy. We also presented at the International Autoshow in Munich, we have been to Automechanika last year, to Autopromotec in Bologna and many other locations, like in France or Switzerland. A pan European approach to communication, both digital and physical. The CEO plays an important role as the ambassador of the company in both worlds, the traditional and the digital.

GG: Talking about your hiring strategy or the kind of people you would hire, do you think that your brand is an important tool for the company to hire the best talent in the market?

AF: We are getting there. People that end up working for us—if they are not insiders—learn most about LKQ from our financial reporting. Because we are not a consumer brand business and have not been around for long as a corporate brand. One of our businesses is celebrating its 100-year anniversary, so we are not a start-up company but through the acquisitions the LKQ brand is still in a process of maturing. It's not like the brand will attract talent by itself, but we have secured talent from companies like Porsche, Bosch, BMW, Microsoft, and Amazon. They are quite excited after they learn more about LKQ, about our mission, and the perspective to contribute taking a six-billion-dollar business that we are today to become "The Leading Auto Service System in Europe" which is our vision for 2030. We've had exciting talent and leaders joining us and we will continue to invest into the further development of our leadership.

There we focus on three different columns: skill development, developing the ability to lead, and very importantly, personal balance. We believe as part of our sustainability program, that people need to be happy with the way they work and be able to balance their job with the rest of their lives. That's one of three pillars which we have installed.

GG: You said that you act as an ambassador of the company toward the external stakeholders. How much do you act as ambassador of the company with your internal stakeholders/employees?

AF: Besides speeches, videos, and other one-way communication, we also have meetings with the core teams in the main locations. That is quite challenging with around 1,000 locations in Europe. But for the main locations and the main regions, every time I have a review there, we provide the opportunity to interact, arranging town hall meetings and other formats. *We also maintain a CEO blog where every employee can ask all kinds of questions as we move along.* Either I will respond to this personally or somebody from the team with more specific knowledge. We have internal blogs which give employees opportunities to post their success stories. There is a lot of communication going on which strengthens our team.

As a leader you can never be close enough to the employees. Therefore, LKQ does an employee engagement survey every year. As we move through transformation, the feedback from our employees is that they would like to know more about this topic. We have permanently closed 100 locations during the COVID crisis as part of an accelerated integration program, so there was quite a bit of change going on and therefore we are monitoring progress in order to be close to our people. The COVID period or the Russian invasion of Ukraine were examples for times when internal communication is very much needed for updates or guidance.

GG: What do you think are the most important challenges about reputation which your company may face in the future?

AF: Internal and external challenges. External are the geopolitical risks, the transformation in the digital space and also powertrain electrification. On both latter subjects, we are trying to be ahead of the pack. This is easily said for a market like us as the automotive aftermarket services older vehicles. Anyway, LKQ wants to be the first to market in electrification and digitalization to serve and support our customers as new products arrive.

Geopolitically we try to be clear. What we do and do not do. Our shareholders emphasize sustainability and therefore it is always good to do the right thing.

We believe that transparency, visibility, and clear communication are important. We will continue to protect our supply chain from geopolitical risks but continue to emphasize the importance of free trade and our code of conduct. Another topic while we talk about keeping your promises is performance and reliability. *Trust and confidence in a leader and trust and confidence in a business come along with reliable performance.* To be clear about what's possible or not possible, but also have the courage to aim high and deliver to that objective. That is a key part to our DNA, and certainly is my goal as the CEO of the business here in Europe.

3.2.4 *"Strongest customer oriented position"*

Dr. Britta Giesen—CEO PFEIFFER-VACUUM AG (BG)
www.group.pfeiffer-vacuum.com
Since 1890, Pfeiffer Vacuum has shaped the vacuum industry with groundbreaking innovations
Turnover 2022: above 900 million €
Employees 2022: above 4.000
and
Prof. Dr. Gabriele Ghini—TRANSEARCH International Partners (GG)

BG: I have spent most of my career within German mechanical engineering companies, after my degree in Mechanical Engineering, a minor in Business and a few years' experience in the consulting sector.

GG: I read your CV. I am very impressed, as in engineering companies it is always so rare to find women in charge, and this is a positive step toward the future.

What do you think is your role as CEO in constructing a strong brand? How do your people perceive your brand? Is it as you want it to be?

In your financial results I noticed that you are growing a lot, despite a difficult period. I wonder if you can tell us if this growth is positively impacted by your brand building activity.

BG: We are in a cyclical economy therefore rises and falls are common. However, what we have experienced within the last year has permitted us significant growth compared to our competitors.

Positive market conditions and internal brand building was essential for this growth. In the past, we have been technologically oriented, so everything was mostly driven by our products. However, for the past year and a half, we have been viewing our brand from a customer-oriented position which has certainly helped motivate people in this relatively difficult time. I have been in this company for a year and a half and been CEO for a year and two months. Reputation is mainly about the customer and keeping them happy, which has definitely contributed to this positive development.

GG: You joined the company quite recently, what do you think that reputation means for your company in the eyes of your clients, or your stakeholders in general.

BG: We are concentrated on being a high-quality supplier through innovation, which is why our customers like to work with us. Our stakeholders were disappointed at the end of the last decade, because in 2018 and 2019, our business community market did not achieve all of its goals. We now have to be more careful in communicating and exceeding what we promised. Personally, I think we have had relatively good development in this over the last few months.

GG: I saw that in your website you put strong emphasis on the sustainability efforts you are making with your products. Was this part of your strategy or something that was implemented before you, and what do you think of your strategy?

BG: Within the last year, we focused extensively on developing our strategy toward customers' sustainability strategies. When looking at social and governance aspects, we have always been 100% compliant with all laws, especially in terms of sustainability and resource consumption. When developing a new product or building, energy efficiency is always a main focus, so we will spend this year developing a global concept on being carbon emission free.

GG: Do you find any obstacles in communicating your brand strategy, any limitations?

BG: We are a very old company, a pride in the area. Of course, when you communicate you want to grow, improve profitability, and I think our community is very supportive and positive about us. Yes, focusing on the customer instead of technology certainly was a change, but actually the main obstacles were fewer than we thought they would be.

GG: Do you measure reputation? Do you have tools to measure your reputation?

BG: The tools toward our customers is cooperation, integrated product development, especially toward the larger customers. We are often on site, working with them. When it comes to the shareholders, this relies on market communications, and we are trying to do our best.

GG: You are the CEO of the company. What is your engagement in proposing yourself as the ambassador of the company and the brand of the company? Do you feel your role in this way in the eyes of the customers, the eyes of the stakeholders, or is your effort more in building the brand of the company as it is?

BG: It goes hand in hand. As a CEO when I want to achieve something it is always attributed to the company. The best way to do this is to give an overall picture of strong customer orientation and reliability. This is important for me, as well as understanding what works well for customers. I think the best we can do is showing the quality of our brand. This applies to CEO communication, brand communication, and any relationships between company and customers.

GG: Are you satisfied with the quality of your team, of your managers? The second part of the question which is probably the most important is how important do you think your reputation is to attract the best talent in the market?

BG: I'm happy with my management. We spend a lot of time recruiting them. I think we have some more work to do on middle management. Ours is an international company which is very appealing. In many cases, the reputation of the company is much more important than the local reputation, such as how stable it is, how we treat people there, etc. Managing an overall positive atmosphere and culture is more important than having a strong reputation as CEO. When I got my first job, I didn't really take into account the CEO of the company.

Coronavirus was a nightmare because as a CEO I had to find a new way to be close to people on different sites. I try to give my people the impression that we have a good internal reputation. This changes company culture and the way the CEO behaves when it comes to problems.

My reputation as CEO outside of the company is very limited outside of Germany, which is why my main impact has been in Germany. But if you ask me who the most important managers in Italy are, I would not be able to tell you. A separate reputation as CEO in public with customers and other stakeholders outside of the company is a different form and different level of reputation.

GG: Let me make a recent example of Giorgio Armani. He made this exhibition yesterday and everybody worked in silence because of Ukraine. When you are in the B2C business you have to expose yourself as a CEO much more, while in B2B you have to do it in a different way. I think your strategy on focusing on the internal communications, in being close to your people and in supporting them in going to the clients is exactly the right way for being successful.

How do you communicate and demonstrate how reliable Pfeiffer-Vacuum is, related to keeping the company's commitments and promises? How is your strategy, you apply for this?

BG: There are a lot of contacts. Yes of course, you have to get the interest of a lot of people, but I have to gain the trust of a much greater number of people. In our industry, it is mainly about trusting our company and trusting me that I will deliver a good product which is innovative and of high quality, reliable, and doesn't cause any issues to the customers. It is really about gaining the confidence of our clients.

GG: Trust is the key word we should use in your case. To make people feel part of a reliable and well-led company.

BG: A lot of what we do relates to quality and the challenges can be a danger for reputation. Anything that is not done well or is not of quality can damage reputation.

3.2.5 *"The 'building with consciousness' idea"*

Mr. Rainer Hüttenberger—CEO Sto (RH)
www.sto.com A complete range of systems & surfaces for creative possibilities
Turnover 2022: just below 2 billion €
Employees 2022: close to 6.000
and
Prof. Dr. Gabriele Ghini—TRANSEARCH International Partners (GG)

GG: The way you work, the way you follow your strategy defines how the reputation is perceived by the market. You are in the B2B business, how important do you believe reputation is to your company?

RH: Various trends which we see in the market, such as digitization, are important in terms of reputation, as we have strong personal relationships with customers and make business directly with our target groups e.g., craftsmen, architects/planners, or investors.

Digitization can create a major challenge because you have to fulfil your promise as a brand without directly being there. Customers today search the internet for relevant information, while in the past they would talk to us to solve a problem or identify solution options. We have to make sure that we fulfil our promise. Topics like sustainability are also important because they are no longer trends but reality. We are a stock listed company, so ratings are also important.

Independent companies want to rate us depending on how sustainable we are in our processes. You have to be extremely careful how you communicate and not to harm your reputation because the criteria is extremely specific. These things increase the importance of having a good reputation and can even strengthen it.

GG: What are the strategies you are implementing to build this kind of brand?

RH: The first is to have a clear strategy and communicate it effectively to the inside and the outside. This is why from 2020 onwards we created a detailed strategy process which is based on reviewing the environmental context and new trends. We clearly observed that there were a few things that needed to be changed.

For example, in terms of Coronavirus, we had to adopt our strategies to be clear to our people and to the outside. We have linked this strategy review to our communication campaign "For the love of building. Building with conscience," which very much focuses on how we want to be as a company and how we want our stakeholders to perceive us.

You do things consciously in many areas, and we wonder how we can strengthen this even further. We have started the campaign which really stresses what we understand and what we can do to build consciousness.

This campaign is not only about the building process itself, but is supposed to underline our way of life at Sto and we need to make sure that everyone understands what we are and why we are doing certain things.

GG: That means that you did not have to renew the claim, but the claim was still the same and it was defined many years ago before issues of sustainability and so. It is good that you have maintained the same priorities and foundations. It is very relevant and interesting because you did not have to renew or change your mission or your claim. You probably had to change the way to communicate this to your customers and the market.

RH: The building with consciousness idea is related to creating and maintaining the value created in the form of buildings and structures.

We are convinced that the claim is more relevant today than it was in 1988. We recognized two things, firstly that we had too many different interpretations in the company by employees, so for example, there were at least four different explanations. Second, there were additional topics that we had to explain in more detail so that people can relate to them.

GG: Can you give us some examples?

RH: We have broken it down to four elements: sustainability, aesthetics, because we are creating the face of a building and need to attract architects, service because people rely on us, and we have to live up to their expectations. The fourth pillar is that we have solutions starting from the design all the way to the purchase. We are communicating these four elements in our campaign.

GG: Do you have any tools to measure your reputation?

RH: We measure it internally, because I think it is important to know what your reputation within your own organization is, and we measure it externally through customer satisfaction surveys, target group interviews, and by looking at independent studies which are done outside. This is where we look for confirmation if we are having issues or if we are strengthening the brand.

GG: As CEO, what do you think is your role in building the brand of your company? What is your participation, your effort, and exposure in building the brand of your company?

RH: Being the ambassador of the brand wherever you are, watching people handle the brand incorrectly and informing them, but also watching people do it well. Encouraging them to use it in the right way. It is pretty much about being a role model, trying to make sure that people understand you are taking it seriously.

GG: That means that your focus is toward the clients, the stakeholders?

RH: It is important internally that the people really understand the value of a brand. The value of the brand is extraordinary. When I started in Sto in 2011, I asked myself in the first 12 months why people buy from us? Why do people specify us? Interestingly enough I always received the same answers which were focused on value and relationships. When someone asks me, what are the main elements, of course there are products, of course there are services, but for me the brand is a differentiation factor for Sto. People link many positive experiences with the brand and the quality of having a personal relationship.

GG: How important do you think is your personal reputation in attracting new managers, new directors, and new talent? What is your engagement in the market in attracting top level talent for your company?

RH: Reputation for that is extremely high. Because we do not only hire people from the market, but due to digitization, competences are even more important. Those people look for formations of reputation. We do not do enough to move close to universities, institutions where we are able to transform the reputation. We are doing regional activities, but we need to strengthen that to give the people an understanding of what we are, what we are doing, and why we are doing it.

GG: This is the difference between Europeans and Americans. When I speak with American CEOS they always use the word "I," but you use the word "We." I do not know what you as a CEO do and feel, so it is a different way of presenting your image as a CEO to attract the best executives in the market.

RH: Years ago, I learnt something about Level 5 leadership (derived from the book "From Good to Great" written by Jim Collins), which is what I tried to do. Talking about myself is not so important but living reputation and values and brand is very important. I think it's important that as CEO you transform what you try to communicate to the stakeholders. I try to spend time with managers, leadership teams, I try to spend time with customers, customer group associations, and so on to let them know what brand means for STO, what STO is all about and what building with conscious means. I think at the end *people don't buy what you do, but they buy why you do something. That is building with conscience.*

GG: What do you think are the most important challenges in your company in terms of reputation in the next few years?

RH: One I already mentioned, which is that we have a brand value that is called "we are humanly close" to our customers. We have to make sure that if the customers are not physically with us, they also feel our value. If they are on their journey we have to make sure that we are with them, even if they are not there to continue to fulfil the promises we make. Other challenges are that we need to manage change correctly, which is a chance to strengthen the reputation, if we do not manage this correctly then we may lose some of our employees. We need to drive the change. We are almost 70 years old, with long-term employees, long-term managers who at times are challenged when it comes to change.

They are not always able to cope with that. Developing the managers, bringing in new talent, this is my key challenge.

3.2.6 *"The unexpected verge of sustainability"*

Mitchel Golledge (MG): Head of East Region Asia Pacific for Continental Tyres
www.continental.com Technologies for future mobility
Corporate Turnover: about 40 billion €
Corporate Employees: 200.000 people
Interviewed by Bill Sakellaris (BS)—Managing Director TRANSEARCH Australia

BS: Thank you for agreeing to speak with us today. As I mentioned in our previous conversations this is a contribution to the book "CEO Branding in the Global Reputation Economy."

Maybe you can give us some context firstly, tell me about where you started with Continental briefly, and more importantly the role that you hold today.

MG: I joined Continental just over 10 years ago as a Marketing Manager, prior to that I had many marketing roles within consumer goods. I joined as the Marketing Manager for the tyre business here in Australia which was at the time a relatively new entry into the marketplace. I joined in that three- to four-year period after Continental had put their own footprint into the market. Shortly after that, I moved to Shanghai to look after the Marketing for the region, with Continental. I spent four years there, after my assignment finished, I moved back to the Australian business and looked after the Australian business completely as Managing Director. At the start of 2022, I took on the role of Head of East Region Asia Pacific for the Continental Tyre business, which manages markets from Japan all the way down to Australia and New Zealand. There are approximately 160 people that report to me in that function, we have sales offices in Japan, Korea, and Taiwan, for example. It is a really growing business and the Pandemic for us was a challenge, but it also gave us some great insights and opportunities to grow the business in all areas and markets.

BS: Fantastic. Are you at liberty to share broadly speaking revenue numbers published in the public domain?

MG: The Continental Corporation published its full-year financial outcomes for 2022: 39.3 billion Euros. Continental Business is broken up predominantly into three different functions, one is the automotive business, one is tyres, and our other is the Conti-Tech business. Within the tyre business, we are broken up into three regions, which are the Asia Pacific region, Europe, which is our home of over 150 years, and the Americas which we took the general tyre business back to in 1987. We are the youngest of all the three regions.

BS: Are you responsible for all three pillars of the business?

MG: I look after tyres, the Australian business here has a shared office, so on a functional basis I have the automotive team, which is a relatively small team since the exit of automotive manufacturing in the Australian market.

BS: How important do you think reputation is for your business today, and based on your experience, can you define what reputation means to you?

MG: Continental trades on its reputation, particularly in terms of a compliance point of view. For example, being an ethical and sustainable business in the way we act is of the most importance to us as a company. The CEO and the Chairman of the Board have an expression that I really love: the tyre business is the people business. Reputation for people is the number one factor, good people usually do not want to work for a person who doesn't have a high-standing reputation in the marketplace.

I place a lot of importance on reputation, and I hope that people believe that my reputation is mostly based on actions, having a vision and a strategy. However, I don't talk much about it, I believe it is mostly about getting on and getting the job done, and part of this is having an achievement orientation.

I suppose that focus, is the reputation that I like to have in the market, and people know that they can depend on what I say, what will get done will be delivered on that basis.

BS: Having established the importance of reputation, what do you think is the role of the CEO in reputation management? Do you take care of this or is there a dedicated team that takes care of reputation?

MG: I like to think that the reputation that I have is bred within the business, for example, that I attract the type of people that are more likely to work well in that sort of environment. It's part of HR's role at the same stage to foster that same culture within the business and support that culture. So yes, predominantly it's me, and the attributes that I have, but at the same time, internally we need to also assist with that, normally with HR that supports in that way as well.

BS: Is there a brand team that also does some work on you specifically, are there brand and marketing teams to look after the brand itself, or your brand and reputation? Do you do anything else in terms of brand management?

MG: I suppose, I did two Master's degrees, one in Business and one in Marketing, a lot of the brand management within my personal self is done by me, just because of my background in Marketing. So I don't have the Marketing team manage me, it's normally me trying to manage myself.

BS: What are the issues, limits, or obstacles which possibly do not allow you to manage this reputation, are there any tools, budgets, skills, or knowledge which limit that brand management?

MG: I work in a business of 39 billion euros, it has 190,000 employees, operating in 60 countries across the globe. In the tyre business itself, we have 19 manufacturing plants. To have a finger on everything that's going on in the market globally is a hard task. I always believe that hard work builds resilience and character, but sometimes it is the amount of information we take on, and working out how to build it within our own brand, in the Australian and Asian market place for example.

BS: Can you think of a time when you as a CEO contributed to the reputation of the company you lead today?

MG: On a weekly or a monthly basis, I send out LinkedIn posts about sustainability, particularly my role on the board for tyre stewardship in Australia. This business looks after the recycling of tires, so this shows an awareness of the focus on making this a more viable and sustainable product. This adds to the sustainability discussion in the Australian market place, and additionally, it globally builds the reputation of the brand. For example,

If I was to ask, how many PET bottles are disposed of on a daily basis globally, would you know?

BS: It would be billions.

MG: If I was to tell you it was 1 million bottles per minute. Continental looked at how to fix that, and they took 40–60 PET bottles and took the polyester, and are now using that to put back into a tyre. Being aware of that type of information is really important, and we do that in so many areas of our business that it becomes hard to keep up with everything. We won a Red Dot design award, for using the root of a dandelion rather than harvesting rubber trees which take seven years to grow around the equator. Instead, you can plant dandelions in other parts of the world, dig them up in 12 months, harvest its root, and achieve the same chemical combination that a rubber tree has. I want to make the world a better place for my children, and these sort of things are really exciting for me.

BS: I love it, that's a great story. What strategies do the organization implement in terms of reputation? Do you have any tools that allow it to be measured?

MG: There are no tools that we have locally, more so on a global basis, I am confident that the Chairman of the Board has an index that rates him as a CEO, but this is not the case on a global level. It is more of my personal ambition that I want to manage it.

BS: What are any platform tools or channels that you see personally or you might be personally involved in, in supporting the company's reputation?

MG: We spoke about the TSA board , where there is a council that is also heavily involved in terms of where the business and industry is heading. For me, I just see this as a part of doing business in Australia and making sure the industry is heading in the right direction.

BS I'm sure I've seen some sustainability advertisements regarding your company and reputation, and how that sustainability link is there. But can you just talk me through this?

MG: There are lots of things that we do in a digital space, either through our YouTube channels or Instagram, Facebook, and LinkedIn. We are fairly predominant in terms of what we communicate on those social media channels, most of those are managed by our marketing team. At the same stage, we try and do those sorts of activities that are distributed in different countries throughout the Asia Pacific Region. Each market is slightly different in terms of what they want to hear and what's important to them.

BS: Does the marketing team have some sort of measures that measure reputation as opposed to say market effectiveness?

MG: If I speak specifically about the Australian market, in terms of journey for Continental, three years ago, just prior to coming back to the Australian market place, if I was to ask 100 people if they knew Continental was a tyre brand, more people would say no it's not a tyre brand, than people who would say yes. For the people in Europe, that would be a hard thing for them to believe. But in the Asia Pacific region, excluding a couple of markets, we're a really young brand. So our brand journey is really at that early adoption stage, early awareness stage, we're just trying to get an awareness of the brand Continental first and foremost. There are executions that we do in terms of sustainability, in terms of being a good business to work for, but it is predominantly around trying to get a bigger awareness of the Continental brand journey. We will get to the stage of having detailed measurements, but at this moment, awareness of the brand within the Australian marketplace is our first priority.

BS: In your opinion, how ready is your organization and you personally to actively manage reputation? Where is the board on the reputation journey? What functions are most involved in this process?

MG: On a global level, there might be different answers. The business supports, carries out media training, investment into people managing their brand reputation. It is at what stage each of those businesses is at, is what we need to be able to communicate, other than a brand message but more about the business, the CEO and what we are trying to achieve on a bigger scale. The stock markets are always interested in financials, so there's lots of information that the business provides, that equips people with managing the financial aspects in the marketplace and one of the four big platforms that we have is sustainability. There are lots of measures, we don't greenwash; it is true factual information. Our CO_2 emissions are 7.8 million tons, so how do measure that, what is our goal, and we want to be carbon neutral by 2050, it currently looks like that will be achieved by 2040. We're still not happy with that, we want to bring it back even further. So lots of those tools are divided as a part of the business to be able to communicate and manage the reputation as pillars.

BS: What do you think are the challenges you and the organization will face in the coming years?

MG: The big challenge I think at the moment is a continuation of the European conflict with Russia and Ukraine. A significant percentage of carbon black that goes into the manufacture of tyres was produced in Russia and supplied to all manufacturers, this is now instead being sourced out of China. So moving from one to the other, are you just transferring the problem, how do you start to spread that around the globe? The semi-conductor shortage is still plaguing the delivery of new cars to different parts of the world. We have started to see some lightening of that, but there are still lots of automotive challenges that we have, and continuing sea-freight transportation as we have no manufacturing plants we need to instead ship those to the 60 locations around the world. This transportation can also be a bit of a challenge.

BS: What are the main competitive advantages in your personal exposure?

MG: I'm a firm believer that investing in people and my job is to make people ready to go but they choose to stay in the business. That's probably the biggest brand that I want to try and promote; is that Continental as a company is a great business to work with, and if I can get a sales-person to stay longer than the average time, then both myself and the individual have got a positive outcome.

BS: On the flip side, if you think of that personal exposure and personal brand, what are the risks that might be attached to that?

MG: There is no work–life balance, there is just life. The blending of that work and life is blurred. My life involves what I do on a daily basis or a yearly basis, and of course what I do at home. I am constantly involved in both the business and its people.

BS: What are the main topics that you have chosen or were entrusted to you when presenting yourself personally? Are there any themes that were either chosen or given to you that said this is the way we need you to protect your brand?

MG: As I said before, the tyre business is a people business, and protecting the people in the business is the one thing that I hold close to my heart. People will make and break businesses, very easily and very quickly, so as long as you treat people well you will have a good outcome.

BS: Where does your brand come into all of this?

MG: It's more about my attributes and how I allow people to make mistakes, and learn from these. Giving people the ability to make mistakes and learn means they are in a comfortable environment, that they will be willing to take upon challenges and opportunities head-on if needed, and if they fail that's okay.

BS: If I did an interview and I were to ask, describe the Mitchel Golledge brand, what do you think people would say?

MG: We do 360 feedbacks with our continental executives, and mine was mostly based on action, achievement, orientation, and people at the center of the strive to ensure the growth of the business.

BS: Are you satisfied with the quality of your managers and how important do you think reputation is in attracting the best in the market?

MG: My success is a direct result of the people that work with me, without their success I would just be another bloke running a tyre business. I am very fortunate that I have surrounded myself with very successful people that in turn have made me successful.

3.2.7 *"One brand for two markets"*

Dr. Norman Goldberg—CEO TESA SE (NG)
www.tesa.com
Adhesive tape and glue for Home and Office—Adhesive solutions for Industrial Markets
Turnover 2022: 1.7 billion
Employees 2022: close to 5.000 people
and
Prof. Dr. Gabriele Ghini—TRANSEARCH International Partners (GG)

GG: You work both in the B2B industry, and the B2C industry, so your efforts must be very different and complex. How important do you think is your reputation as a company for your business?

NG: Indeed, we are both, a consumer- and industry business-driven company under one brand. In my opinion, reputation is very important but for Tesa, it is not identical for the consumer business and for the B2B business. For the B2B business, I think in many ways, we are a typically engineering-driven company. We have 500 engineers and chemists who continuously work on creating new solutions, e.g., for the automotive industry, driving innovations, and enabling progress. Here we built a good reputation for customers. I am always very proud of our biggest customer—one of the most famous electronics devices producers in the world. Companies like this believe in the power of technology and innovation. On the consumer side, it is a bit different because we are quite well known in German-speaking regions and in Italy, thanks to our European setup, but more for the quality of our products. In Germany in particular, we have this very strong asset of the brand, and it even has become part of our German language, you can look it up in the way to name tape. Thus, you are posing me a very simple question, reputation is very important, but for us, it has two different arms.

GG: What are the issues with building the right brand, the brand you would like to have, in the two different markets?

NG: The biggest issue to a certain extent is the strength of the company which can be also a weakness. We have only one brand: Tesa, only Tesa. Now that we are trying to develop the consumer brand strongly because we believe we can stand for more, we have a new board member who is focusing on doing more with our brand. We are repositioning the consumer brand, and this may potentially contradict with the B2B brand. If you try and drive the consumer brand in one direction, it potentially has indications for the Tesa B2B brand. A lot of other companies are umbrella brands. We are a mono brand, which is sometimes a blessing, but sometimes also a curse, trying to drive the companies in different directions. Managing the different entities can be really a challenge.

GG: Absolutely. What is your strategy to build the kind of brand you want to have on the market? Do you have a clear strategy, do you follow this, and do you have a clear group of people working on it?

NG: Yes and no. We have identified over the past 20 months that we have a challenge with our brand strategy. In the past, the strategy was to be externally focused and find the least conflicting common denominator. For example, if the B2B organization had derived, let's say, a brand slogan, for the business and engineers, and it was "Tesa is great to work with," the employees working in the consumer segment believed this didn't work well for them. Now the only brand building that we did for the past many years was basically a brand ambassador that made sure that the company cared for its appearance, branding, etc. Now that we are building the consumer brand and pushing this a few months, I am struggling to approach building the brand further beyond that. I have some teams discussing this and a brand communication manager who is also working on this. The strategy is currently setup, because we know about its importance, but to this point it is not there yet.

GG: If I can add just a thought, I read your website very carefully and I found a lot of very profound contents within the website, but I did not find the right match between the headlines: "We create sustainable adhesive solutions" that improve the work and life of our customers, with the contents of the website. I thought that the contents were much deeper and well thought than the headlines.

NG: The headline you are referring to "We create more sustainable adhesive solutions that improve the work and life of our customers" is our mission statement which we defined a few years ago. This has to work for everything we do at Tesa. Whether referring to our consumer or industry business. Of course, the way we leverage our mission in consumer and industry is different, but it serves as a very good connecting piece of our different entities. It describes the core of our business, e.g., creating adhesives on the one hand, and it covers our severe and strong commitment to sustainability. And the content we provide on our website and basically on all our touchpoints then goes down more deeply by explaining how we leverage our mission around the globe.

GG: What do you think is and will be your role in building the brand of the company, both internally and on the market?

NG: Let me give you a little bit of a historical excursion first of all. The Tesa company is predominantly family owned. The majority of the shares are family owned. With that comes some clear evidence that it is directed particularly from the family members. They like their management to not be that visible. In the past, the theory has been to stay out of the limelight, no views are good views, and we don't want CEOs becoming super CEOs who are displayed publicly. That has been and is somewhat the common denominator. This is also a bit of philosophy, perhaps what German companies are like. When you trade a lot, you don't necessarily talk about it a lot. This is a cultural aspect. Having said that, of course I know that nowadays with social media, etc., and social media acting with businesses, such as LinkedIn it is becoming more and more important for the CEO to be a public and political figure, and to be recognized for people who associate with him. I personally try to find a compromise, as I communicate the values of the company internally and externally. I try to shine away from the limelight, except for LinkedIn. This is unusual for Tesa as nobody would ever do that before.

GG: I think, if I can give you the flavor of other interviews and studies. The culture in Germany is very shy of not exposing for the reasons you said. This is very clear compared to cultures in America, or even Italy, where the culture is much more open and expressive. But, as you said, and I would like to investigate more on this aspect. You are internally focused on building your brand and keeping your people motivated, etc. What do you do for this? Because internally to have a very strong and motivated team is equally important.

NG: I do a lot of communication internally on various channels, which is a large change vs. before. I think that it is more important to drive the culture of the company proactively, to give you one example, I do interviews on our internal communications, and give presentations or situation updates. Yesterday, I wrote a long letter to all of our global team on the situation in Ukraine. I have a communications manager helping and assisting me there. Every two weeks, I have an hour with people called "Meet the CEO" both physical and virtual and we discuss topics which interest them, about Tesa, the culture, and so on. Those are the main activities, but of course I do try and interact with my people as much as possible because I think it has been particularly important in these past two and half years of crisis, that they feel a sense of belonging.

GG: How much do you think the way you build your reputation internally is useful to attract the best talent on the market?

NG: I think it is important, especially among young people, even more nowadays than it was for our generation in the past. We still have the luxury of looking for an employer that has the right mindset and the right culture, this certainly has a lot of purpose. This is what we strongly associate with the CEO.

I like to engage with younger people, and I believe that if someone has the right mindset that they associate each other with, that will also have a benefit in terms of brand and employers.

GG: What are the three most important challenges in brand building that your company will face in the next years?

NG: Maintaining and dealing with the fact that we only have one brand despite being in many different business sectors, consumer vs. industry. How to deal with this is an important challenge. The second challenge is building a brand beyond Europe. We are present in Asia, and in America, but I would argue we are not a brand there yet. This is because as a consumer brand, we have focused on Europe exclusively before. Now, internationalizing and localizing the brand is a big challenge for us. The third challenge will be finding the right values which are associated with our brand's engineering, quality, and moving it more into a sustainable brand. Transforming it in this direction will be a challenge.

GG: It is probably difficult to find what is special about your company in terms of environmental concepts. Your website already contains a lot of very good things, but they are not so well developed.

NG: We have tightened our strategy this year, with it we want to align ourselves more sustainable in the long term. We will go all out in the transformation to make our production and products more sustainable and environmentally friendly. To do this, we will invest heavily. Both in the plants and in experts who will help us further develop product sustainability. An important partner in this is our customers and their needs. Here, we are already experiencing high demands that need to be managed. Our employees are enthusiastic and committed. But before we talk about our progress publicly on the website, we first want to effectively initiate change. We have 500 engineers who will be able to innovate in a short period of time.

Presenting, driving, and developing this is also my job. Of course, I hope that people will be able to identify with this and thus also with the Tesa brand.

3.2.8 *"The brand around the person is becoming stronger"*

Ole Kristian Jødahl—CEO of Alimak Group—https://www.alimak-group.com/it/
Alimak Group is a world-leading provider of vertical access solutions for professional use. Global reach spanning over more than 100 countries, Founded in Sweden 1948, the Group has its headquarters in Stockholm, 24 production and assembly facilities in 15 countries and approximately 3,000 employees.
and
1. Lars Tegelberg (LT): TRANSEARCH—Partner, VP Northern Europe, Global Council Member
2. Prof. Dr. Gabriele Ghini (GG): TRANSEARCH International Partner

LT: You have been in the company for three or four years now, and you have done a fantastic job with Alimak Group. Now it is a truly global company.

OKJ: We have had a big turn around and changed the group completely. It has been a lot. I think everything has worked out for the best, and of course the pandemic has also given us an opportunity for change and growth.

GG: This project involves exploring the different approaches within CEO branding taken by CEOs across the world. I have interviewed people in Australia, Germany, Spain, France, Italy, and several other countries. The first definition I will talk about is the difference between brand and reputation. The brand is the promise you make to your stakeholders, while the reputation is the perception of what you have done from the stakeholders. I have read your profile and description of your company, and the first question I have for you is what did you do to increase the brand and the image of the company when your first joined? Was the brand a tool in which you invested?

OKJ: This is a difficult question! First, I think cultural differences are important to mention, such as the CEO brand and perspectives of how important this is. But that said, I think that the brand around the person is becoming stronger because it is more normalized and accepted today that CEO's need to be more present and visible, so this is certainly an important part of the identity of the group as a whole and all stakeholders. At the same time, I think that this is not really what I am trying to drive, as I am not focusing on myself personally. Instead, what I believe is most important is that the group performs, and obviously that I am aware of the way I act and how I show myself in relation to the organization and its people. All these things matter. I do not do it for myself, but to create a good culture in the company.

GG: This is more related to the internal culture and brand. I looked at your LinkedIn profile and websites, and I found your focus on diversity very interesting. What have you done to increase the brand of your company toward your client?

OKJ: It is very similar, it's about simplicity, and an idea which sticks, and which people can relate to. It needs to be a strategy that people understand. We found a good name, the New Heights Program, and this is something which I have used since Day 1. As a group we talk about this program, and it has built a clear communication in understanding what we achieve, what we have been doing as a group, and where we are at in this process. From an investor perspective, this is very important, and our stakeholders understand this. We have had the same strategy for three and a half years, and we have now reached our targets and have raised the bar, so we have recently updated our financial and sustainability targets to reflect that. The market appreciates this because it helps them understand what we are doing and creates transparency which gives them confidence in us. We have been true to this communication both internally and externally. The cornerstones of our brand are also important to consider, our methods involve three steps with constant communication. Then we have our core values, which have been the same for three years and which form the culture of our brand. Therefore, our company members have learnt and consistently used six strategic drivers and four core values. I strongly believe in simplicity, as it means you are not dictating, and people take responsibility. It all ties very well together. These are our cornerstones, which people hold on to in terms of stability and creating a safe space. In this way, we enhance and maximize our performance and we can dare to go beyond our expectations because we have created a safe and stable foundation.

GG: I found this very fascinating because you are treating your company, which works in the B2B business as one which works in the B2C business. Other companies in the B2B business have very complex mechanisms, and the focus is very rhetorical in terms of sustainability, diversity, environment, and so on, that it is hard to understand what type of product they make.

OKJ: We take this to the next level; we are a company where we all need to understand what we are doing and need to drive things in the same way. It needs to be easy, to make people understand your company and then give responsibilities within your company.

GG: You arrived in a company with a lot of history, a lot of traditions, and roots. What difficulties did you find to change the culture and give new inputs in the business? What were the obstacles? Did you find any resistance?

OKJ: Yes, there were many obstacles and resistances, in all areas. Some of these were for good reasons, some for wrong reasons. Good reasons came down to matters of safety, and what people knew and were familiar with. However, we had to create that type of environment where people were open to new ideas, and this was my responsibility as a Leader. As Einstein said, doing the same thing and expecting a different result is the definition of insanity. Creating a safe space, where people had the opportunity to flourish and develop was my goal. There was also a lot to do in terms of personal assistance, managers for example had something to protect and wanted to maintain their power and not let anything go. This is why I wanted the company to see me as one of them, and not someone special. Of course, there were people I had to take out, but throughout these years, I have consistently maintained my transparency. In an organization, people need to see that if you talk about things, but you don't act upon them, or approach them with the wrong behavior, others around them will understand this to be acceptable, and might similarly do the same. They may think that not doing what you are supposed to do is okay. I need to ensure we don't have this culture. If I see things that are not working, I need to act on it, and set an example for the people around me.

GG: I saw your communication in your LinkedIn post, and it looks to me that your communication is strongly based on the results of your company, focusing on your successes to gain trust. Is this your strategy?

OKJ: Yes absolutely, because again, we also need to realize that we are here to deliver results. I sometimes use the pension system as an example. Everyone expects a pension in the future. Pension companies invest in companies like ours. If we don't develop, pensions could be at risk, and people need to understand that there is a connection. It is not one singular individual collecting money; it is all of us collecting pension money through our work. We have a license to operate because we are supposed to deliver results, in this way people are the most important asset. We give responsibilities, we do what we can for everyone, but we have clear expectations that people bring us results and perform. Results are crucial. We take care of the customers because if the customers are not willing to pay for what we are doing, there will be no results for us.

GG: Have you ever thought about measuring your reputation in the market?

OKJ: In our divisions, we are measured on our reputation depending on the satisfaction of our customers. However, this is from a customer perspective. There is also the stock market where this is measured everyday, but other than that, not really. We set new financial and sustainability targets, which you can say is a form of measuring reputation, but we do not have a specific method.

GG: I interviewed 22 listed companies in the Italian stock exchange, and we sent a survey with various questions. The first question was how important reputation was for every companies, and 80% of them replied that it was very important. Twenty percent of them replied that it was important. Our second question was whether they were measuring reputation, and they all said no. There are companies specialized in measuring reputation and analyzing the increase of decrease in their reputation. This is a way of taking a step further in defining the strategies behind brand building and their reputation in the market.

OKJ: It's being measured in many ways today, and there are also more regulations being initiated. For example, we need to measure the sustainability and diversity side of things. When we updated our targets this summer, a lot of it had to do with sustainability as well as financial targets. We are a safety company, so health and safety are also important, for example doing surveys of our suppliers to see if they comply with our measures. Promoting women as engineers, for example, is important in increasing our diversity and encouraging women in this field of work, to show that we actually take action.

GG: I would like to use this opportunity to gather your feelings about the Scandinavian culture on personal brand. At the beginning, you said your focus was to develop the brand of the company rather than your personal brand as CEO. I am Italian, and we have a different approach, we tell that it is like yours, but realistically we promote our own personal brand. I would like to explore this difference in cultures.

OKJ: In this time of social media, it is very different compared to the time when you only read about companies in the newspapers. But what we see more across social media is a focus on results, rather than the company itself. On LinkedIn for example, we put my face there in talking about the results of the group. This is something that is coming more and more. This is a way of saying that our focus is on our people, and it is the CEO who creates this culture. I have made a lot of changes in our company, but I am just a small part of its results, so it is certainly not just about me as CEO. A leader is instrumental, they can destroy a lot, but can also create a flourishing and successful environment.

GG: Do you see the importance of the attraction of yourself as a brand, in terms of talent and executives? How easy is it for you to attract the type of people you want in your company?

OKJ: This is becoming more important, because people today are very different. The younger generation coming into our workforce have different values, perspective, and expectations. They really need to feel like they are in a place where they fully belong, they need to believe in their core values. In a way they have more demands on everything. I think this is right, and I think it's good to focus on this. The people in this group are the most important asset. Today, people have more options, which is why the idea of people is more important than it was before. They are more aware of what happens in other places, and it is easier to move or find something else. There are simply more choices to make. Of course, this means that the CEO must take responsibility to create this culture. If I am unapproachable and difficult, people will be more hesitant to join. It is about how I run the company. I like to focus on how we work together, we are a big family and spend a lot of time together. For this reason, we are like a dinner table, we need to feel safe and similarly to a family. You don't always like what your children or what your wife is saying, but you need to stick by them and show support. You love them, and they are part of the family, and most importantly they have the freedom to speak their mind. If they have a bad day, you help them and hopefully make that day better. It is the same in the office. We need to help each other, and this is part of the culture which I want to achieve, for people to perform while feeling safe. Additionally, we have a diverse and international team, where we value and respect each individual and their own different cultures. This is also essential to create a workspace where our workers feel safe and valued.

3.2.9 *"The long term investment: reputation is everything"*

NAWAL OUZREN—CEO SENSORION PHARMA
www.sensorion.com "Find solutions for hearing disorders"
and
Prof. Dr. Gabriele Ghini—TRANSEARCH International Partners (GG)

GG: I studied your company, and correct me if I am wrong, you are still in Phases 2 and 3 and you are listed, so you collect money from the stock exchange, promising them that once you will have the products you will give the money back?

NO: Yes, that is correct.

GG: You have been in the company since 2017, almost six years. How long will it take to get to the market with your first products?

NO: We expect it to be another five years. When I took over the company, they changed the CEO. What they were doing was raising capital from what we call technical investors. So the first two years, it was very tough as we were almost on the verge of bankruptcy. What we did to save the company was we signed a strategy agreement. So we started in 2019 on a blank sheet, and next month we will hopefully be signing for clinical trial agreements.

GG: Listening to this story, I think that reputation is crucial to you.

NO: It is everything, because that was the only thing I had in the lowest moments of the company. We had no money, but what I had was a very good relationship with the professor who was leading the team. I told her, I don't have money yet, but I would like to get exclusivity for six months on your data, and based on this I will raise money. She said, if you go to the board, I will support you. So thanks to her, her trust and support was important.

GG: And how deep do you build your brand, during this time?

NO: I don't think I did it deliberately. There are a few things that really drive me, the first thing is that I really care about our patients. When I first joined the organization, I asked the doctors if I could just shadow them, so I could immediately understand how it all worked. I think this mindset is really helpful because the doctors see that you are not solely focused on the economical side, or getting something for yourself, but see that you are really trying to bond with them and build a relationship. The other thing that I tried to do was constantly build bridges, with the patients, other organizations, the doctors, and the other companies as well. There are things where working together is so important. I have noticed that when you do something like this, you are seen.

GG: Do you manage your private brand, your private social network, and the professional social network, what is your strategy? Do you consider them important?

NO: I have both a private and a professional social network. As you can see with Adele, we met in a professional setting, we were somewhat colleagues and because we nurture the relationship, we work well together. This is a similar attitude I have with my professional networks, so with colleagues I have met 20 years ago, we still keep in contact. At the beginning, I really had nothing, the only thing I had was people I knew. A noticeable feedback I get is that I am very resourceful; this is because I always think, who can help me, who knows this thing that I don't know, I am not scared to ask for help.

GG: How difficult was it to build the brand of Sensorion? To connect the brand of Sensorian with yours? Did you focus on yourself, or on the company, on the product?

NO: If you look at the network of people who want to work with us, they are the best in class. As the CEO, I carry the weight of the company, but when I hear the doctors say, we have a very good reputation, I know that this is what would save the company at the end of the day. Because if we work with the right people, and the investors still believe in us, we will have a good outcome. I try to focus on things where I have control, but it is true that the stock prices are a burden on my shoulder.

GG: You feel very responsible for this?

NO: I do. I feel responsible for the investors and how they spend the money for us.

GG: I work with companies like Ampliphon here in Italy, and the market is booming, because both the older and the younger generations have problems with hearing, so I think you are in the right market. Depending on the kind of solution you propose, but in principle this is a very interesting market.

NO: It is an interesting market, and as you said there are huge opportunities among the young, the N.O.t so young. I do believe in synergies, because for example a big problem with these vast companies, because there could be drug device complications. This is the reason why I also try to build bridges, with the many distributors.

GG: Yes, the distributors control the market. What do you think are the main challenges you and your company will face in the next few years in terms of reputation?

NO: The first thing that we have to do is finance the company. If we are unsuccessful in doing that, the company goes down. So, probably raising capital and executing everything successfully. There are a few milestones that we communicated to the market that need to happen within the next few months. The second thing we hope will never happen to us, but you never know how because we are dealing with drugs and clinical trials, is for example if something goes wrong and happens to the patient. Right now we have a team of medical doctors who make decisions, but this is something that keeps me awake at night.

GG: I read the news on your side from the investors, I must admit that I found them more compelling from the scientific point of view, but a bit vague from the financial point of view. I don't know if this is something that you wanted because you have no clarity about the potential earnings and business, or if this is just by chance.

NO: That's interesting feedback actually. Regarding the potential earnings, it is too early to guide the market right now, because as you said, a lot of things need to go right before we focus on the marketing, but maybe we can do a better job in educating the potential size of the market. When you are talking to investors in biotech, they are interested to know about the strength of your data.

GG: The other impression is that you are building your brand based on a very sophisticated, high-level, technical, scientific aspect. To me, this strategy was very clear.

NO: This is correct. Our focus is on the medicine.

GG: Seeing this situation, do you feel like you are able to with your own reputation and the reputation of the company, able to attract the best people in the market to collaborate and work with you?

NO: Wide feedback that we are getting is that sometimes we look too French. This is certainly true because most of the management team is French. I know that for the successful deployment of the company, we canN.O.t be a localized company. We can't work and focus only on one market. So, this will be something that will be hard to change to attract more international people.

GG: Do you have a strategy in mind for this?

NO: One of the biggest strategies is money because once you have money, you can attract more talent. The challenge today is finding someone who will deliver good work with one year of cash, especially when they don't know you. This is why a reputation must be very strong externally, and why we need to deliver good data. So I need to raise capital, and I need to execute.

GG: Thank you very much.

3.2.10 *"170 years of reputational heritage to feel young"*

Dr. Joerg Pohlman—CEO LOHMANN GMBH & CO. KG (JP)
www.lohmann-tapes.com The Bonding Engineers
Turnover 2022: close to 900 million €
Employees 2022: 1.800
and
Prof. Dr. Gabriele Ghini—TRANSEARCH International Partners (GG)

GG: The goal of our book is to understand how the CEOs work on their own brand to enhance the brand of the company, investments, measurements, etc. How important do you think reputation is for your company today?

JP: Reputation is important in so many ways—not only among our customers but also for recruiting employees in the war of talent. Continuously reviewing our brand, products, and services is essential, because this determines whether we have long lasting relationships with our customers. Whether they will come back and engage in new projects with us. This is something they will only do if both our services and products are reliable.

Another crucial element besides the product quality is that if something goes wrong, we act immediately. I have always viewed failures also as opportunities.

If there is a problem, it is an opportunity in which we can show if we are truly customer and service oriented, and especially whether we can quickly solve problems and turn such events into something which will instead increase our brand reputation. We turned 170 years old last year, so we are truly interested in long-term relationships with our customers. This is the essence of what we do.

GG: You lead a company with a strong family name. You don't have the same family name. Are you more interested in developing your own brand as a CEO or to link your name with the brand of a long-lasting family name company?

JP: Before I joined Lohmann, I had a nice job in Munich as CEO of a fantastic brand, going to film festivals around the world. Lohmann wasn't on my mind from the beginning. But I'm a family member (fifth generation) and have been a shareholder for decades. I was actively involved as Chairman of Lohmann's Advisory Board, however, in a non-executive position. Three years ago, I looked at Lohmann and decided I was not happy with the development of our company. As a family member I felt responsible, so I decided to take the risk and make the jump. I am determined to make the necessary changes. This is also a personal matter. If a few years from now I can look back and say "I managed to turn this company around and gave it a future," not for my own sake, but for the family and the tradition we established, well then I will have accomplished my mission.

GG: In terms of brand, your own brand and the brand of the company, what steps are you taking toward this?

JP: The priority is making sure that from a product point of view we lead the company in the right direction. For example, five years from now, I want to be able to progress from being "bonding engineers" today to "smart bonding engineers." This is because the solutions we sell offer not only bonding, but other technologies such as thermal or electric conductivity, which give the company a product portfolio that will lead us to the future. In terms of brand, I want us to be recognized as a high-tech company.

Furthermore, I believe the focus on our environmental impact is our chance to become a leader in this area. We are already moving in this direction, e.g., we laid the foundation to significantly reduce our carbon footprint by an innovative solvent-free adhesive technology—we call it TwinMelt®. Furthermore, engaging with others is essential. For example, we are active in helping sports clubs and non-profit organizations, using the revenue we generate to do something good for the community and environment we work in. Our employees value that too—I'll give you an example: Last year, we had someone applying for a job for director of marketing and communications, a highly qualified individual. During the interview, I found out that one of the reasons why he was attracted to our company was that he valued how engaged we are in social projects in the area.

I am convinced that a company that acts responsibly will be a more attractive employer, especially for the younger generations.

GG: How much do you expose yourself to this project? Do you put the company in front or are you the one who leads and appears and makes statements?

JP: It is more about the company than about me, but you truly have to engage personally. Authenticity is key. It's not something you do because it is expected or because it is what everyone else does, but you must make sure all actions are honest and authentic. As a CEO you are one of the few or maybe the only person who can ruin the reputation of a company in next to nothing. This is why I have to lead by example.

GG: You are in the B2B industry. Do you have any tools to measure your reputation? Do you check your reputation with your clients or have an external agency which checks your reputation?

JP: Yes, we monitor what our customers think of us in the segments we're involved in. The markets are highly diverse though: We work in hygiene, medical, automotive, building and construction, household appliances, and flexo-printing. Our tapes are literally everywhere, for example, in cars, mobile phones, or even Covid test kits. In many different projects and among many different clients around the world, we want to get the feedback and learn from them in which areas we are good and which areas can be improved.

GG: You are one of the few, too often CEOs and managers say that reputation is important, but this doesn't mean that they measure it.

JP: I believe the most important thing is that we have to live up to the expectations of our customers every day. If I want to do a better job, I have to know how to improve. I have to listen to my customers. It feels good to hear we are doing certain things well, but much more important is to know which areas we can improve in.

GG: You said that you have been working as CEO of this company for almost three years, did you see an improvement in attracting talent because you are there and because you work on reputation?

JP: I think so. I don't want to sound arrogant or be misunderstood. But I think this is a consequence of the new leaders in the company, it is not just me but also my fellow colleagues. We managed to get people onboard who in return attract new talent. For example, we hired someone from a highly respected university for the area of printed circuits. We also hired a female engineer, who was involved in 3D printing for Adidas. The two of them went to customer meetings and did presentations. As a consequence of one of these meetings, we got a job application from another young professional who wanted to work for us despite us not having publicized job openings. These new employees left a mark on people and brought new talent to the company. People who would have never considered coming to our company a few years ago. I am a very strong believer that our company can only be good if we hire and retain great people. And my main job is to establish a good team.

GG: What do you think are the three most important challenges in the brand and building in the next years? Your challenges and strategies. What are the three main pillars for your brand building in the next years?

JP: If you are in our industry, it's all about being innovative and not just to follow. We constantly need to be creative in terms of adding value for our customers. This starts with quality and continues with smart products, which enable our customers to go beyond their own expectations.

Another challenge is that we want to be a global company serving global customers, with increasing demands in terms of supply chain, quality, and service. We want to create a highly flexible European network to best serve our customers. My big challenge will be to create this. A true sales network, a true European production network. It starts with a mindset—and it will result in our customers experiencing better technology, better quality, and a seamless supply chain. That should turn into a win–win situation for our customers but also for us in becoming a better company, therefore a more profitable enterprise.

3.2.11 *"Emotional builders"*

José Luis Ramon Moreno—CEO NEOLITH (JLRM)
www.neolith.com Emotional Beauty
and
Prof. Dr. Gabriele Ghini—TRANSEARCH International Partners (GG)

GG: I studied your company and I saw that you are owned by Private Equity Funds and the Management, is that correct?

JLRM: Formally yes, we sold the company last year. CBC is actually the main shareholder, CVC, and management. We have our own 15% and CBC is a majority shareholder and previously it was Investindustrial, the Italian Bonomy Family and extended family, alongside management as well.

GG: The figures I got are more than 150 million.

JLRM: Our last number was 180 million Euros in Revenue. We have an EBDA of around 32%, making us one of the most profitable companies in our industry in the world, as well as one of the fastest growing. I like to think we are doing many good things, the reality is that new material and pioneer material, as well opportunity among the market being insanely high. Our opportunity on the market is concrete space vs. other materials such as natural stones, quartz, glomerate, glass, and more. We can use the material from kitchen countertops, wall panels, and you can also use it for furniture businesses. The company is very young, thirteen years old, and it was founded from scratch, with hard work in its product and process development. From this time, we have gone more international, more direct, and we take care of the integrated way in which different stakeholders organize the logistics of the supply of goods. At the same time, the most important aspect of working with different influencers to generate its people, from architects to designers because the material is in fact being used is that of a building material company, high-end material of large format. It is very versatile both in functionality and design. It is very strong in terms of sustainability, and this has been in the core of the company since its inception. Our goal today is activating money in different segments within different countries. For example in Italy, this is the most active within the kitchen industry. We are near 8% penetration, bathroom is below 1%, but in other parts of the world this could be the opposite. This is a very dynamic company, growing at an average of 20% or more year after year. Our presence is in more than 100 countries, and we have 970 direct employees. We can talk about the center stone revolution, since it's one of the best materials, and can substitute other materials depending on its need and application.

GG: You are in a pure B2B business?

JLRM: No, not only. The company started in the B2B, and reputation is crucial because in B2B professionals definitely deal with the business in a continuous way, but we do not sell. Imagine how a kitchen countertop works, you must be finally landing in a kitchen of different users, with different rates. Imagine we have one store in the world, we need to convince a family to change the kitchen and install it nearly every 45 seconds. This is the actual rate worldwide. To make this happen, you need to activate so many different things at the same time, and the material needs to be available in different locations. When the family goes to the shop, they must see this material. Typically we work with different brands, such as Scavolini, Lube, Bennett Magazine, or Stosa. These are examples which might be familiar to you, but we also build collections with appliances such as Samsung, fridges for examples, or panels for LG. Then you start working with brands which will be cooperating within the same space, to join collections. But then, you need to activate the different stores one by one, training the different people promoted within those stores and any kind of designer who designs your kitchen, because each kitchen is unique. The most important thing at the end, is this whole process. This is the demand generation end to end, but its fulfilment is completely different. Very large slabs going to the fabricator, to someone that processes stones and marbles, to complete the holes, do the finishing and later install in your home at an appropriate time. This is very complex, yet we also do facades. The last important facade we did was the stadium in San Francisco for the Warriors. Doing a facade outside a stadium is difficult, you need to calculate the structure, therefore the stakeholders can be completely different. You need to work with a building company or the technician part of a company. The most important, however, is showing up the beauty of our material, not only on the technical side, but playing more and more with emotions. This is our business. So if someone tells me, what is your business about? It's definitely not about building materials, but about emotions. This is why we are by far the most expensive in the world. If we sell slabs, we can deliver dreams and many things can happen within this process. It's so important in this business to take care of this.

GG: Of course. When I teach at University and talk about reputation, I always mention how it is an emotion, and often based on emotional instead of rational aspects. So my question for you is how important is reputation in your business?

JLRM: It's crucial. It's crucial because we have a fantastic product. We provide a fantastic service, but so are many others and we have more than 200 competitors. This is why when you demonstrate things consistently, this is what matters. Delivering a promise is what our business is about.

GG: So what do you think is your role as CEO? How much do you invest your time and effort in building the company's brand?

JLRM: First, let's talk about this in an economic way. Even though we are a B2B business, we interact more and more with who is in contact with the end users. We talk a lot about influencers, because they are connecting the end user and representing you, so I dedicate a lot of effort to this, almost 10% economically. In fact, our branding is marketing tools, because building a brand is the future value of our company. My main mission is the Bill Equity Value, not necessarily performance, which yes is important, but not always the most important. I need to dedicate time and care to commercial sales and industrial production, which is always very complex yet remains transactional. What differentiates us is innovation and branding, dedicating 10% to innovation and 3% to branding within our revenue scale. We are closer to a Looks brand in terms of rates of investment on these aspects, rather than a building company.

GG: Do you have any tools to measure reputation, and do you invest in measuring the reputation?

JLRM: Of course, we have Opinion Leaders continuously talking to different stakeholders, even with customers or indirect customers. We put a lot of focus on differential aspects and continuing the evolution. You need to be active in searching for what's next because businesses are dynamic. We challenge ourselves by putting other brands in our questionnaire directly and following up with much detail. Sometimes, it is not easy to get Opinion Leaders, so typically we run surveys which may reach thousands of different stakeholders. Barriers, fabricators, installation companies, builders, architects, designers, and one of the key questions for us is whether you recommend our brand. Most professionals highly recommend our company. It's very interesting however, because there is always room for improvement and training, there are always aspects that need further dedication. It's important to be direct and communicate openly with clients that are perhaps a bit more critical with you. So we do this in a consistent way, especially in a country where the company is new. It's important to start the methodology, start the improvement process, and work toward the right metrics.

GG: In the book there are interviews with Brunello Cucinelli and Riccardo Illy, and they present themselves alongside their brand in a way of always being present and being ambassadors of the brand. What do you think about this? Do you do the same thing? Do you bring your name and your competence and image to the forefront of the brand? Or do you prefer to bring the name of the company before yourself?

JLRM: As an industry in some cases it could be a choice, but in our case it cannot be a choice. The CEO is definitely connected, because they are a reflection both internally and externally of our brand, and internally may take priority because this is important to the rest of the team and the professionals. Showing that confidence and vision to them is essential. We do this first hand in many different ways, for example organizing meetings with my team globally, consisting mostly of open questions. This is not only for myself, but the senior leadership team. One of the definitions of the roles we put within the company is Bing Bing, a brand ambassador for the company. This means that you need to feel okay and breathe. At the end of the day, we are building a brand for life, and building it together. I am also happy to use my image in order to participate actively, including on social media. In fact, the digital arena is very important.

GG: You say that you are an ambassador of the brand and you like to expose yourself to the market and the stakeholders, in order to create a strong brand. So you use your influence, presence, and efforts to build the brand. Do you think there are risks?

JLRM: There are risks, but people are looking for authentic testimonials. This is my main point, working personally and with passion. We use third parties as well, and we love that third parties talk about us. For example, if we consider the kitchen, we work with so many big chefs around the world, we are sponsoring a Michelin Guide. Importantly however, is that we have 550 Michelin Star restaurants around Europe that use our material. However, the real reputation comes in when a chef calls you to install a kitchen in his own home. Again, participating and bringing authentic testimonials is important, participating professionally in forums and interviewing architects that use specific materials or products. We certainly dedicate a large extent of time and resources to this.

GG: I have your website in front of me and one of the first things I'm noticing is sustainability. What are the main pillars of your brand building strategies?

JLRM: The material itself is powerful, but so is the final product because of its design and functionality. These are essential, but so is sustainability, which may look as if it's simply a current trend, yet this is not how we view it. We were the first carbon neutral industry, but this does only stand for environmental aspects. Sustainability also means taking care of your employees, partnerships, and distributors. Design and innovation can therefore become our main drivers. We are not big fans of loans, instead we support making creations. There are lots of cooperations, to finalize materials and solutions. Building branding together in the innovative aspects supports creative makers.

GG: Terrific. One of my last questions for you is how easy is it for you to attract the best people in the market? How important do you think your reputation is in attracting the best talent in the market?

JLRM: It's certainly very important. Our attitude is the most important, whatever experience people have. Because anyone can develop and positively contribute toward our company. The rotation is high and we have more and more professionals joining us everyday. In a new market, it is a little challenging because our brand is still fairly unfamiliar. In these cases, it is important to collaborate with the local leader, perfect the business and familiarize the rest of the team. People are attracted to our company globally because we are fast growing and put our own mark on the rest of the industry. We are a mix of a startup and a startup corporation, which also helps us attract the best talent because people join who are typically engaged in our common project. It will be intense, but people will be willing to work hard. If I consider North America, we can find that we have some retention problems. North America is complicated at the moment, we have around 30 employees, and our target is to double this in the coming year, which may prove extremely hard, to retain employees and keep professionals motivated. We have a system to carry out employer branding campaigns, and this certainly is important in helping.

GG: Thank you so much.

3.2.12 *"Building a family owned trust"*

Dr. Michael Radke—CEO HÖRMANN GROUP (MR)
www.hoermann-grouppe.com Technology specialist, always at the forefront of innovation
Turnover 2022: around 700 million €
Employees: close to 3.000
and
Prof. Dr. Gabriele Ghini—TRANSEARCH International Partners (GG)

MR: The Hörmann Group is a business of many cultures, as we have more than 26 individual companies. I think it is wonderful representing the role of CEO.

GG: I was told that you are a CEO who does not want to stand in the middle informing about his performance—instead you focus on your team's work and let your team shine. You let your people work, who are proud of being members of your team. At the end of the day, the family relies on you because you are at their service. Therefore, you were recommended for this interview. Now let me start the interview with my first question: How important do you consider reputation is for your business and company?

MR: I think reputation is a very important factor in all businesses. Most decisions from customers, investors, shareholders, or bankers focus on the reputation of the company. I believe there is a strong emotional factor in decision-making, for example employers' decisions to join the company or stay in the company. From this point of view, reputation is very important.

GG: Do you know how to overtake the reputation obstacles you face, and do you have the resources to do so?

MR: Firstly, I would like to give my interpretation to what reputation means to me personally. Reputation within business means trusting a CEO. Trust is the most important factor in a family-owned business. Investors and banks make financial decisions based on figures but also on positive long-term experiences dealing with companies. Can they trust you? What you promise, what you have achieved in the past, and what you may achieve in the future?

I think trust and confidence are essential in defining the reputation of the company as well as the CEO.

In terms of limits and obstacles, I think the most important is to maintain and create an excellent reputation for the company which I am working for, not optimizing the reputation of the CEO as a person.

I believe our task as CEO is to serve the organization, the company, and the shareholders which we are working for. I have this philosophy because I have been working for more than 20 years for several family-owned companies. My view about reputation and management philosophy are related to family businesses.

All these family businesses share a culture strongly influenced by the family and founder of the company, because in many cases the company reflects the name of the family. Members of the family can also be employees in the company or be involved in management, therefore the family takes an important role in the supervisor's report.

The reputation of the company is more important because it represents the family and owner of the company. Based on my own personal experience, it is not wise for a CEO of a family-owned business to focus marketing on his personality, or even strengthen his own reputation as this can come into conflict with the family. Therefore, my approach to improving the reputation of the company is closely linked to improving the reputation of the family name.

GG: So, your strategy is to create a brand of the company which positively reflects on the family, therefore you remain behind the curtain, driving the machine but being careful not to appear too much in order to give a positive image of the family brand.

MR: Companies who successfully own a good reputation are helped both by stakeholders and the family name. I worked for a stock listed company for a long time, which has helped me understand that in terms of risk assessment we should discuss the company based on the CEO. The life of a CEO within a specific company has become shorter in a stock listed company. The relationships of all employees are related to the CEO, so there is a significant risk when and if a CEO leaves, as several managers may follow the CEO and the company could be put in a dangerous position. Other CEOs may become too confident and decide fully which direction to go in without any advice from other members of the company, which is also a danger that companies may face.

GG: What type of strategy do you and your company put in place to build the brand of the company? Do you measure the reputation of your company in the market with your stakeholders?

MR: We established a corporate communication in marketing when

I joined the company in 2007 as a way of improving its brand. This was done through typical measures, such as a new home page, creating an employee journal and generally improving our appearance on social media. Furthermore, we created a new corporate design with very strong future oriented colors to attract as many people as possible through a modern look. These can all be considered normal marketing and corporate communication initiatives.

We have more than 2,700 employees, and more than 600-million-euro turnover, and I had not heard about this company until I was asked to join. One of the ways to improve recognition of the Hermann group name is through possible applicants, as this is our main challenge at this moment: obtaining workforce, talented and qualified people of all levels. In terms of measurement, we do not really have one to measure our reputation, but one approach could be to look at a public evaluation platform where we obtain responses from employees or possible candidates, which can help us optimize our work. Another approach could be applying for awards which recognize our work.

Currently, the main response or feedback we achieve is from investors or banks which inform us of our positive figures.

GG: What you said is important, when you joined the company, you put effort into increasing the knowledge and reputation of the brand, as you were the first person who did not know enough about the brand of the company. Based on this, you decided to later invest in the brand?

MR: The Hörmann Group has quite a unique philosophy. We have 26 subsidiaries, 35 different managing directors, and they all lead the company as more or less independent. We are active in 43 different business fields, so they act independently as well. As CEO I ask myself, what does my role mean? Am I just the administrator which puts together all of this, therefore do I need to have a specific strategic approach, or shall I introduce new approaches? It is a matter of convincing people, as I do not have the right to make directives completely by myself.

GG: Are you satisfied with the quality of your managers?

MR: Like in any other company it is necessary to have strong managers and others who need further coaching or support. A company is all about variety, with 35 managing directors we have some who are running a company with 80–100 people, and others who run 200-million-euro companies, so there is an important difference between their priorities. We optimize this step by step, as this could be the change of generations.

GG: Do you think that your reputation can facilitate the hiring of talent? A figure which has come to light is that only 6–7% of candidates are clearly aware of the reputation of the CEO of the company they are applying for. Furthermore, there is a 20% increase in the willingness to join the company if they have the knowledge of a CEO's good reputation. The brand of the company is therefore fundamental when joining a company, so there is a reliance on the CEO and the image of the company. This can be seen as a win–win situation, because when the brand of the company is strong, the brand of the CEO is strong.

MR: The percentage of the people who know me or know my name might not be that high, because there are so many of our companies in Germany. There is not much focus on marketing my name, being on LinkedIn is sufficient enough. We refrain from advertising my role as CEO in newspapers, journals, or other forms of advertising. My visibility is therefore limited, but the approach to attract candidates for the company becomes an increasingly fascinating storyline.

I have interesting challenging tasks, future-oriented projects, and we try to inspire candidates through interesting projects and tasks. Of course, during the interview process, the CEO plays a very important role. In the end, my role is to inspire, attract, and convince people to come onboard by selling the advantages of the Hermann group. At the end of the day, reputation is trust and confidence, and the candidates must feel confident and comfortable with the CEO. The CEO is therefore more interested in the feelings of the candidate.

GG: What are the three most important challenges in building your brand and reputation in the future?

MR: Our first challenge is the significant increase of our fluctuation rate. There has also been a significant change in work attitude, particularly among younger generations. Many young employees change their jobs depending on their life experiences. I would say long time employment is now history. People enjoy changing their jobs every five years or so, particularly the younger generations. We have a significant lack of young staff. Right now, almost 10% of our positions are vacant, and we are searching for 200 people on all levels, starting from electricians, mechanics, project managers, etc.

I think the reputation of the company is built on its people, its employees, more frequently, the change of the staff means that the reputation of the company will also be in continuous change. There is a constant need for renewal of reputation to keep it on a good level. People are changing, and there are new people onboard with different cultures, backgrounds, and experiences who need integrating.

There is a need for more investment in corporate communications, corporate culture, and work ethics which is what companies such as Google, Facebook, and Microsoft are implementing. This is essential for the future of companies, keeping people happy and keeping them as long as possible.

I expect there to be a significant acceleration in the change of technologies in the next 10 years driven by climate protection and mobility, which will have a huge impact on our businesses. Our biggest challenge will be to reinvent ourselves, to speak up, and implement new technologies, and to successfully achieve this, companies need qualified and creative people who can drive this process.

If you cannot follow the change of technology, the company will lose its reputation. Who wants to work in an old-fashioned company rather than a future oriented business?

Issues of stability, family, and work are more important than they were in my time. This has deepened further through the Coronavirus pandemic because people are becoming more used to mixing their private and work life. How to accelerate this process will also be a big challenge, even if it is a positive change in attitude. Companies need to reinvent their business systems, find new solutions, and create a new reputation regarding their work.

3.2.13 *"The passion for sustainability value chain"*

Mr. Andreas Ronken—CEO RITTER SPORT (AR)
www.rittersport.com Doing the right thing to create really good chocolate
Turnover 2022: in excess of 500 million €
Employees 2022: close to 2,000 people
And
Prof. Dr. Gabriele Ghini—TRANSEARCH International Partners (GG)

GG: With some colleagues at the Milan University, we wrote the book "CEO Branding in the Reputation Economy" interviewing Italian CEOs or CEOs working for Italian Companies. Now we want to expand this into an international perspective, interviewing CEOs from different parts of the world. We are interested to see the different approaches taken depending on various countries' cultures, as well as the culture of the specific company. We want to see what the policies of the companies and the CEOs of the companies are in building the brand. This morning I viewed your post, but I could not read your replies because they were all in German. You put the double language, and all others replied in German. However, I read very long replies, so I think this is very emotional. In the end, reputation is an emotional factor, it is not a rational fact, so we have to accept this.

I will start with three definitions to define a common ground. Brand is the promise you make to stakeholders, reputation is whether or not they perceive that you keep this promise. Brand is built from inside out, and reputation is built from outside in. Reputation is what the stakeholders understand, feel about you. You are in the B2C business. The first question is, how important do you think reputation is for your business?

AR: Reputation is of course important. The importance of reputation differs with the kind of business. It makes a difference if you are running a non-branded commodity business or e.g., a family business with well-known consumer brands.

In my view, the reputation of a CEO running a branded business has to somehow fit with the brand and company values/reputation. If you are selling spare parts for machines, then the importance is a different thing. Reputation is important for our company. Ritter Sport is a well-known, highly emotional brand with high reputation scores. The brand is furthermore a dialog brand, which means the consumers and fans like to interact with the brand e.g., make their own editions of chocolate on the online variety creator. We started our journey four or five years ago to follow up the purpose. If you call it, let's say in management terms, we are a mission driven and purpose driven brand. Our purpose is doing the right things to create good outcomes. Our main focus is based on the supply chains.

We are a chocolate brand which is well known in many countries for its colorful variety, good taste, and square format. We are now putting all our efforts into using our purpose in one direction, so the people discover not only our good chocolate but also the good in terms of our big passion for sustainability in the cocoa value chain.

The families owning the company are actively supporting us in terms of doing the right things to make really good chocolate in terms of sustainability. It is important to them, to me, and to all employees that there is good use and purpose behind everything we do.

GG: You have been working in Ritter since 2005 in different roles. Have you seen an evolution in the strategies for brand building and for the reputation of the company?

AR: Yes, for sure, it is always a journey. We are also part of the chocolate industry, in the past nobody talked about cocoa because nobody wanted to make consumers aware that there are problems in the cocoa supply chain. The chocolate producers are therefore also a bit guilty that people do not have a strong link to cocoa—like wine grapes do have for wine consumers. The average person knows a lot about wine and its production, but not much at all about cocoa.

For most wine drinkers, it is clear that they want to buy wine from a wine maker who has its own vineyard and has 100% control of the wine making process. Very often I get asked: Why do you have your own cocoa farm? Nobody would ask a wine maker why he has his own vineyard.

In wine, the real transformation started in Germany and Austria after a quality crisis in wine. Looking back, it was a good thing for the wine makers. Transformation in cocoa chain is complex. Producers, Governments, and NGOs have to work together to make a real impact on the life of the cocoa chain and we have reached already a lot in the last 10 years.

GG: You are the CEO of a family-owned company, where the chairman is quite present in the press.

AR: Yes, that is true. The name of the brand is also the family name.

GG: Yes, but his image, if you look on the web you find the image and name of the company and so on. I would like to understand if there is a policy to use and to leverage the name of the family in favor of the brand building, or are you involved in this strategy, are you putting your own personal brand to leverage the brand of the company?

AR: In my case, I have worked only in family companies. The family name is also the branded name. So of course, if you take Ritter: Ritter Sport is the brand, the family name is also directly related to the brand which is of course always an emotional thing. It was always natural that the family name was, is, and remains part of the brand.

I learnt very early in my career to never go unbranded if you can link your values with the brand. It's a personal attitude. Of course, my personal values and how I am communicating on LinkedIn and within presentations should be in line with our purpose. Because otherwise, this is something you cannot trust. If the CEO tells you something different from what the brand is telling you, this would not be purpose driven.

GG: Do you use the image of the chairman with the surname as a front man or ambassador, or do you do this in the name of the brand?

AR: We all, from chairman, to CEO, to doorman we are working for our company to do the right things to make really good chocolate.

As persons we are all temporarily in charge—the brand hopefully lasts. So, we should always link to the brands.

My intention is to be transparent and to live the company and brand values as the CEO of Ritter Sport. I am not doing it for my personal reputation or my career. There are people who are interested both in me and the brand, but I am a manager, and my job is to make the brand and the company better. I personally am not important and in 5 or 10 years, there may be a new CEO. The company will go on, but it is important that the company stays with the same important values.

Company values and company culture are much more important than strategies.

Strategies can be changed rapidly if needed, but changing values or culture is almost not possible short/midterm. A good company reputation and good company culture are the fundament of successful business in the future.

GG: How much do you take part in building this culture?

AR: Building culture is a day-by-day process.

We need to internally make a conscious journey in terms of culture. This needs a culture analysis—what are the good aspects we want to keep and what are the aspects we want to change. This is a long-term transformation.

We are also sometimes forced to make hard decisions.

In our case we are facing a dilemma between purpose and responsibility, when it comes to our Russian business.

GG: I think the dilemma between reputation and responsibility is something really new which we did not expect.

AR: You cannot 100% control reputation. In the past, it was easier to control the reputation, but now with social media it became a lot more difficult. Someone with about 50,000 followers is constantly in the public eye, they don't necessarily have to meet the press. Twitter for example is the most aggressive social media channel. Bad news is always selling better than good news.

GG: How much is your own personal brand important in attracting the best talent in the market?

AR: In terms of attracting top management this is important because our industry is relatively small. Salary, location, and reputation are of course still the main important factors, but flexibility of working hours and office environment become more important. In terms of home office, we allow two days per week in home office, we have good experiences so far—we believe in this hybrid model for white collar.

GG: So, you are saying your reputation is important because you are known in your specific market, and to attract the best talent you need to listen to their needs and comply with them?

AR: We want to attract talent who can fit to our values and who are helping us to drive our purpose. That is the most important thing. We offer flexible working hours in a very modern and inspiring office environment and a human-friendly cultural environment.

3.2.14 *"The racing side of reputation"*

Andrew Westacott—CEO AUSTRALIAN GRAND PRIX CORPORATION (AW)
and
Bill Sakellaris—Managing Director TRANSEARCH AUSTRALIA (BS)

BS: Andrew good morning, and thank you very much for joining me today. As you know, we are going to be talking about brands, or rather the CEO and the role that reputation plays. I'm going to ask you to please introduce yourself and then we can dive straight into our questions.

AW: I'm Andrew Westacott, Chief Executive Officer at the Australian Grand Prix Corporation based here in Melbourne, Australia. We run the Formula One Australian Grand Prix and the Australian motorcycle Grand Prix, commonly referred to as Moto GP. These events have been in Melbourne and Victoria since 1996 and 1997 respectively. They've got a long history of boosting our tourism economy, and I have been the longest serving CEO in the history of the corporation.

BS: Congratulations, what wonderful events you've put on year after year. The first thing I'd like to ask you is how important do you think reputation is for businesses today and based on your experience, can you define what reputation means to you?

AW: The reputation of the business is closely aligned to the reputation of the products that you have, and also the reputation of the public facing nature of a CEO. In a business like ours, we are an instrument of government and are essentially owned by the people in Victoria. This means that everyone has a right to comment or critique what our events are doing, how they are portrayed in society, the responsibility that we take, and how we act and behave. Everything from ticket pricing to our interaction with the community, as well as clearly our ability to raise revenues. To generate income and to deliver and sustain our events, reputation remains sacrosanct. It is our number one attribute. If you want to sustain the growth of a sport such as Formula One or Moto GP, you need to be making sure that brand and reputation of the corporation, and my role as CEO is up there as number 1.

BS: Fantastic, thank you Andrew. Yes, I do appreciate the importance of reputation for the CEO. So then, after having established the importance of reputation, what do you think is the role of CEO in reputation management, and do you take care of that yourself or is there a team?

AW: Reputation is linked to the culture of a business as well. You know, we have an independently appointed board that is responsible to the Victorian Government and our responsible minister here in Victoria. They oversee the business, and that's got to be led from the top. As the CEO, I have to embody the right values and approach to our brand, the way we're portrayed. We're a business of 100 employees, occasionally swelling to 230 at event times. We rely on the successful delivery of events through around 600 independent businesses, and about 12.000 staff over the weekend. So we need to keep developing an approach to reputation management, brand management, culture, and customer service which is going to be led from the top.

BS: No doubt, those numbers are incredible. When you think you could go from 100 to 12,000 in the space of just a few weeks.

What do you think of the issues, the limits, and the obstacles that possibly affect a management of reputation?

AW: The first thing I'd say is that we are in an increasingly digital- and social media-oriented world, for example we are dealing with products of a global nature, Formula One and Moto GP. It is very easy for the media to jump onto something, sensationalize it, and use it as clickbait. You have to take a strong, uncompromising approach to make sure that the actions and activities of the business stand up in this court of public opinion. In Melbourne, we have a few daily newspapers, which include the Herald Sun, and we refer to something called the Herald Sun test. Would the actions and behaviors of us in this corporation stand up to the Herald Sun test, which is more neutral and non-branded? The issues, limits, and hindrances come down to making sure that the culture of business is fully aware of the obligations of the corporation and that everyone has a role to play in it. This doesn't mean we always make easy decisions. But we must be aligned with what we do, how we behave, and how we interact in a manner that is appropriate.

BS: Thank you, I appreciate the difficulty and the balance required there. Could you describe a situation when you as CEO contributed to the reputation of the organization?

AW: Well, you know, there's a number of angles you can look at it from, for example, the contribution to the reputation of the corporation. I think that this can be in positive times and also challenging times. And I think at all times the role of the CEO is to never shy away from being accountable. When I started here as CEO in 2011, there was often a degree of reluctance to face the media who would critique aspects of our events.

The 80 throw away line was the event which costs taxpayers a lot of money and, this money could be better spent on hospitals, education, and infrastructure.

If you do not stand for something and believe in something, then you can let those sorts of things slide over you, so I think it comes down to being strong in, in positive times, strong in negative times, and if you're always strong, accessible, consistent with your values, and stand for something, then over time those values, will create a strong brand, which develops a set of attributes. Now I think the contributions I've made in the corporation has helped with its growth. We consistently deliver events to people, this helps boost tourist and economic branding. This means providing them with excitement, entertainment, and value for money through a day out as an experience. It also means that in periods of downtime, we need to deal with events such as cancellation of sessions, rain delays, dealing with adverse criticism, or issues relating to our event. You have to be on the front foot and deal with this in a public manner, such as the cancellation of our event due to Covid. This was probably one of the first events to cancel globally on the March 13, 2020, and this again comes alongside strong leadership, courage, and at the end of the day doing what is right.

BS: I remember that day, I think everyone was shocked, but you were very steadfast. You were very strong in your commitment and saying, yes, it is disappointing, but you know we'll carry on and I love that about you and I think that that talked very much to your brand and your reputation, so well done.

What strategies do you and the organization implement or have implemented in terms of reputation, what tools have you used, and how have these been measured?

AW: We have a like business a very strong strategy that has multiple facets. But I think the key one I'd say in this area is to be aligned and aware of the changing trends in nature of your customer base.

In Formula One in particular, that customer base is constantly changing. We're seeing a younger demographic, an increase in females, many new people being attracted to the sport through the virtues of Drive to Survive, a Netflix series that has existed for about five years.

People have been attracted to Formula One for over 70 years, but more recently the attraction is becoming more obvious with newer fans. Now the ticket to entry for those newer fans is about different sets of values than what the older aging traditional fan of Formula One or even Moto GP motorcycle racing would want. So, we have to adapt and adjust to the needs of the consumers and do so in a manner that's real and authentic. And that might stem down to things like sustainability, accessibility, and inclusion at our events. You know, we take it very seriously. For instance, at events in a public park, we do our best to make sure that the venue is accessible for persons with a disability, whether that be a wheelchair access disability, visual disability, or maybe disabilities associated with autism or special needs. But we wanna make sure those sort of things are front and real and are addressed by the business. So I hope that addresses the essence of the question

BS: It does, but if we take that a little further, what tools do you have that allow you to measure that accessibility for example?

AW: If you can't measure things and if you can't get that feedback, then you don't know actually where you stand. Formula One and Moto GP are businesses and sports that are recognized and based very much on data and feedback. They get it within seconds and milliseconds. We get feedback through customer surveys, we get feedback through our own research. We do focus groups at the event.

We send people into our event to observe and provide feedback across a variety of different areas.

You've got to be attuned to what's happening in the marketplace, so we'll use our tools, get feedback in those variety of ways, but then also in another way as we always benchmark what we're doing. We only get two chances a year to deliver events. One for Moto GP and one for Formula One, so it's a long time between events. So what we've got to do is adopt an ethos of continuous improvement, so there's another set of inputs where we will look and benchmark our own operations and observe our own operations and implement whether it's in motorsport or major events in the city or its entertainment and hospitality or even international events will take all those inputs. We'll make sure we're always critiquing and debriefing our events on an annual basis. We make sure we take the feedback very seriously, and it comes back to what I was saying earlier about authenticity.

BS: Thank you. And I think that's very, very relevant, Andrew.

What are some of the platforms or the tools or the channels? And are you personally involved in supporting the organization's reputation?

AW: If you're the CEO of a business that's in a public forum, it has to be a full commitment. You know within my role I see it as broader than just delivering and running the business here. I don't want to overplay it, but it's the role of a statesman. It's the role of an AA leader. It's the role of a spokesperson and it's got to extend beyond just being a motorsport event. We are a tourism and branding entity and as a result of that the networking that we can do within the tourism industry is vitally important because you've got to have a level of inquisitiveness. And you only get that level of inquisitiveness by mixing with groups and individuals and peoples who are beyond your sphere. If you're only looking inside motorsport, then you could have a very, very narrow view of what the reminders of our event is. So the platforms and tools, as I'm a researcher and in the sense of always wanting to understand what other events are doing, I'm a networker in terms of wanting to make sure that we are dealing with everyone who's associated with our industry and the salesperson is wanting to look to new opportunities to align with Moto GP and Formula One. And he knows there's a level of social tools, there's revenue tools, and there's business networking tools I guess.

BS: If I think about some of the other platforms and channels, I mean, obviously we see the media, whether it's radio or television above the line, we see banners in the city, we see websites, and we see magazines. I see you on social and business platforms shaking hands with, you know dignitaries and others. I mean that's all part of the platform that you use to promote I guess the organization, the event, and your reputation.

AW: Yeah, it is. And what I've noticed more and more is the way that the business has changed. It's the way I've also observed things in the early days of being the spokesperson of the business. And I think the spread and growth of us was wholly and solely our chairman, the original chairman of a big, larger than life character in Melbourne, Rob Walker. Then it broadened to Ryan and myself and now we're broadening to make sure that different members of our staff and business are the mouthpiece of different aspects because if we're out the selling our appeal and selling the virtues of the event to a crowd who wants to come along and listen to, you know, rock bands and music that are popular with a genre for the 19–27-year olds.

The net message is going to be better delivered by people in our entertainment team rather than myself, who are not necessarily going to associate with either the audience or be the product. So you have to be able to adapt. And I think also social media and the different aspects, you cannot just rely wholly and solely now on the strength of your products or your brand at once as it needs to be multifaceted.

BS: Yeah, fair enough. I understand that. So just changing topic for a second, in your opinion, how ready is your organization and you personally to actively manage reputation?

AW: How ready are we to manage reputation? I think we are. We are always ready, because at any particular time. Given the variety of interactions that we have, there might be something that's going to go wrong when you work in the events industry, and when you're working in Moto GP and Formula One, you need to have contingency plans, you need to have backups. You need to have gone through readiness through simulation through preparation through what if scenarios. And you need to be adept, and there's a level of alignment to the politicians, although I'd say we probably give more authentic and real answers sometimes. But you need to be prepared for the good and the bad.

And that can happen at any particular point in time. It might be, at its worst, it could be a death on track. It could be something interacting when we're entertaining 130,000 people on race day. Potentially there's a lot of things that can go wrong. And so you've always got to be prepared in this manner and you've got to therefore have a strong approach with your communication team, with your corporate affairs, brand management, reputation management, and what I'd say is you've got to be very, very aligned and have very strong connections with your stakeholder group and your core stakeholders.

BS: Yes, and I imagine that the board would be very supportive of what you've just said. Is that a fair assumption?

AW: Yeah, you know the changing nature of governance, industrial manslaughter laws, and reputation management. We have a volunteer board, so people have involvement on our board for the love of the sport, the love of the corporation, and what we stand for. Sometimes that might be similar to someone being on the board of the school they attended, or something like that.

Reputations can be damaged very, very quickly by the performances of a business and so the board is acutely aware of the importance of government governance, compliance, reputation management, due diligence, appropriateness, probity, and process. And therefore they're the things that people don't necessarily see when you've just got the core delivery of a Moto GP.

BS: Thank you, Andrew. What do you think of the three challenges that you and the organization will face in the coming years?

AW: There are always short-term and long-term challenges, but immediately if I look at Formula One, one of those challenges is actually to capitalize on the sweet spot that Formula One has at the moment.

To grow the audience and sustain that audience for the future. We can't control the excitement of the sport, but we can control the excitement and the offering of the event. So the first one is that we've got to make sure that we're capitalizing on this to preserve and protect future growth. Second, when it comes to our audiences for Moto GP and Formula One, there's an increasing interest in the authenticity and the public positioning of that event or that sport when it comes to anything from modern slavery and working practices to the environment, it's level of inclusiveness, the diversity of the audience, and the morals upon which the sport is based. And that is a non-negotiable.

I do GP and Formula One and taking strong approaches to the sustainability area as we are at the Australian Grand Prix Corporation.

That's just non-negotiable. The third challenge, I would say is, you know organizationally, continually ensuring that staff, training, development, cultural alignment, succession planning are all very, very fertile, that they're all paid attention to. When I started here in 2006, there was a wonderful team of individuals.

As I am now in 2023, there's an equally capable team of individuals. You have to have the mix of experience and new ideas, but you also have to have the right alignment to the organizational values and therefore you've got to ensure that through the recruitment process you're getting an alignment of individuals who know what they're getting in for, but then can combine to produce a wonderful team effort. And I think we're seeing that with the record crowds that we've had at Formula One and Moto GP.

BS: Andrew, what are your main competitive advantages for your own personal profile?

AW: I haven't had much thought on that one. The competitive advantage of my own personal profile, I think I'd say one of them is if I could run.

Businesses are becoming very much about agility, businesses are becoming more and more complex there are so many different things that CEOs and leaders have to deal with during any particular day, any particular week, or any particular part of the business cycle. As CEO, you've got to be across everything and know the interactivities between each of those things. First one I'd therefore say is agility. The second one from my perspective is a competitive advantage of my profile. I think it would be my ability to interact with people in a very natural, authentic way. Everyone wants to come to work and enjoy it. You want to enjoy working and mixing with nice people. You want to be able to smile. You wanna be able to have fun. But you also want to be stretched and stimulated in what you do. I feel that my interpersonal skills and my ability to motivate, but also to, you know, not compromise on the standards, I mean.

Sometimes that's a balancing act, because if we're to deliver a product at the globally highest level and Moto GP and Formula One are the globally highest levels in their sport and so you strain Grand Prix Corporation needs to deliver at that, then you need to be able to balance standards with an interpersonal capability. Third, I think I've got a knack of knowing what our customers want, knowing what we have to tailor to give our fans a product that is going to be sustainable and grow into the future.

BS: On the flip side, what is one of the main risk factors that might impact your personal profile?

AW: I'm a task-oriented individual, while I've spoken about my interpersonal skills I am very conscious that I'm a task-driven individual and that could be a risk to how I operate, and I have to ensure that as leader I'm leading a high performance team of leaders themselves. I think over the course of the journey, when you look at the development of the individuals that have worked here, and the capabilities they have, it is something I have got to watch. It is important to have balance, sometimes it's important to ensure that this level of fun is not confused with it being all fun and games. You need to be aware of not only when the game is on, but also when to turn it off. Outwardly, it might look like I am a bit complacent to newer staff who try and adopt this approach.

BS: When you first started what were the main themes or topics which were entrusted to you to protect your reputation and that of the organization?

AW: One of these I picked up from Norman Schwarzopf, leader of Desert Storm in the US armed forces. He had a saying which was to adopt a rule, which was to do what's right. I learnt that being at the front piece of the organization meant being critiqued, or often interviewed by the media, and through that the public was getting an insight into how this business operated. You had to be authentic and honest, you could not mislead, misdirect, and create distrust within the community because the community funds the business. Therefore, ensuring that we do the right thing, preserve our reputation by actions, words, and staging of our events. Ultimately, reputation builds because people associate it with the right set of values. It was something that my own upbringing and respect in treating others served me, as well as the way in which I would want to be treated myself.

BS: Good foundational values. Final question. Are you satisfied with the quality of your managers and how important do you think your reputation is in attracting the best profiles of talent in the market?

AW: First, when it comes to my managers, we've recently had some restructuring. The restructuring and adjustment for several of those roles was actually done from within because in a business of our size, one of the things that we need to create is the ability for people to develop their careers.

If we're a stagnant structure and a small business, if you happen to hit a ceiling very early on in your career you'll be lost to the business, so backing people with experience is important. Yes, they might have some development areas. What we've now done is retain the IP and knowledge, the understanding of our events, the DNA, what essentially makes the business tick. And we've been able to create, therefore, opportunities for others in the business to move into those particular roles. When it comes to the reputation that I've created and the way of working the values of the business, people have been attracted to the corporation because they've seen that even during their interview process, it is very easy to hear what the CEO has to say about the business, how the CEO conducts himself, and this is something people have recognized. This is appealing and I think that the brand and the way we're viewed by candidates do not directly affect the CEO in our leadership team. People are attracted to the corporation because they can clearly see that it's a business that they want to work in.

4   CEO Branding as an Asset to Attract and Retain Top Managers and Talent

by Gabriele Ghini

4.1   On the threshold of a new "war of talent"

From the yearly CEO Outlook conducted by the company KPMG[1] on 1,300 CEOs active in 11 of the world's major economies, (2019, 2020, 2021, and 2022), it has emerged that talent management is one of the main risks perceived by the CEOs of the world's largest companies.

The Covid-19 pandemic that has hit the world has certainly brought an unprecedented period of uncertainty, and the war in Ukraine has demolished the sudden rise of the economy after the end of the pandemic. CEOs today face a new scenario and new challenges, their greatest concern being not having the necessary talent to deal with the difficulties and return to growth. Furthermore, the new focus on sustainability and corporate responsibility issues leads organizations to review their contribution to society and review their goals.

In the investigations prior to the pandemic, the CEOs relegated the risks associated with the difficulty of finding new talent on the market and keep them among 12th place of their concerns; instead, today, this voice is at the top of the list and is perceived as one of the main threats for the business of companies, in front of other themes such as supply chain, the return of nationalism, and environmental and climatic concerns.

In KPMG surveys from 2017 to 2019,[2] there were other priorities in-

---

[1] KPMG 2020, 2021, 2022 CEO Outlook.

[2] KPMG, *Agile or irrelevant. Redefining resilience*, 2019 Global CEO Outlook; *Growing pains*, 2018 Global CEO Outlooks; *Disrupt and grow*, 2017 Global CEO Outlook, https://assets.kpmg.

dicated by CEOs. In 2017, the top positions were listed: disruption as an opportunity, growth of uncertainty, change in the geopolitical climate, and penetration strategies on consolidated markets. In 2018: cyber-attacks; generational change with the arrival of Millennials as consumers; return of localism to geopolitics as a threat to business. In 2019: agile or irrelevant, that is being too slow can lead to failure; the need to introduce a culture capable of accepting errors as part of the innovation process in the company; rebuilding the leadership to be more resilient.

Jumping into 2022, the priorities are: Employee value proposition to attract and retain the necessary talent (25%); Advancing digitization and connectivity across the business (25%); Increasing measures to adapt to geopolitical issues (21%); Inflation proofing capital and input costs (19%); Execution of ESG initiatives (10%). In my view, that means finding a way to combine the attraction and retention of the best people in the market with the increase in productivity of the whole company thanks to digitization.

If the preoccupation of identifying, hiring, and retaining talent has become the main concern of so many CEOs on a global level and it is lasting many years, this book could not miss a thorough reflection on this, also because we think this situation will continue over time, affecting many of the years to come.

To respond to the difficulty in attracting and retaining talent, companies will have to put in place all possible tools to be attractive and motivating toward the best profiles on the market. Through concrete and discounted tools such as remuneration, roles, and career, we analyzed the impact of the company's reputation and its leadership on its attractiveness in the labor market. Knowing how to use these intangible assets can give you a fundamental advantage over the competition and present itself to candidates as a company capable of satisfying the needs of professionals and managers both in the choice phase and in the decision to stay in the company and guarantee the best performance.

We compared the research data on employer reputation carried out by the RepTrak Company in Italy[3] with a survey carried out within Federmanager to verify the main attracting factories of a company and draw conclusions on the most effective practices that CEOs can put in place to convince and retain the best talent on the market.

---

[3] "Italy Employer RepTrak 2019: da employer branding ad employer reputation", www.affaritaliani.it, October 23, 2019.

4.2   From employer branding to employer reputation

The RepTrak Company studies 200 companies every year in Italy from the point of view of job seekers (those active in seeking or evaluating a new job) to understand what the reputation of a company means in terms of an employer, and what it is driven by.

This study is known as "Italy Employer RepTrak 2019" and is available, as other studies cited in this paragraph on the website www.Rep-Trak.com.

The study highlights the following:

1. As reputation grows, the desire to work for that company also increases. Therefore, if the reputation of a company improves, the willingness to consider that company as a potential employer becomes higher. For companies with a poor reputation, less than 10% of potential talent would be willing to accept the job offer. For companies with an excellent reputation, this figure would be over 70%.

2. Companies with better reputation have lower recruitment costs, lower entry salaries on average (if willing to choose a company even with a slightly lower salary), and lower turnover (less willing to leave the company that enjoys a strong or excellent reputation).

3. What guides the candidates' choices are purely intangible elements. In fact, the choice of going to work for a company is not exclusively based on hard aspects (reward, compensation, career, etc.), but it relates instead to aspects of responsibility of the product and, in this case, we are talking about social role, transparency, vision of the future, and company leadership. All of this is represented by the CEO.

Reputation in the field of employer reputation is based on the emotional bond that candidates have toward the future employer. This bond of trust, esteem, and admiration is completely guided in a positive or negative manner by rational factors that mainly look at:

1. *Total rewards (weight of 17% of reputation):* everything related to benefits and compensation as well as work–life balance.

2. *Professional development (accounts for 19% of reputation:* the perception of what career this company can offer.
3. *Work environment (worth 15% of reputation):* Flexibility, safety at work, and physical and social environments. With the arrival of the pandemic, these elements are increasing in importance.

From the RepTrak Company studies, these three elements are the so-called HR areas and are also those that are mainly reported by Human Resources/Recruitment functions when wanting to attract new talent for a company.

There are also two areas that are not traditionally part of the HR function, and these are:

1. *Product and responsibility (accounts for 27% of reputation):* Meaning marketing, responsibility, and the impact on society.
2. *Market leadership (worth 22% of reputation):* How much a company is a market leader (not necessarily in terms of volume but also of thought), alongside the vision of the future and its leaders, precisely the CEOs.

In recent years, companies have started working on employer branding, that is, the promise they make to the candidate. Promise is one side of a medal and is under the control of the company. The other side of the medal is employer reputation, that is, how much the company is able to meet the expectations of the candidate in terms of its promise.

From the "Italy Employer RepTrak 2019" study, a series of key points emerge, strategic to compete in attracting the best new talent: There is a statistical correlation between employer reputation and the strength of the brand as an employer—therefore the company's ability to improve its promise as an employer allows the candidate to increase the reputation that he will attribute to the same company in a constant cycle, in which the company is able to go through with its promise meeting the candidates expectations and the candidates will prefer that company more and more. Therefore, companies can directly influence their employer reputation by fully understanding what areas guide it most, set a promise, and subsequently a professional experience on the principles that influence their needs and expectations.

Everything reported may seem logical. In reality, working for over 30 years in the Executive Search Field, the evidence I am confronted with on a daily basis is that a large number of companies in Italy and globally very often have not even formalized that promise, in other words they have not formalized an employer value proposition. Other companies that have formalized it very often have done this by looking carefully at their own business. A correct approach radically changes the nature of the corporate promise, and instead of relying on its interior, it arises from the needs today and tomorrow's candidates, without forgetting the employees who are already operational.

The process must therefore begin by asking ourselves what candidates expect from our company and reconstructing the promise based on what emerges. How can we then increase the attractiveness of a company and consequently promote the choice of that company as a future employer and the related business benefits? It is necessary to improve the employer value proposition, that is, the ability to fulfil the promise that companies make as employers, which directly impacts the increase in reputation as an employer. Naturally, this value will need to be quantified, so that human resources can translate typical tactical actions with a strategic vision, thanks to data and numbers, and communicate with corporate leadership in terms of medium-term strategic objectives.

4.3 Company leadership in attracting talent and motivating employees: the Federmanager survey

Corporate leadership is itself a formidable asset to improve the ability to attract the right talent. The personification of leadership in this case, its main representative, the CEO, is fundamental in transmitting that promise and making it concrete and personifying it because people trust people.

Also, from the "Italy Employer RepTrak 2019" study, it emerges that when a company adopts an employer branding strategy making the most of its corporate leadership (in particular its CEO), it then multiplies the positive behavior of its stakeholders, such as that of recommending the company in terms of employment, going to work there and speaking of it positively. The study makes it clear that on average these positive behaviors increase by more than 20% when you come into "contact" with the company's CEO.

Essentially, it is important to not be ashamed. It is interesting to observe how long there is still to go on this issue, in fact only 13% of candidates are familiar with the CEOs of the companies, therefore the remaining 87% who are unfamiliar with company leadership and its CEO are much less likely to choose the company as an employer.

We wanted to test and compare the research results of the RepTrak Company directly addressing the company leadership represented by Federmanger shareholders. With about 180,000 executives, top managers, and high professionalism in service and in retirement, Federmanger is the most representative association in the world of management, of which they take care of contractual, institutional, social, professional, and cultural aspects (Figure 4.1).

We launched an online questionnaire to 20,000 Federmanager members subscribed to the association's periodic newsletter, and they responded in 4,690.

The sample managers who participated are expressed by the following elements:

In Figure 4.2, they are divided into the following age groups:

1. Up to 40: 3.2%.
2. From 41 to 50: 24.5%.
3. Between 51 and 60: 49.5%.
4. Over 60: 22.8%.

Figure 4.1   Managers who answered the questionnaire divided by gender

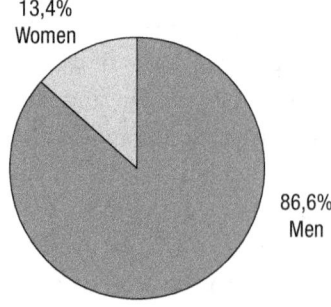

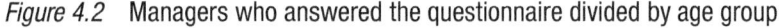

Figure 4.2   Managers who answered the questionnaire divided by age group

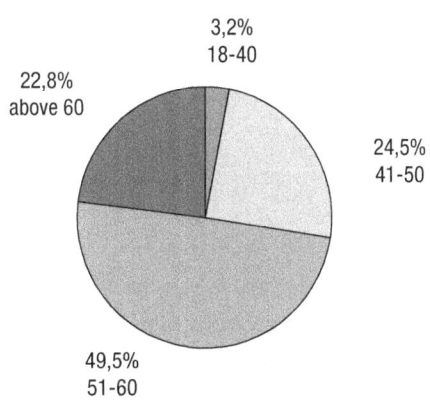

In Figure 4.3, the work area is significant:

1. North: 73.8%.
2. Centre: 17.7%.
3. South and Islands: 5.3%.
4. Abroad: 2.2%.

The vast majority of managers who responded already held a top position within the company (Figure 4.4):

Figure 4.3   Managers who answered the questionnaire divided by working area

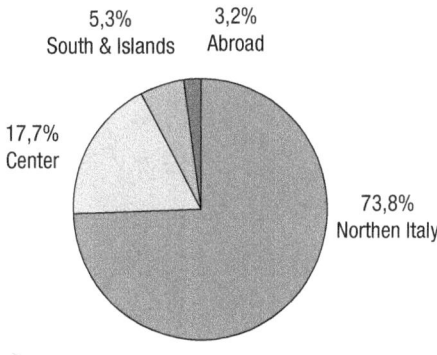

1. CEO: 10.2%.
2. General director: 14.9%.
3. Operations director: 24.7%.
4. Commercial director: 17.7%.
5. CFO: 7%.
6. CIO: 7%.
7. HR Director: 4%.
8. Middle Manager: 7%.

As for the type of company (Figure 4.5), 86% of managers who responded to the survey work in a private company, 5% for a public one, 1% in non-profit, and 8% in consulting.

The last two indicators of the Federmanager sample are related to seniority (Figure 4.6) and educational (Figure 4.7) qualification.

Ninety three percent of respondents have been working for more than 15 years, 4% from 10 to 15, and only 3% less than 10.

Unsurprisingly, 59.1% hold a degree with the old system, 17.1% have a Master or PhD, 4.2% have a three-year degree, and 19.6% have a diploma.

We are therefore examining a highly representative sample of the class of senior managers in private companies in Northern Italy, the type of manager who falls under the magnifying glass of headhunter specializes in Executive positions.

Figure 4.4   Managers who answered the questionnaire divided by role

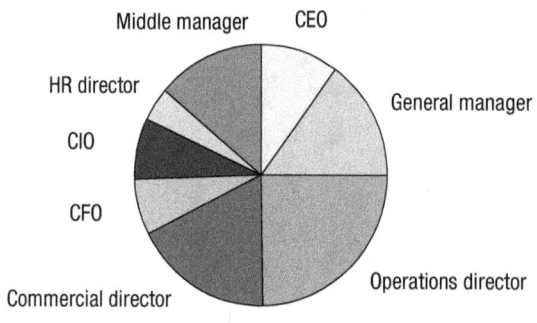

Figure 4.5   Managers who answered the questionnaire divided by type
of company

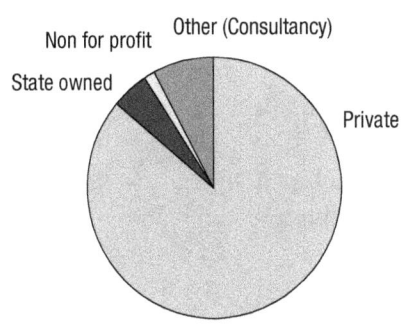

Figure 4.6   Managers who answered the questionnaire divided by seniority

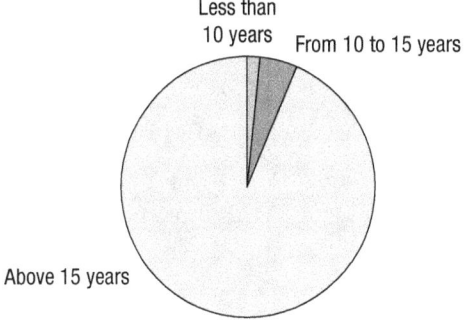

Figure 4.7   Managers who answered the questionnaire divided by educational
qualification

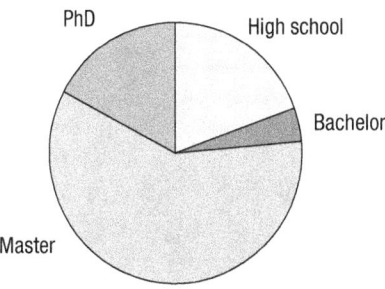

To facilitate and encourage them to fill in, we limited the questionnaire to five questions, the first three formulated to understand the most important reasons for choosing the company:

What are the most important aspects for you when choosing a job?
Managers were asked to rate the following aspects:

1. Quality and reputation of top managers.
2. Economic and financial solidity and vision of the company's future.
3. Has a positive impact on society, a company that behaves ethically minded.
4. Offers reliable products and services.
5. Operates in an interesting sector with stimulating job duties.
6. Is an innovative company.
7. A positive environment and culture within the company.
8. Stability within the workplace.
9. Guarantees adequate salary.
10. Offers equal career opportunities.

By summing up the most important parameters ("influential," "very influential," and "essential"), the ranking of the choices (Figure 4.8) was the following:

1. Economic and financial solidity and vision of the company's future.
2. Adequate salary.
3. Reliable products and services.
4. Reputation of top managers.
5. Operates in an interesting sector with stimulating job duties.
6. Positive impact on society.
7. Positive environment and culture within the company.
8. An innovative company.
9. Equal career opportunities.

The lack of interest in innovation and equal opportunities seem to flex the composition of the sample, male managers with high seniority, while the other parameters are enclosed in a handful of points of difference with the exception of the search of solidity and vision of the future

Figure 4.8   Ranking of the most important parameters in choosing the workplace

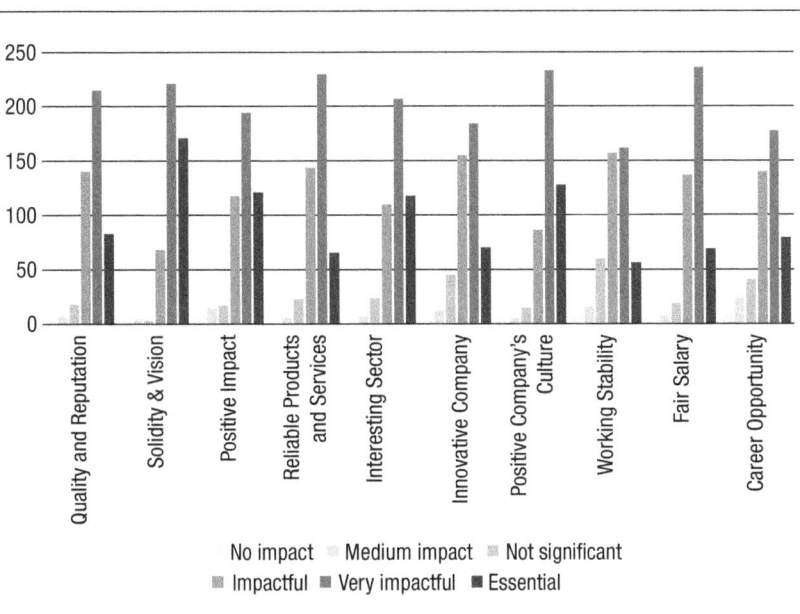

of the company, parameters for which our sample shows a particular sensitivity.

In any case however, a company that aims to attract and retain the best talent available has the responsibility of paying attention to all these factors, since on one hand they have now become essential to be able to compete in the markets in an adequate manner, and on the other hand, these are elements that play a fundamental role both from a reputational point of view and from a recruiting perspective since, in many cases, they constitute real differentiating factors.

How much does the reputation of a company influence your choice to work for it? With this question, we wanted to verify in a timely manner the impact of corporate reputation in choosing a manager to work for this specific company.

In Figure 4.9, the weight (expressed on a scale from 1 to 10) is reported that managers attributed to the reputation of the company when they decided the organization for which it was appropriate to apply. As can be noticed at first glance, the majority of managers have attributed to this

Figure 4.9   Weight attributed to the reputation of the company by job
             candidates

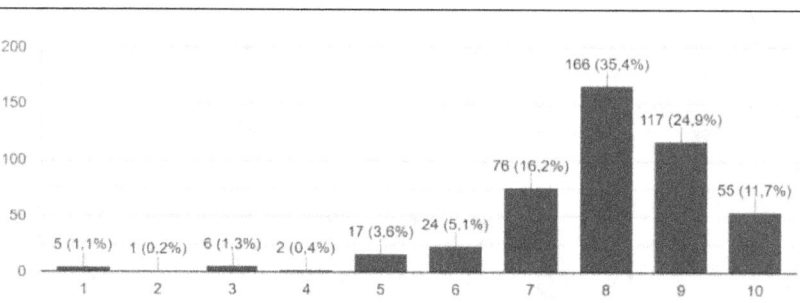

aspect a weight higher than 5, therefore confirming that in many cases, they informed themselves and were influenced by the reputation of the company they wanted to work at. Consequently, they were well aware of this factor in the moment in which they made that choice. It is ulteriorly confirmed how the reputation of a company is important in attracting the best talent, therefore constituting a strategic drive in the process of recruiting.

How much does the reputation of a CEO influence a person's choice to work for a particular company?

Figure 4.10 also refers to the role of reputation, but in this case, the focus shifts its weight (always expressed on a scale from 1 to 10) that the CEO of a particular company has in directing the interviewed manager to apply for one open position within the company itself or to accept a job proposal.

As already found for the previous question, most of the respondents attach considerable importance to the reputation of a CEO in the selection phase, although this time the managers who expressed a weight less than 5 are slightly more numerous than those who have given little weight to the reputation of the company as a whole. The possible reasons for the lower weight attributed to this aspect could lie, for example, in a lack of knowledge of the personal reputation of individual CEOs (the reputation of the company in many cases is more important), or alternatively in the fact that respondents attribute a lower incidence to the CEOs reputation than that attributed to corporate reputation regarding the effects that this can have both on the working life of collaborators and on the general

Figure 4.10   Weight attributed to the reputation of the CEO by job candidates

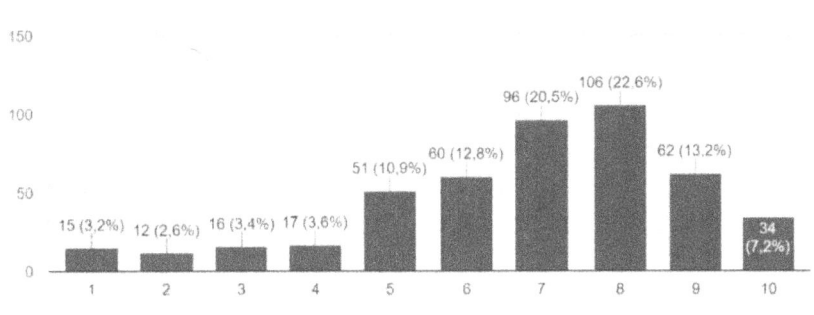

mentality of organization. With the following question, we entered the personal sphere of managers in terms of their reputation and areas to invest in their career.

How important is your personal reputation for your career or to get a new job?
Regarding the importance attributed by the interviewees to their personal reputation when they present themselves in a new company or career the answer is unanimous: Figure 4.11 clearly shows how almost all of the sample gives personal reputation a weight between 6 and 7, therefore corresponding to the maximum score that can be attributed to this answer. Only 1.4% attribute little or no weight to this factor.

The importance that the interviewees give to their personal reputation testifies how this issue has now been widely understood and constitutes further proof of the growing importance which this element has to be able to become part of the best companies.

In support of this claim, it should be emphasized that headhunters carefully scan (and thanks to social networks have ample possibilities) privacy aspects and personal reputation of all candidates, especially those for top positions.

Such attention to this aspect is more than justified by the fact that, always referring to a work perspective, it has now demonstrated various times how the reputation of various collaborators and in particular the management team is able to reflect and influence that of the companies they work for and vice versa.

Figure 4.11   Weight attributed to one's personal reputation for career
              and a new job

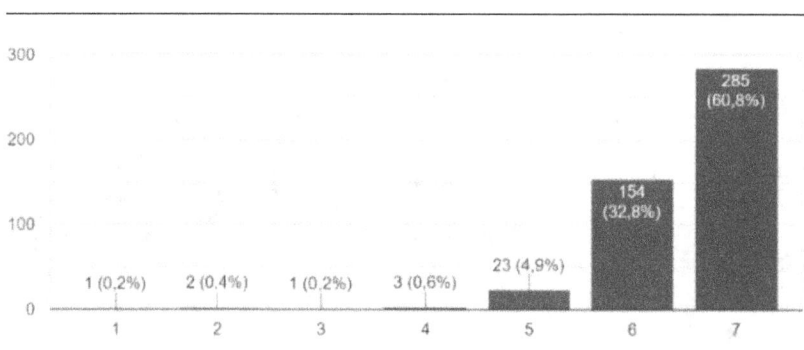

*What are the areas in which you feel you need to invest to further consolidate
your reputation as a manager?*
In examining the answer of the interviewees to this question (Figure
4.12), we find ourselves in front of four drivers which come into play for
the construction and consolidation of the reputation of managers. The
drivers in question are leadership, responsibility, management, and influence, which are used to distinguish the various areas in which the managers who are interviewed consider it important to invest with the ends
of consolidating their own reputation, just as the weight they attribute to
each of these factors. The weight is expressed through a scale formed by

Figure 4.12   Areas to invest in to improve your reputation

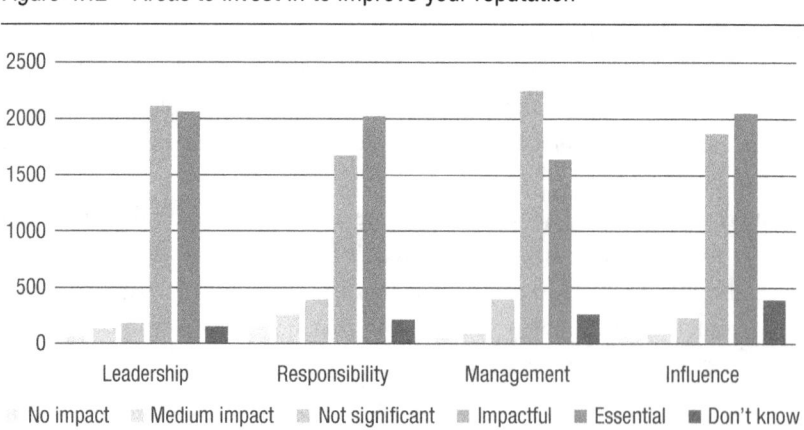

five different indicators, which go from "not relevant" to "essential," to which one can answer that they do not know.

As for leadership, that is, the ability of a manager to accurately perceive their image in the company, to adequately transmit their strategic vision and manage in an optimal manner change, most interviewees have attributed the value "important" and many "essential." Even taking into account the management factor, so the ability to manage the business and create value, the trend of replies is fairly similar despite being in this case the gap between "essential" and "important" being broader.

As for responsibility, which refers to working ethically and transparently, influence, that is, the ability to build relationships, influence choices, and build vision, the majority of managers interviewed attributed to these two aspects the rating of "essential." It is important to consider however, that the rating "important" was also expressed in many cases.

At this point, wanting to provide an overview and comment from the data just listed, it is immediately evident how a manager's awareness of the elements that they are able to significantly influence their reputation has been acquired in most cases.

Such an important weight attributed to elements such as responsibility and influence could constitute an important indicator about understanding the new trends of the workplace which from now on, also due to the growing attention that stakeholders give them, will influence in a continuously determined manner the reputation of manager and company and that therefore will be considered with further awareness. Some particularly fitting examples in this regard could be the increasingly important role of sustainability in companies' processes, the positive contribution which managers and companies must provide to society through their operations and acting ethically in a transparent manner, a factor which is now essential for companies and managers who desire to be successful.

4.4   Headhunter, corporate reputation, and talent attraction

From the above, we can affirm that even from the managers themselves, the CEO and company leadership are considered fundamental assets in the attraction and retention of senior managers and talent and must be an integral part of this strategy. An expectation exists (that of talent) and a strong awareness (that of managers) of "using" this asset to construct a competitive advantage.

Furthermore, the concept that CEOs must construct a strong brand to attract and keep the best professionals on the market is reinforced.

In the work of a headhunter, ideal target candidates are successful managers, satisfied with their position and career, with important growth prospects in the current company.

Nobody asks us to look for mediocre, frustrated, and underperforming managers. Therefore, attracting the best implies an activity of "selling" the position and company that undermines the candidates' certainties and leads them to carefully evaluate the proposal. If we want to further investigate the complexities that emerge during the persuasion of the candidate, from research on the field and personal experience, the priorities on which to act differ between men and women. The men are generally more motivated by salary, career, and hierarchical power inherent in the role, while the latter also carefully evaluate the climate and corporate culture without obviously neglecting the more practical aspects. But all candidates who are considered from headhunters are willing to face an often articulated and time-consuming selection process only in the face of a company that has an impeccable reputation, a leadership that guarantees and communicates a clear vision, and knows how to talk about itself in a convincing and authoritative way.

In complex times such as those we are experiencing and which will affect all sectors of business for many years to come, the attractiveness gap for executives and talent between companies with strong reputations and led by market-recognized CEOs and companies that lack those assets will be even wider. We are experiencing this daily in our headhunter job when we have to face uncertainties, resistance, and fears of change on the part of the candidates.

A large part of our role is also to act as career counselors. One of the recurring phrases when analyzing a resume or recommending a choice is: "This company makes curriculum," to indicate that an experience in a company with a strong and recognized reputation guarantees visibility to the manager also in view of subsequent steps career wise. Equally important is being able to mention having worked alongside a CEO with great imagination and reputation, and able to transmit a high level of experience, knowledge, approach, and vision. In my experience as headhunter, I have also encountered cases of top managers being able to put their careers at risk to follow a CEO with a particularly strong reputation in company situations that appear impossible to be recovered. In fact, it is not infrequent to encounter CEOs that present careers that are not very comprehensible. Frequent changes—entrance in society which present the necessity of strong reconstruction to leave situations of crises, lateral, and non-vertical passages. Deepening the motivations that have driven the manager to construct this particular career path, the minimum common denominator is the reputation of the CEO with which they have decided to establish a strong collaboration. CEOs which are able to overturn the destinies of companies bringing them back to being successful even in situations that seem apparently incurable.

4.5   The best practices for attracting talent

At the end of this chapter, we are able to indicate some best practices that will make it possible to achieve the desired objectives in attracting the best talent and motivating those already present in the company.

The reputation of CEOs is based on the emotional impact that stakeholders, in this case, managers and talent manifest toward the four drivers of this role: leadership, responsibility, influence, and management, and their definition is given in Chapter 3. The effective and truthful narration of how the CEO uses these four drivers consistently with the values and mission of the company is able to guarantee a reputational return of great depth. It is necessary to integrate the brands of the CEO and corporate leadership with specific company issues, company positions, and staff policies, defining a communication strategy with the HR tactics implemented in the company. In other words, building a fluid and collaborative process among employer branding, marketing, and corporate communication activities.

HR Directors will increasingly be required to adapt personnel policies both in the recruiting and in the retention phase, to the evolution of the labor market and to the generations of workers present in the company. Too many companies still think in terms of rigid pay grids, logistical constraints, and predefined working hours when instead, the reality and the experiences originating from the pandemic have caused a total revolution in the world of work. The speed and flexibility with which HR Directors will lead new business organizations will be fundamental parameters in the construction of a new image and attractiveness to the best professionals on the market.

Our experiences as headhunters have verified how a new approach in the management of human resources is successful in emerging from the pandemic, defined as two-dimensional leadership. On the one hand, empathy and support, that is, being accessible and listening, giving trust and space to people, enhancing the uniqueness of individuals, encouraging emotions and suggestions, developing collective and collaborative intelligence, and spreading hope and propulsive energy. On the other hand (and at the same time), assertiveness and authority that imply favoring rigor among people, demanding respect for rules, spreading a sense of individual responsibility, assertively indicating the direction to follow to avoid confusion, communicating with authority to stimulate performance and leave no room for alibis, connecting elements of the internal and external context, giving a strategic meaning that cannot be freely interpreted and a clear direction.

The communication levers on which to act in the construction of employer reputation are the following:

1. Distinctive and characterizing corporate objectives.
2. Consistent and recognizable communication in corporate conduct and its leadership.
3. Maintaining promises.
4. Sharing values with people you want to attract and later keep.

It is therefore crucial that companies become increasingly capable of focusing on the figure of the CEO and the entire leadership team to communicate their promise to the market and internal staff, by defining an employer value proposition that impacts the rational and the emotional aspects of the target audience.

We know there is still a long way to go to integrate the attractiveness toward the labor market between communication, marketing, and HR management to leverage the image of corporate leadership, but we have also shown how these strategies can guarantee a rapid return of effectiveness, efficiency, and savings in recruiting and retention of senior managers and best talent.

5 CEO Branding Strategies in Small and Mid-caps

by Gabriele Ghini

5.1 Small is not beautiful anymore. Italian small and mid-caps that want to grow on the stock market

Small and medium Italian businesses, indicated as corporations with a turnover which is inferior to 50 million euros, employ 82% of workers and represent 92% of active businesses. We are talking about 5.3 million SMEs (Smal and Medium-sized Enterprises), which employ more than 15 million people and generate a total revenue of over 2,000 billion euros. We found it important to give a specific focus on the perception of the value of reputation in the superior part of this important segment, and how much CEOs of this type of businesses are sensitive to the subject.

With the collaboration of Borsa Italiana, we have identified a significant sample of companies, identified in corporations, which after becoming part of ELITE, have chosen the market of Borsa Italiana as the privileged to support one's own projects of growth.

ELITE is the international platform born in Borsa Italiana in 2012 with the collaboration of Confindustria, which facilitates the encounter between companies and sources of capital to accelerate processes of growth, through an innovative model based on technology and a continuous development of products of alternative finance at the service of the company. ELITE accelerates opportunities for visibility and networking at an international level, supports decision-making processes and strategic planning, contributes to equip themselves with a more sophisticated managerial structure and to compete at a global level.

The stock markets of Borsa Italiana allow businesses of all sizes to collect important financial resources. Resources to accelerate development, diversify funding sources, and involve domestic and international investors. The best price improves the profile and visibility of the company and helps to motivate and involve management in business results. The sample selection is born from the hypothesis that the construction of CEO branding could have a different priority for corporations in different phases of their development cycle (Table 5.1). The corporations that decide to enter ELITE usually do this to further comprehend the

Table 5.1   The investigated companies

Company	Region	Listing date	Market
MASI AGRICOLA	Veneto	30/06/2015	AIM Italia
GIGLIO GROUP*	Lazio	07/08/2015	AIM Italia
TPS	Lombardy	28/03/2017	AIM Italia
WIIT*	Lombardy	05/06/2017	AIM Italia
FINLOGIS	Lombardy	09/06/2017	AIM Italia
PHARMANUTRA	Tuscany	18/07/2017	AIM Italia
AQUAFIL	Trentino-Alto Adige	04/12/2017	MTA
DB GROUP	Veneto	14/12/2017	AIM Italia
SOMEC*	Veneto	14/05/2018	AIM Italia
CAREL INDURSTRIES	Veneto	11/06/2018	AIM Italia
MONNALISA	Tuscany	12/07/2018	AIM Italia
GUALA CLOSURESS	Piedmont	06/08/2018	MTA
FINE FOODS & PHARMACEUTICALS	Lombardy	01/10/2018	AIM Italia
EDILIZIACROBATICA	Lombardy	19/11/2018	AIM Italia
POWERSOFT	Tuscany	17/12/2018	AIM Italia
TECHEDGE	Lombardy	19/12/2018	MTA
ANTARES VISION	Lombardy	18/04/2019	AIM Italia
ELES	Umbria	19/06/2019	AIM Italia
PATTERN	Piedmont	17/07/2019	AIM Italia
SHEDIR PHARMA GROUP	Campania	23/07/2019	AIM Italia

* The companies marked with an asterisk are listed on the main market, after market transition. Giglio Group and Wiit currently listed on the STAR segment of MTA; Somec on MTA. On December 12, 2020, Pharmanutra debuted in the STAR segment.

dynamics of growth by considering different factors, entering into contact and confronting themselves with other entrepreneurs who face the same challenges of crisis.

ELITE presents itself as neutral regarding structured financial tools to support the growth of small and medium companies, aware of the fact that finance comes later and is at the service of who does business. There are many corporations which after entering the ELITE platform decide to undertake a listing path as a choice because they have analyzed profoundly all the possibilities of finance and support to available growth and have decided that the support offered by the listing in terms of raising capital, refining of governance, and application of the maximum levels of transparency is preferable to realize their own ambitions of growth. The choice however, to quote one's own company, even more so if at the end of training, indicates with strength the attention of the company toward the themes of governance and transparency.

We are therefore talking about companies which have already undertaken an evolutionary path, including in cultural terms, from which the construction of an adequate CEO branding should not be separated.

The analysis has been focused on separate levels: the awareness of the importance of reputation; the level of use of reputation; the strategies of constructing the CEO branding. From the results of the survey, it clearly emerges that awareness has become an important part of the industrial sector in Italy. Small and mid-caps also demonstrate the same level of awareness that is found in companies of great dimensions.

5.2 The importance of reputation for small and mid-caps and their leaders

The first question of our survey was the following: *How much do you believe reputation is important nowadays for the business of companies?* In the answers to this question (you can also see Figure 5.1), we can see that almost 80% of all people interviewed consider it fundamental and the remaining 20% consider it important. So we can definitely say that in the minds of small and medium Italian caps, quoting reputation not only is an important element, but it also had direct and tangible impacts on the performance of business. This awareness has increased considerably compared to even five years ago, so much so that we can see an increase

Figure 5.1   Importance of companies' reputation for the business

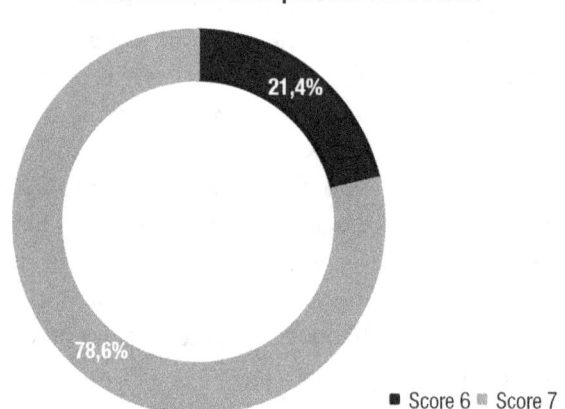

Today, CEOs consider the reputation of companies to be very important for the business: all respondents voted 6 and 7

21,4%

78,6%

■ Score 6 ▩ Score 7

of almost 30% in comparison to the *Reputation Leaders Study 2015* conducted by the RepTrak Company.[1]

The second question aimed to verify the willingness of small and mid-caps in measuring the impact of reputation on business.

How important is reputation for the business of your company?
From the responses expressed in Figure 5.2, an element of reflection emerges. Almost 40% of small and mid-caps don't measure reputation, in other words they are not aware of how much this intangible asset impacts on their own business, and therefore, we notice a strong distance between awareness and the use of the reputational tool.

Therefore, it is determining for the business but not determining enough to be measured? The risk inherent in a qualitative approach is making strategic decisions on the base of sentiments and not of objective parameters. Therefore, the accepted and shared principle of the importance of reputation does not yet have the need to define an approach structured to its measurement, the only one that allows reputation to be used in a scientific manner as a strategic asset for the development of business.

---

[1] The RepTrak Company, *Reputation Leaders Study*, 2015.

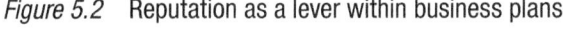

Figure 5.2 Reputation as a lever within business plans

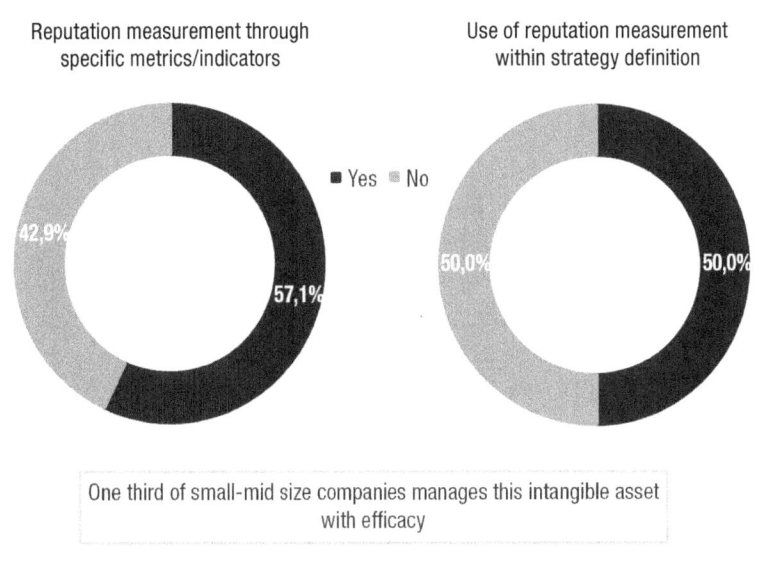

In this book, we try to bring to our readers some elements that allow them to understand in a detailed way which are the factors that guide, determine, increase, or erode the reputation of a company or its managers. In this complexity, even its own measurement seems to be an unclear element, often confused with the simplest indicator of Net Promoter Score (NPS) or with online sentiment indicators that do not allow a clear understanding of the entire ecosystem of the company and are limited to observing positive or negative comments. We realize that a more sophisticated intermediate step is required to move from awareness to measurement with respect to the complexity of this topic.

Focusing now on the use, if 57% of companies claim to measure their reputation in different ways, only 50% of this 57% declare, however, that they use the measurement by including it within the definition of business strategy, that is, using reputation as a leverage within business plans.

The result is that only a third of small and mid-caps manages to leverage on this intangible asset effectively, while 70% of companies don't yet do this. If we want to see the glass half full, in 2009–2010 only 15% of companies in Italy and the world had a clear reputational strategy, and therefore the awareness of its importance is in any case a strong increase.[2]

5.3   Reputational management toward stakeholders of small and mid-caps

When we talk about corporate reputation, we must ask ourselves the question: reputation toward whom? There are multiple reputations of the company since they are based precisely on the expectations of different audiences (*the different stakeholders)* which bring with them different interests and expectations. On this issue, we further wanted to compare ourselves with ELITE companies who then decided to go public on the markets organized and managed by Borsa Italiana, and understand, from their perspective, which are the most important, those on which a reputational strategy must be built and managed at the level of corporate strategy with a strong and specific engagement toward them.

Questions related to this topic were as follows:

1. In your branding strategy, what priorities do you give to the various stakeholders?
2. What do you think your reputation is with various stakeholders?

Figure 5.3 shows on the left the weight of the corporate roles responsible for creating reputation, and on the right, the stakeholders toward which the message is addressed primarily.

The panel of companies involved in the survey operates in disparate industrial sectors which are not linked to the institutional, political world which is judged to be of little influence in determining their reputation.

As for internal stakeholders in the same company, it is interesting to note that the CEO and the top managers are indicated as the main managers in conveying messages that affect reputation, but the weight that company employees as a whole can bring toward external stakeholders is not overlooked.

Moving on to stakeholders that are external to the company, research

---

[2] The RepTrak Company, *Reputation Leaders Study*, 2009.

Figure 5.3 Reputation to whom?

INTERNAL STAKEHOLDER	
1. CEO	85,7%
2. Top management	85,7%
3. Employees	57,1%

EXTERNAL STAKEHOLDER	
1. Clients	92,9%
2. Public opinion	64,3%
3. Investors	57,1%
4. Institutions	14,3%

Customer is the main stakeholder

brings with it ample room for growth in reputational investment in public opinion, investors, and institutions, even though the latter are considered uninteresting. The most important are therefore the customers. This seems obvious given that the goal of a company is to sell, but the percentage difference in respect to other stakeholders is decisively marked and requires a broader reflection on public opinion and investors.

Even if this does not emerge from the survey, all studies converge in defining public opinion as the stakeholder by definition, which is also of strategic importance within the B2B and small- and medium-sized sector businesses in the communities in which they operate. The company has a social impact, regardless of whether it acts locally or nationally. The companies on our panel correctly attribute a certain weight to public opinion, they are aware that their work is judged by a wider audience than their customers, and therefore know how to act consequently, but only 64.3% consider this important. It is useful to underline that public opinion also influences investors in a descending process, which if managed correctly can multiply the positive returns for the company.

Institutions, on the other hand, are a separate chapter and are affected by a general opinion that considers them unimportant when not disqualified (one would write: sometimes harmful) in business management and our panel of companies believes that they do not require special attention.

From a reputation building perspective, the CEO and top management are definitely responsible for building corporate reputation, while its management is the responsibility of the company as a whole, from the CEO to his leadership team, to the colleagues in customer service and sales. Everyone has an important role. The interesting and encouraging data is that almost 90% of all CEOs believe that reputation and management are on their own personal table.

5.4   The role of the CEO in small and mid-caps with a strong vocation for development and growth

The areas that characterize the reputation of a CEO are:

1. Leadership (the CEO has a strong image, a clear strategic vision, and anticipates change).
2. Responsibility (acts responsibly, works ethically, and supports good causes).
3. Management (an effective manager who understands the context of business and builds values for stakeholders).
4. Influence (has good communication skills, a global perspective; and their vision has a strong influence).

We asked ELITE listed companies to give a weight to each of the above drivers in building their CEO's.

The question was formulated as follows:

In your opinion, how important are the following drivers to work on the reputation of a CEO?
The answers are shown in Figure 5.4.

The responses of the panel show a certain uniformity of judgment without a strong prevalence of one over the other. Responsibility, that is behaving in an ethical and socially conscious way, was the most popular, but the difference in percentage compared to leadership is minimal, similar with other parameters. The inherent risk of this assessment is to tend to overestimate the perception within the company, compared to the reputational judgment expressed by stakeholders.

Figure 5.4   Drivers for working on CEO reputation: responsibility and leadership
are the main reputation drivers for a CEO

Results Elite Companies

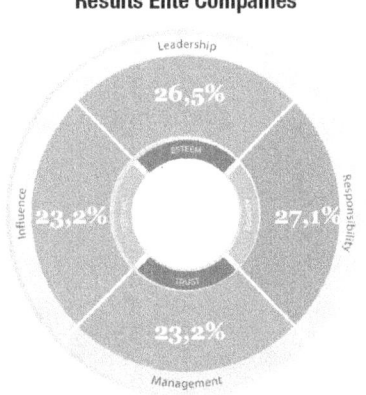

5.5   The degree of satisfaction in the management of corporate reputation

As for the satisfaction in managing the reputation of your company, the question was the following:

How much do you manage your company's reputation strategy as you would like?
The answers are shown in Figure 5.5.

If even a third of these companies are satisfied with their reputation management strategy, the large percentage of those who declare themselves unsatisfied is however surprising. Forty three percent believe that they have a large room for improvement on this strategic aspect, which we should not forget to mention, was considered fundamental by the whole panel. Unsurprisingly, this percentage coincides exactly with that of the companies who do not measure their reputation quantitatively. Therefore, the sensitivity toward the importance of reputation is clear, and an important number of companies realize they have ample room for improvement in order to be satisfied, but probably, they are still searching for the tools that allow them to measure it and master it to the fullest.

Figure 5.5 Level of satisfaction with the management of the reputation
            strategy in the company: the majority of CEOs responded positively

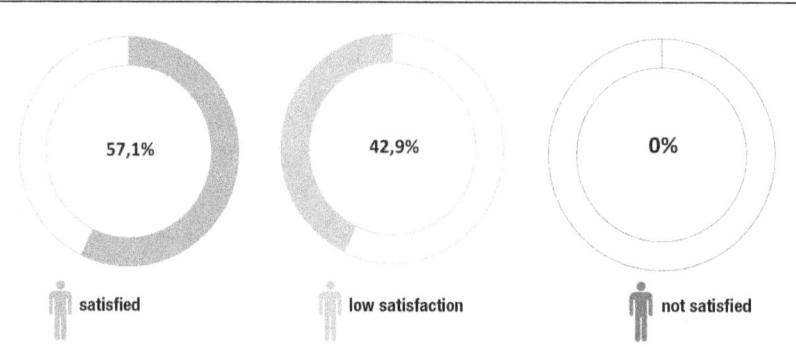

5.6   The CEO's reputation for attracting talent

Entering the part relating to the reputation of the CEO as a tool to attract the best professionals on the market, we have formulated the following targeted question:

*How important do you consider your reputation in attracting the best profiles
on the market?*

From the responses in Figure 5.6, it emerged that 64.3% of the CEOs
of companies surveyed believe that reputation is very important in attracting the best talent.

Figure 5.6 CEOs today believe that their reputation is very important
            in attracting the best profiles on the market

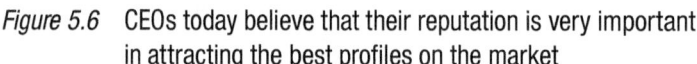

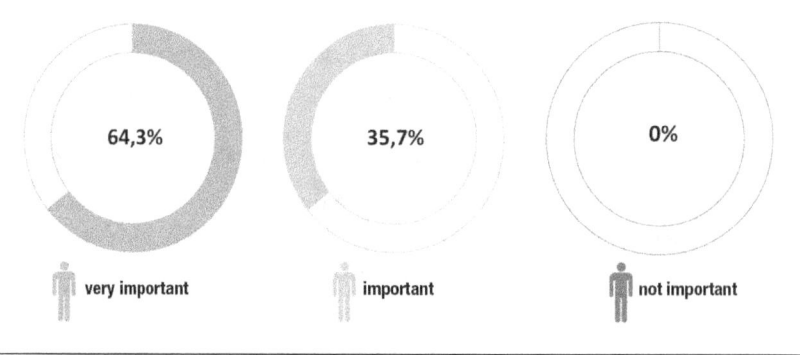

Therefore, it can be seen how CEOs recognize how relevant their own actions are and how much one's reputation can influence the company's attraction of the brightest managers and professionals on the market.

The importance of the CEO's exposure is confirmed to demonstrate the solidity and prospects of the company and as a safe leader for its current and future employees.

In this perspective, the theme of CEO branding is an extraordinary opportunity to consolidate the reputation of companies.

But it is a potential that is hard to express because today, from in depth studies, only 13% of people looking for new job opportunities know the CEO of a company, its history, and its successes. Those who know them, would go to work for that company in 22% of cases.

In this book, we considered it important to dedicate a specific chapter on this topic, to indicate the most suitable practices to achieve the expected results.

5.7 CEO activism

Finally, we wanted to deepen the theme of CEO Activism. In recent years, several CEOs have expressed themselves publicly on social issues of great resonance (for example Rose Marcario, CEO of Patagonia vs. Trump on the environmental issue). This phenomenon, better known as "CEO Activism," is profoundly transforming the public role of the CEO.

An emblematic example of the impact of CEO activism managed in a disruptive way is in the strong stances Giorgio Armani took in the middle of the Covid-19 pandemic. After quickly converting some production lines into the production of hospital gowns, Giorgio Armani wrote a letter to *WWD Women's Wear Daily*, a magazine that is a point of reference within the world of fashion. A premise is important because it expresses the disruptive force of an intelligent example of CEO activism. Giorgio Armani had a turnover of 2.9 billion euros in 2019. In the same fiscal year, other international groups of this same sector presented the following turnover: LVMH 53 billion euros, Kering 15, Richemont 14, Chanel 10, Ralph Lauren 5.5, Tiffany 4.6. Despite having an important name and reputation, Giorgio Armani is not in the top 10 brands worldwide in terms of turnover. With his letter and position, Giorgio Armani has however demonstrated a sensitivity and ability to read the changes in global sentiment toward fashion, which is now leading to a profound review of the production and marketing models of the entire industry.

Obviously, the technical times to see this revolution being fully implemented have yet to be realized, but the way is marked.

The letter cited above is the following:

The decline of the fashion system, as we know it, began when the luxury sector adopted the operating methods of the fast fashion cycle of continuous delivery, with the hope of selling more. I no longer want to work like this, it is immoral. It doesn't make any sense that a jacket or suit of my design will live in the store for three weeks, then immediately become obsolete and be replaced by new merchandise, which is not very different from the previous stock. I don't work like that, I find it immoral to do so. I've always believed in the idea of timeless elegance in the creation of clothing, which suggests a single way to buy them: so that they last over time. For the same reason, I find it absurd that in the middle of winter, there are linen clothes in boutiques, and in summer alpaca coats, simply because the desire to purchase must be immediately satisfied. Who buys clothes to put them in a closet waiting for the right season to wear them? Nobody, or very few at least. However, this system, driven by department stores has become the dominant mentality. It is wrong, we must change, and this story must end. This crisis is a wonderful opportunity to slow down everything, to realign, to draw a more authentic and honest horizon. No more spectacles, no more waste. For three weeks now, I have been working with my team so that after the lockdown our collection will remain in boutiques until early September, as it should be. We will work like this from now on. This crisis is also an excellent opportunity to restore value to authenticity: We have had enough of fashion as a communication game, enough with the fashion shows around the world with the sole purpose of presenting bland ideas. We have had enough of the entertainment with shows that today turn out for what they are: inappropriate and if I can say, vulgar. Enough with the shows around the world, which only contribute to pollution. Stop wasting money for shows, they are just brushstrokes of enamel over nothing. The moment we are going through is turbulent, but it offers us the truly unique possibility to fix what is wrong, to remove the unnecessary, to rediscover a different human dimension. This is the most important lesson we can take from this crisis.

In this open letter, we find many of the themes that were expressed strongly by various stakeholders: respect for the environment, a return to authenticity, social responsibility, and a new humanism. In the following days, a new open letter is released, with 40 signatures, a group of designers from all over the world including: Thom Browne, Dries Van Noten, Altuzarra, Tory Burch, Erdem Moralioglu, and Gabriela Hearst, but also large department stores which were strongly hit by the pandemic, such as Nordstrom, Bergdorf, Goodman, and Selfridges. Italian names include the multibrands Tessabit, Tiziana Fausti, Antonioli, and La Rinascente.

This is the content of their letter:

We believe that the current crisis represents an opportunity for a fundamental and positive change that will simplify our activities, making them more sustainable from an environmental point of view and ultimately aligning them more toward customer needs. We want to achieve these objectives by adjusting the seasonality and sales in male and female sectors, starting from the autumn/winter season of 2020/21. We must bring the Autumn/Winter season back to Winter (August–January) and the Spring/Summer season to Summer (February–July), creating a more balanced flow of deliveries throughout the year to always offer new products, keeping the sales only at the end of each season, so in January and July. We will also work to increase sustainability along the supply chain and sales calendar through less waste, less travel, digital showrooms, and a review of fashion shows. As we can see, this is the beginning of a worldwide movement which, stimulated by the pandemic, and above all from Giorgio Armani's position, will cause an epochal change in the world of fashion. With these premises, we asked our panel how much it recognizes itself in this behavior, or whether it considers it risky, if not harmful. The answers are shown in Figure 5.7.

It was found that 64.3% of respondents do not recognize themselves in this behavior and believe it is risky for the CEO of a company to adopt this approach. Those who are very active on this issue are, in fact, only 35.7%. The answers to this question very clearly reveal the need to raise awareness of the importance of this exposure for small and mid-cap CEOs listed in line with emerging and most successful market trends. CEO activism, judged risky by the vast majority of the panel, has instead, as shown by the initiative of Giorgio Armani, become one of the keys and differentiating drivers in reputation-building strategies by major global companies.

Figure 5.7   CEO activism: the CEO interviewed does not recognize himself
in this behavior and considers it very risky

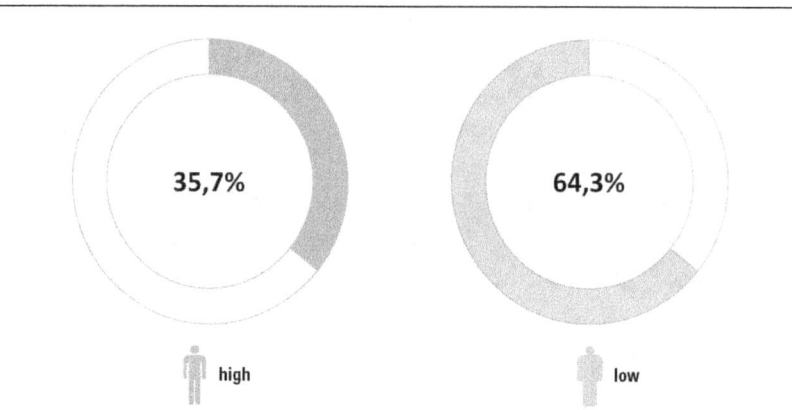

CEO activism carried out in a consistent and courageous manner increases the benefit of the doubt of stakeholders in times of difficulty,
crisis, or exponential emergencies. There is a suspension of judgment
in order to verify in more detail the true actions which were carried out
by companies, offering a competitive reputational advantage that can be
decisive in crisis situations. Having the time and opportunity to present
one's own version of events while being listened to on all levels has been
vital for numerous companies which have been accused of causing environmental damage, negatively affecting health, etc. On the contrary, we
have numerous concrete examples that show how many companies have
irrevocably lost their reputation for the inability to be listened to objec-
tively by the market. When put on the index, the effects on the value of
a company and business can be fatal.

CEO activism is strategic for growing your reputation with the public
and must be guided by a strategy that allows you to influence and express
yourself on what interests the public. The complexity of CEO activism
is related to the need for consistency between statements and actions,
easily identifiable in an era of transparency such as the current one. We
think that the degree of awareness of the importance of this approach in
the small and mid-caps interviewed has ample room for improvement on
which to set punctual and concrete strategies.

5.8 The reputational differences between large companies and small and mid-caps

To conclude this chapter, we will focus on four aspects that could make the reputational difference between large companies and small- and mid-sized companies, that is, size, investments, leverage, and leadership.

Dimension. Reputation has no correlation with size; large companies with a global presence are not subject to different reputational criteria than small and mid-caps: reputation is owned by stakeholders and regardless of size, attention to stakeholder expectations must be the same. Obviously, a global multinational lives a dimensional complication related to the number and heterogeneity of stakeholders, but the attention to be paid to them must be comparable.

Investments. Reputation has no correlation with the absolute amount of investment in communication. We see companies investing billions worldwide in constructing their brand yet are not the best in terms of reputation. On the contrary, small and mid-caps may be able to obtain a better reputation than large companies, thanks to the quality of their investments and their ability to transfer relevant content which adheres to the real needs of stakeholders. Therefore, it is the investment quality that defines how much a company is able to transfer propositions deemed important by stakeholders, not the quantity of resources invested. It is obvious that a large company, capable of investing significant amounts of resources and communicating in a relevant and appropriate manner, will see its brand emerge and its reputation becomes excellent. The real issue, however, will be the quality of the stakeholder engagement, not the simple amount of money invested. The secret lies in the ability to invest in relevant and impactful channels for my stakeholders, by transferring a message in line with their expectations. Investments make a difference when it comes to fueling notoriety of the brand, but reputation is based on the relevance that people of the desired target attribute to the company's promise.

Leverage. Here is where working on the Corporate Social Responsibility (CSR) becomes a lever to multiply the value of this reputation. This leverage can be activated both for small and mid-caps as well as large companies. Therefore, it is strategic to identify and act on the reputational levers relevant to the stakeholders of the individual company. A small company will be able to have a strong reputation toward its local community on the same level that a global company will have toward larger communities. Understanding and acting on the expectations of its stakeholders, companies of any size can be effective on a wide audience of consumers, as well as on a single, important customer.

Leadership. People trust people. Therefore, leadership is essential and equally essential is that leaders tell relevant things. The attention of leaders and management team must be focused on transferring the image of the company beyond the products or services sold. The CEO is ambassador, testimonial, and custodian of values and the broader purpose of the company, and this applies to companies of any dimension. In global companies, it will be necessary to identify local ambassadors to get the message closer to consumers, while in small companies, the CEO will act personally. Reputation is *local for local* because it depends on the expectations of specific communities, and communication must be segmented to adequately reach the desired stakeholders. CEO activism fits into this aspect, as it is one of the most powerful levers to significantly increase reputational weight, and which we have seen from our surveys, had yet to be understood by small and mid-caps. Still seen as a risk, it could instead constitute a fundamental tool for a communication strategy capable of differentiating the company from competition.

The ELITE Platform, by Marta Testi, CEO of ELITE
ELITE represents a new way of looking at small- and medium-sized enterprises, at their needs and challenges that, thanks to an increasing use of tools of finance complementary to traditional tools of finance, can be dealt with and brilliantly overcome. ELITE itself is a tool for defining and strengthening the reputation of companies, of which the CEOS represent the top. In these very words, ELITE, are summarized the characteristics that from the very beginning are the basis of this idea, which then had the strength to become a company: Excellence, Leadership, Innovation, Talent, Ecosystem. ELITE is Excellence. What has always guided us has been the continuous and tireless pursuit of the highest possible level of quality, precisely excellence. ELITE is Leadership. The

ability to lead to changes, to seize the opportunity that emerges from every moment of complexity, is one of the great values that only true leaders manage to demonstrate every day. ELITE is innovation. We believe that every company should have the opportunity to access the best resources on the market to grow and innovate their business. ELITE is talent. It is only to thank people that every business idea can take shape and exist. Only through research, management, and continuous attention to talent can companies make the most of favorable moments and courageously overcome the most complex ones. ELITE is Ecosystems. Before anything else, ELITE is an eco-international system at the center of global finance.

The reputation of a company and its CEO are based on multiple factors, and membership of the ELITE team, summarized in the five values I have just described, is increasingly considered among the elements that positively influence it.

The release of this volume in a context like the one we are experiencing, certainly gives importance and visibility to businesses, because it is from businesses, from their growth, and also from their reputation that we can all restart. We must continue to invest, we must return to grow, and we must resume work to facilitate those who everyday do business to restart the entire country.

Appendix. CEO Reputation in Small Mid Cap

by Cristiana Brocchetti[3]

Discussing corporate reputation, such as top management and a CEO's can be very complex, and certainly falls within the context of intangible corporate assets. In a way, it could be included in the definition and factors which contribute to a start-up.

The simplest way to understand this is to understand it's definition. There have been many varied definitions over the years, and the one

---

[3] Founder of ACE & Co. Financials in 2009, advisory company focused on investor relation, business development, corporate and investment services for PMI, VC and financial institutions. Independent Board Member for Alba Private Equity Spa. As of today she is also of-counsel advisor in IR TOP and venture partner in Kobo funds.

which I prefer is the following: 'Reputation is the ability, by a physical or legal entity to keep faith to commitments made, in an implicit and explicit manner towards the stakeholders' (Riccardo Taverna).

This is a definition which intrinsically includes many other topics:

- Ability: Responsibility, leadership, technical and organisational skills, which can be understood as a good management of the tangible and intangible resources available.
- Keeping faith: being able to provide a delivery on what has been declared, being credible and equally align interest with the stakeholders.
- Commitment: implicit- implementing the correct behaviours – or explicit – through the declaration of corporate growth objectives.
- Stakeholders: an enlarged cluster which identifies the community of carriers of interest in which a subject operates internally and externally to the company itself.

Regarding companies, especially listed ones, the ability to remain faithful to commitments made undoubtedly lies in the CEO's role, within the expression and actions of top management, and in the guidelines provided by the Board of Directors, which can be seen as the sovereign body. Regarding companies listed independently of market capitalization, 'keeping faith' can undoubtedly be declined in the ability to align interest between all financial stakeholders, whether understood as non-significant minority financial investors, reference shareholders, creditors of various levels or financing bodies.

A further consideration I propose is to evaluate whether a CEO themselves are a shareholder/entrepreneur, whether they have stock option plans (and whether this also exists regarding top management), or whether they are a manager elected by the Shareholders Meeting. This diversity is essential because it intrinsically brings a different propensity to risk in management choices and a sensitivity to the concept of reputation, personal and corporate brand, as well as alignment of interest with other stakeholders. This difference is evident if we analyse the composition of CEOs in large companies compared to small or medium sized ones, in which frequently the CEO themselves are also a reference shareholder as an entrepreneur or the expression of the entrepreneurial family they helped grow until listing the company, for example opening the capital to third-party shareholders with a financial and non-business managerial program.

If an entrepreneur uses financial and non-financial resources to carry out their financial work, a manager uses their human capital with limited expenditure of other types of resources, although it is often incentivised through stock option plans precisely for alignment purposes (i.e Marchionne Case). The value that an AD Manager attributes to their reputation and business compared to a CEO-entrepreneur undoubtedly remains a subjective factor. In small to medium companies, it is the minority shareholders themselves who request for the CEO to remain in the company for a matter of continuity, but this is less frequent in the case of larger scale companies. If a CEO of a large company moves towards another business at the end of their mandate, they will bring with them leadership, organisational skills and responsibility of their ability to create value. There are few historical cases in which this could generate a shock, which the market prices between 10 and 12% of market capitalisation at its announcement. Differently, if the CEO of a small to medium scale company withdraws their mandate, this represents a high level of discontinuity for the market, especially if the CEO's reputation was highly valued. The company now faces a period of generational transition.

At an empirical level, the consideration, value and weight that a CEO of a small to medium company provides to the concept of reputation is often aligned to the companies itself, yet it is often subjective, as there is not always the developed sensitivity to understand how intangible assets such as reputation can generate positive influences.

Take a person who takes care of themselves, by going to the gym, going on daily walks, observing a balanced diet, possessing few vices which consequently prevents the onset of certain diseases and slows down aging. Thus, generating fewer costs and contributing towards the economy in their own way. This is similar to taking care of a business effectively.

Without a doubt, corporate sustainability which can also be understood as the optimization of resources available, is a tool which alongside corporate governance contributes to the achievement of a company's reputation and its awareness on behalf of top management and relevant shareholders. Well defined corporate processes, especially in small to medium companies where the free float is less than 50%, and the reference shareholders are the entrepreneurs themselves, contribute significantly to the creation of corporate reputation, especially from a perspective of risk management. This can be understood as a deviation, both in a positive and negative way. The ability to communicate effectively and efficiently in a punctual and transparent manner contributes to creating the reputation of both the corporate brand and CEO, making them both reliable.

The credibility of the CEO is even more identified with the companies brand especially in small to medium sized companies, whether they are a key shareholder or if they have spent their lives working in the company or sector. The consideration and esteem that financial stakeholders towards them generates positive consequences regarding the market itself, which will be inclined to positively evaluate what has been communicated or evaluate in the long-term any shocks which may occur (such as Covid). Equally, competitive advantages can be found in the ability of the CEO to attract new capitals and investors, and in obtaining interest rate financing.

From this point of view, the reputation of a CEO and of the brand of the company becomes almost a prevention and protection factor in the management of any crisis or emergency situations.

In my opinion, the reputation of a CEO and their ability to strengthen the company brand in a dynamic and multifactorial asset, which must be kept updated in a constant manner and be almost, so to speak, automated in its ability to engage with all clusters of stakeholders, not only the financial ones.

Let's talk about the credibility that a CEO should have within an extended social group, both internal and external to the company and the territory in which it operates. At the corporate level, we could think of the brands reputation as a summary of actions of response from individual clusters of stakeholders. I tried to summarise in the following way the different groups of stakeholders of listed small to medium companies, and the positive consequences which derive from credible and responsible behaviour of the CEO (Figure 5.8):

- Institutional investors – Long term investors.
- Banks and financiers– Better access and conditions.
- Partners – Attracting new partners.
- Providers - Loyalty, procurement savings.
- Human resources – An increase in motivation.
- Clients – Loyalty.
- Prospects – Attraction of working with the company.
- Collectivity – Diminishment of local conflict.
- Media – Improved image in publicity.

Figure 5.8 Positive consequences of credible and responsible behaviour of the CEO

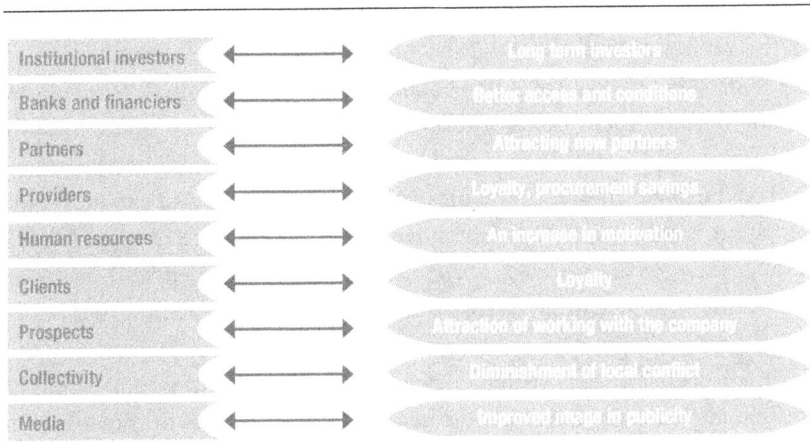

This holistic vision of the company's life towards its stakeholders certainly contributes to strengthening the reputation of CEO and the brand itself, in aligning their beliefs, and improving the sustainable management of available resource, whether they be financial or otherwise. Certainly, in speaking of intangible assets and reputation, corporate communication, sustainability and brand awareness play a role in the creation of value.

The point remains that despite the marked sensitivity towards these issues by the company's top management, when referring to intangible assets such as sustainability, the first consideration which emerges is how much it costs to invest in such assets or how to measure the return on investment in them. How to maintain them over time, and what synergies are obtained.

If we wish to focus our attention on the entrepreneurial structure of Italian fabrics, we can observe the composition of the price list in various segments, such as the picture painted by Borsa Italiana through companies listed on Euronext Milan is rather reliable.

There are 418 companies listed in the various Euronext segments with a capitalization of approximately €755 billion (March 2023). Almost half belong to the growth segment, but represent only 1% of total capitalization, with an average per company of €57million. In the Star segment there are 75, 7% of the market capitalization, with €707 millions of average capitalisation. Only one in the MIV. The 149 from the main list of Euronext cover 92%.

From 2018 to today, 208 companies have been listed, 163 in the Growth segment – 78% of total IPO and 39% of the total list. These companies represent respectively only 29% of the capitalizations of listed companies in the reference period, and 1.5% of the total market capitalization at the end of February 2023. If we look at listed Italian small to medium companies and focus our attention on the segment of Euronext growth and Euronext Growth Pro, which represent almost in numerical terms half of the listed Italian companies, but only 1% in terms of capitalisation despite representing Italian fabric, we can certainly state that the CEOs reputation is recognised as a corporate value. Entrepreneurs who choose the listing route themselves are all in agreement in affirming that being listed first is a reputational factor, a goal. This is because by choosing the listing process and reporting financial obligations not in the direction of stakeholders means that the company must start a process of transparency and credibility which leads to positive external consequences, increasing credibility of the top management, such as towards credit institutions.

A confirmation that sensitivity, at least on a theoretical level exists. The crucial point for small to medium companies is that there may be a lack of resources to allocate towards a process of continuous engagement, as well as building reputation, which however must remain listed over the course of a company's life. Sometimes it's unclear how to undertake the process of reputation management in a dynamic and continuous manner that contributes to the start-up of the business. Small to medium companies can be limited to the resources needed for communication, descriptive in terms of product and finance, or which may also include a path dedicated towards the reputation of a CEO, to their credibility or their ability to create guidelines which fit towards the commitments given to their stakeholders. It's not often considered a priority. When a company chooses the path of listing, it implicitly chooses transparency rules that a private company can choose not to adopt. This step is fundamental in the growth of reputation management, and how much it can be used in engagements with stakeholders to build the company's brand.

The measurability in economic terms of the investment of the creation of reputation and sustainability remains the Achilles heel on which many entrepreneurs or top managers remain sceptical about. A challenge for the future, of budget, reclassification, changes in reporting methods and allocation costs when comparing profitability levels at the same perimeter over a medium to long term period.

Conclusions: A Leader and Ambassador CEO

by Gabriele Ghini, Stefania A. Vitulli

The writing of this book and the interviews of CEOs took place following two events that have, quite literally, changed the world: the Covid Pandemic, and the Ukraine War. We have experienced firsthand the valid concerns of various CEOs regarding their operations in Russia, alongside the need to change both organizational and management models and reassuring investors regarding the return of their investments.

The goal of this book was to convey to top managers an approach, a model and the best practices needed to successfully build and protect the reputation of companies, aided by capitalizing and focusing on the impact of the CEO, as well as the definition of elements which are relevant in the construction of CEO branding, even and above all in moments of difficulty or great uncertainty. This is when the CEO figure becomes a point of reference both inside and outside of the company.

We started from a theoretical analysis of the elements that are at the core of building reputation: we deeply explored the strategic choices of CEOs of global companies, we have analyzed the behavior of small/midcap and later presented the best practices to attract and retain the best talent by capitalizing on the company's image, and the CEO's reputation as an intangible element. In a rational and emotional way, the mantra underlying a strong brand was confirmed and strengthened: esteem, admiration, trust, and positive feeling find its correspondence in a "two dimensional" leadership. On the one hand, they must show the ability to indicate clear and credible strategies that reassure stakeholders of their capability to lead the company in difficult, if not dramatic times. On the other hand, however the CEO must appear as empathetic, close (even individually) to the managers and employees of his company. They must be able to support them emotionally, of making them feel consistently supported. At the same time, thanks to a comprehensive and distinctive communication strategy they must be able to withstand public exposure and express strong opinions which at times may oppose the mainstream, which certainly characterizes a unique and recognizable position.

Earning the trust of stakeholders daily, whether they be public shareholders, a family-owned company, employees, customers, or the market has emerged as one of the top priorities in the actions of the CEO. This trust is earned and maintained, thanks to an ability to listen and interpret changes in the market, and the needs of their own employees, as well as presenting themselves as a credible point of reference who is ready to modify approaches in the short term, but within a continuity of strategy in the long term.

These are therefore leaders who earn esteem, credibility, and thus consequently a positive impact upon their own reputation due to their sensitivity toward social issues, which make up for the shortcomings of various institutions whose reputation is at risk. On August 19, 2019, when the pandemic was not even imaginable, the CEOs of 181 of the largest American corporations, associated with the Business Roundtable (in-depth analysis[4]), announced that they had signed a declaration in which they were committed to guiding their companies in the interests of their stakeholders. This was a profound cultural change compared to the traditional historical approach, which saw stakeholders as the priority recipients of the company's vision. In further detail, in the declaration of new company objectives, we can read: "Since 1978, Business Roundtable has periodically defined corporate governance principles. Every version of this document since 1997 has strongly supported the principle of 'shareholder primacy', or that corporations exist primarily to serve their shareholders. The new declaration replaces the previous one and aligns itself with the new and modern standards of corporate responsibility."

In July 2020, after a series of open letters to global CEOs written by CEO Larry Fink (letters in which Fink strongly encouraged paying attention to the impact of climate change upon their activities and behavior), BlackRock has identified 244 companies that are "making insufficient progress in integrating the risk of climate change into their

---

[4] https://www.businessroundtable.org/business-roundtable-redefines-the-purpose
-of-a-corporation-to-promote-an-economy-that-serves-all-americans

respective business models information." BlackRock voted against in meetings of 53 companies, and for the remaining 191 it "notified the state of surveillance and the risk of casting judgment toward management if they do not make substantial progress by 2021." A BlackRock spokesperson cast his critical rating toward 53 companies, compared to only 6 in 2019, which indicates a stricter global approach.[5] With over 7 trillion dollars under management, BlackRock holds a large influence within the boardrooms of Corporate America. Under pressure from clients and activists, BlackRock had said it would bring new attention to concerns over climate change after only supporting shareholder resolutions on the topic only around 10% in the past. This position is continued in following years by using a long-term strategy, expressed by Larry Fink as: "We focus on sustainability not because we are environmentalists, but because we are capitalists and trustees of our customers.[6]"

Our testimonies show a radical change in the vision of companies caused by the changed sensitivity of international public opinion regarding social issues. Regardless of the effects of the pandemic and war, the focus must be on the new reality that emerges after emergencies. Therefore, we believe it will be useful for CEOs to consider some questions that may help us improve our actions in the near future. We ask you them with the certainty that not many will have definitive answers but instead will be able to consciously observe the mass transformations of your companies and adopt the necessary tools at the right times which will help to build a sustainable future and communicate this with all your stakeholders. They who do this, and do it confidently and honestly, will have what it takes to win the reputational challenge.

1. What actions have you undertaken in this period which you have never thought of before, which will redevelop the organization and business?
2. What were the impacts of the last emergencies upon your stakeholders?

---

[5] Blacklist of non-sustainable companies: https://www.momentofinanza.it/blackrock-blacklist-societa-non-sostenibili/

[6] 2023, letters to investors and CEOs on behalf of BlackRock CEO: https://www.blackrock.com/corporate/investor-relations/larry-fink-ceo-letter

3. What are the new behaviors and how have they changed your business practice?
4. Is your mid-long-term strategy clear to all your stakeholders?
5. Do you constantly measure the trust you earn from your stakeholders?
6. What actions have had a positive impact upon your stakeholders?
7. How will you redefine your organization to be ready to face new crises?

At the end of asking yourselves these questions, one certainty remains: Whatever your business and your company, one element will not change during the crisis, and this is the importance of the behavior and reputation of the CEO. This reputation is earned through *credible and responsible actions at the core of its business, to contribute to the overall well-being of society through competent, professional, and long-term management of its own company.*

CEOs who act as leaders within their own companies, always close and available to their people; and who act as external ambassadors, representing the companies' values and objectives with honesty and transparency.

www.ingramcontent.com/pod-product-compliance
Lightning Source LLC
Chambersburg PA
CBHW062350220526
45472CB00008B/1758